sex & DEHUMANIZATION

Social Policy and Social Theory Series
David Marsland, Series Editor

Transforming Men, Geoff Dench

The Australian Nation, Geoffrey Partington

Darwinian Evolution, Antony Flew

Sex and Dehumanization, David Holbrook

David Holbrook

Sex & DEHUMANIZATION

*with a new introduction
by the author*

Transaction Publishers
New Brunswick (U.S.A.) and London (U.K.)

Library of Congress Catalog Number: 97–27082
ISBN: 0–7658–0402–6
Printed in the United States of America

Library of Congress Cataloging-in-Publication Data

Holbrook, David.
    Sex and dehumanization / David Holbrook ; with a new introduction by the author.
        p.   cm.—(Social policy and social theory series)
    Rev. ed. of: Sex and dehumanization in art, thought, and life in our time. 1972.
    Includes bibliographical references (p.   ) and index.
    ISBN 0–7658–0402–6 (pbk. : alk. paper)
    1. Sexual ethics. 2. Sex (Psychology) I. Holbrook, David. Sex and dehumanization in art, thought and life in our time. II. Title. III. Series.
HQ32.H64   1997
176—dc21   97–27082
                                                              CIP

For my children

♅♅♅

. . . Sex isn't something you've got to play with: sex is *you*.
It's the flow of your life, it's your moving self, and you are due
to be true to the nature of it, its reserve, its sensitive pride
that it always has to begin with, and by which you ought to abide.

Know yourself, O know yourself, that you are mortal; and know
the sensitive delicacy of your sex, in its ebbing to and fro,
and the mortal reserve of your sex, as it stays in your depths below.

And don't, with the nasty, prying mind, drag it out from its deeps
and finger it and force it, and shatter the rhythm it keeps
when it's left alone, as it stirs and rouses and sleeps . . .

Sex isn't Sin, D. H. Lawrence

Contents

	Introduction to the Transaction Edition	ix
	Preface	xvii
	Acknowledgements	xix
1	Introductory: on my 'attitude to sex'	1
2	What is happening: the sadist revolution	18
3	Philosophy, science and meaning	50
4	Psychoanalysis and sex	74
5	The dangers of moral inversion	81
6	The truth about perversion	94
7	Ethics and sex	112
8	The delusions of sexology	132
9	Sex and culture	165
10	'Enlightenment'—a new imprisonment?	195
	Glossary	213
	Bibliography	218
	Index	223

Introduction to the Transaction Edition

This book was written about a quarter of a century ago, yet I feel I can still almost totally endorse it: certainly I would not want to alter it substantially—though, as will appear, I should like to give the argument a further twist, one which I feel will illuminate my concern and perhaps enable us to understand what has been happening in Western civilization.

During the intervening years since 1972 the situation has hardly improved. The concept of sex has become increasingly separated from the rest of existence, especially in the realm of discourse. Meanwhile what must be called sexual casualties have increased, in some areas disastrously: the spread of AIDS has brought an ominous and deadly manifestation into the human picture, yet at the same time the response to this menace has often become that of manic denial. What is important, it seems, is the preservation of the myths of modern emancipation, even at the expense of certain doom. As the taboos on the reporting of sexual casualties have been relinquished, I find the current reports on sexual casualties—consequent upon child prostitution, rape, sexual perversion, and murder—and such indications of increasing hate in this sphere so unbearable that I shrink from them, fearing for my belief in human potentialities for goodness. Whatever statistics one takes—whether those of sexual activity among young children, or abortion, or sexual disease—one finds a grim antidote to any hopes of progress in the sphere of human dealings with the sexual.

One would have expected, in the face of such a mounting tide of grim consequences, that it would have become fashionable to express concern, for the human condition, in the face of current trends. Yet, if one examines the way things have been going in the realm of culture and entertainment, one finds a deepening of what seems to be a cynical assertion of prurience. The language and content of novels, plays, films, and even poetry, with some honorable exceptions, seem to indicate something of a frenetic stampede, towards ever-increasing explicitness, an ever-increasing exploitation of perversion and the dynamics of hate. Even in poetry the display of extreme sexual language seems *de rigeur*, and much in the area of writing and the arts seems to belong to the pursuit of false solutions, for profit.

There has been, of course, during the three decades since my book appeared, works purporting to represent the view of women, the feminist viewpoint. This body of work awaits its comprehensive valuation, but it seems now too enormous, too varied to summarize, certainly to find in it any representative theme which manifests new and radical insights. Much of it seems to belong to an impulse to demonstrate that women can be as false to their experience as men. There is also a vast literature in social science on the nature of the exploitation of sexuality in the media and examination of its social effects. But too often, like feminist writing, this disappoints, because it fails to examine the fundamental assumptions behind one's interest in sexuality in the first place. In attending, as I do, to certain psychoanalytical studies of the underlying meanings of sex in our culture and thought, I believe that I have enabled myself to discuss the problems that arise without needing to attend to these commentaries, which themselves will require re-examination, if my premises are agreed.

As will appear, my book was originally prompted by a feeling that much of what is written about sex in our era is nonsense, and "belong[s] to a complex of certain false assumptions about man in our intellectual and cultural life which are leading towards dehumanisation." I therefore undertook to write it, against my better judgement, and so put myself against the predominant fashions of our time. I became, because of it, something of a pariah, since I was felt to set myself against certain predominant tendencies in our culture—to be "open" and "frank" about sexual matters, which was taken to be "realism" and "freedom." Alas, to the bewilderment of the public at large, such "openness" has gone with increasing catastrophe in the sphere of personal relationships—besides the huge increase in divorce, an increase in sexual behavior among children, and other such manifestations of moral decline in the sphere of personal relationship.

Perhaps among many couples there is a feeling that their lives together have gone dead, and that they are living a lie. But one also suspects that many of the disasters that are indicated by the statistics are the consequence of false solutions, rooted in feelings that solutions to life problems are to be found in the sexual sphere because of the elevation of sex to its predominant position in the whole pattern of existence. More adequate solutions seem too complex to confront, while our civilization lends little or no support to efforts to solve the problems.

The clue to the whole false process which is affecting our civilization is to be found in a grim and disturbing book which follows on from the work to which I try to draw attention in the present volume. I found here a chastening position in the writing of the New York psychotherapist Rollo May, to whose work as an existentialist practitioner I make reference throughout my book, especially towards the end. A book from the same publisher, Basic Books of New York, refers to Rollo May and represents a direct development from the same discipline: *Existential Psychotherapy* by Irvin Yalom. Indeed Yalom pays generous tribute to those psychotherapists whose wisdom I have often referred to—Leslie H. Farber, and May himself. He is professor of psychiatry at Stanford University School of Medicine.

Yalom presses the problem of the quest for a sense of meaning and identity in the modern world beyond the examinations of will and identity pursued by Rollo May, in such a way as to be liberating and at the same time deeply chastening. I also found his chapters on the general problems of living in our civilization deeply disturbing. He is, it seems to me, unflinchingly realistic about human nature, and especially about our capacity to deceive ourselves. I realized, reading his book, how much I was struggling, in writing *Sex and Dehumanization*, to find my way out of a falsity which our culture largely imposes on us, to hold us in thrall. And he forces us to confront the real problems of existence to which our attention to sex is taken to offer us an escape.

Freud himself, says Yalom, warned us that a cigar, in the symbolism of our consciousness, is not always a symbol for a penis: "sometimes a cigar is just a cigar." Yalom goes on:

But Freud does not go far enough in his warning. It is possible that sex may be a symbol of something else. If the deepest ultimate concerns of the human being are existential in nature, and relate to death, freedom, isolation and meaninglessness, then it is entirely possible that these fears may be displaced and symbolised by such derivative concerns as sexuality.   page 382

Sex, he asserts, may be used in the service of repression of death anxiety. He gives as evidence of this comment several instances of patient behavior which seem, by his perspective, grotesque. He reports that married couples, where in each case one spouse had terminal cancer, spoke to him of little else except their sexual maladjustment:

At times, in the heat of this discussion, during the recriminations and counterchanges, I forgot entirely that one of those individuals was facing imminent death. Such is the success of the defensive manoeuvre.   page 382

Earlier he had discussed the case of a young woman with advanced cervical cancer who found that her disease not only did not discourage male suitors but, on the contrary, seemed to increase their number or their sexual appetites. And he refers to a colleague, Ella Greenspan, who describes research which demonstrated that women with breast cancer, by comparison with an age-matched healthy cohort, had a higher incidence of illicit sexual fantasies. He says, "There is something gloriously magic about the lure of sex. Sexuality seems to have 'a force of its own' and seems 'bigger than life'."

So, we may see the emphasis on sex in our culture as representing a manifestation of isolation, and the failure to sustain caring and relatedness.

Compulsive sexuality is also a common response to a sense of isolation. Promiscuous sexual "coupling" offers a powerful temporary respite to lonely individuals. It is temporary because it is not relatedness but only a caricature of relationship. Compulsive sex breaks all the rules of true caring. The individual uses the other as equipment. He or she uses, and relates to, only a part of the other.   page 383

To some people it is "an advantage not to know the other and to keep most of themselves hidden." The sexually compulsive individual neither knows nor engages the other. He does not exist "between" but always observes himself. And here Yalom quotes Martin Buber's description of "erotic man":

Many years have I wandered through the land of men, and have not yet reached an end of studying the varieties of the "erotic man." There a lover stamps around and is in love only with his passion. There one is wearing his differentiated feelings like medal-ribbons. There one is enjoying the adventures of his own fascinating effect. There one is gazing enraptured at the spectacle of his own supposed surrender. There one is collecting excitement. There one is displaying his "power." There one is preening himself with borrowed vitality. There one is delighting to exist simultaneously as himself and as an idol very unlike himself. There one is warming himself at the blaze of what has fallen to his lot. There one is experimenting. And so on and on—all the manifold monologists with their mirrors, in the apartment of the most intimate dialogue!

Between Man and Man, pages 29–30

Yalom goes on to finish his book by discussing the philosophical basis on which to combat, through therapy, the existential isolation which underlies such manifestations as the invocation of sex to evade the problems of life:

Individuals who are terrified of isolation generally attempt to assuage their terror through the interpersonal mode: they need the presence of others to affirm their existence; they long to be swallowed by others greater than they, or they seek to alleviate their sense of lonely helplessness by swallowing others; they attempt to elevate themselves through others; they search for multiple sexual bondings—a caricature of authentic relating.   page 393

This widens the perspective, in recognition that the particular obsession with sex in our era is a generally false solution to problems of deficiency in social and personal relationships—an impression that is deepened by Dr. Yalom's final chapters.

To examine our approach to sex is thus an index to the nature of our civilization. And this is reinforced by the way and the degree to which the "media" have worked on consciousness—"sex" being one of the headings, in his prescription for financially successful journalism, of Lord Northcliff's original program. By promoting this hypnotic fixation, he and his followers have transformed Western society, breeding such harm out of our more vulnerable weaknesses, so that, in the age of television, mankind has been lured into the grossest falsification ever, by what is called the "sexual revolution." Of course, we must distinguish between what people in our society think and believe, and what is manifest in the media—in newspapers, film, radio, and television. No doubt people are influenced by other cultural pressures, in which we must include religious beliefs, books, and school instruction, as well as the natural inclinations of good conscience. But we also have to take into account the formation of their personalities in early nurture, especially at the hands of their mothers and fathers, and other members of their families, including siblings. Anxieties are crudely exploited by the media under the headings of sex, death, violence, money, disaster and war. The newspapers rely still on the precepts of Lord Northcliff, and the advent of television has merely deepened the methodology of such appeals, to the "lowest common denominator." So, there is no chance of a child today growing up innocent, since besides explicit sex scenes on television, there is explicit discussion of matters of perversion, sexual misconduct, rape, homosexuality, and sexual murder on radio and television. Behind this "freedom" there is presumably some kind of enlightened belief that "open" knowledge of the direct human proclivities must be beneficial: yet as the plethora of distorted modes of behavior is presented, even an experienced adult must sometimes feel contaminated by news of modes of behavior which fall upon us from the "media." Is it really beneficial to air every perversion, cruelty, and manifestation of destructiveness, every false and harmful mode of behavior, without reticence or a sense of outrage, from such powerful instruments? This process has gone on by subtle developments, under the impulse of certain figures who seem to thrive on the corruption of sensibility, who seem to seek to bring about a world that is as coarse as their own souls—which, to speak more plainly, thrive on corruption.

What this "revolution" has brought about, by subtle progress, is the locking of our civilizations in the West, into the inversions of hate. The predominant mode, in our present-day emphasis on sex is, without there being any widespread recognition of the fact, rooted in hate. Perhaps the dominant feeling today is that we are not in control of our lives. Our lives are governed by impersonal forces, which are, as Freud tended to think in his theory, beyond our control, and ungovernable in the interests of society and healthy growth. Our lives are run by those who essentially hold us in contempt. This in turn promotes a feeling that we are alienated, and so, to protect ourselves, we take further resort to behavior itself rooted in hate. This, as I have tried to point out in my analysis of the effect of James Bond films, leads to a deep falsification of our modes of existence.

In this situation, as I try to say in this book, "the prevalent obsession with sex in our culture will turn to increasingly destructive and nihilistic modes...one of the worst effects will be that of damaging the arts themselves as a source of meaning," and this at a time when the loss of a sense of meaning in life is already severe. As I say in my book,

What is threatened by the dehumanisation of sex is a threat to our whole perception of the world. What is threatened is the banalization of sex in the destruction of creative potency, meaning and effectiveness.   page 211

The recognition, as is grimly indicated by Irwin Yalom, that the obsession with sex in our culture is a screen for a necessary confrontation with the problem of death, and the loss of meaning in general, is chilling. But as a road to the recovery of our senses in this sphere its unmasking may perhaps prompt some form of recovery.

Which brings me to the question of how our civilization could ever escape from its obsession with sex. Yalom can only recommend what he calls "engagement":

Engagement is the therapeutic answer to meaninglessness regardless of the latter's source. Wholehearted engagement in any of the infinite array of life's activities...disarms the galactic view.

It should perhaps be pointed out that Yalom confronts what he calls the "galactic view":

From this vantage point, which philosophers refer to as the "galactic" or the "nebula's-eye" view (or the "cosmic" or "global" perspective), we and our fellow creatures seem trivial and foolish. We become only one of the countless life forms. Life's activities seem absurd. The rich, experienced moments are lost in the great expanse of time. We sense that we are microscopic specks, and that all of life consumes but a flick of cosmic time.   page 478

Yalom, in combating this view of existence, takes on the pessimistic Schopenhauer and asserts against his views a sense of the value of "engagement" as the basis of a grasp on commitment and action, rooted in his engagement, as a therapist, with the problem of meaninglessness, quoting Tolstoy: "It is possible to live as long as life intoxicates us" (though pointing out that the great author went on, "as soon as we are sober again we see that it is all a delusion, and a stupid delusion"). He goes on, however, to urge that "engagement"

enhances the possibility of one's completing the patterning of the events of one's own life in some coherent fashion. To find a home, to care about other individuals, about ideas or projects, to search, to create, to build these, and all forms of engagement, are twice rewarding: they are intrinsically enriching, and they alleviate the dysphoria that stems from being bombarded with the unassembled brute data of existence.   page 482

He ends his book by declaring that "one must immerse oneself in the river of life and let the question drift away."

As Yalom's book demonstrates, the problem of reaching beyond the preoccupation with sex and its lures in our society requires immense resources, and a critical determination to examine the predicament of modern man. Few of us have the capacities to engage in such a struggle, not least when the whole tendency of civilization seems against any such exposure to the truths of existence. But at least we can arm ourselves against the more false persuasions of our time, and I hope that the book that follows will help at least some of us to resist the worst falsifications of our time.

Preface

The suppression of sexuality reached its height in the Victorian era and the emancipation from this evil has been hard, slow and painful; indeed, in some respects, it is by no means achieved. A revolution is never a simple process, for the drive towards a truly creative new form can easily be submerged by the sheer need to counteract the original fault. And the sexual revolution is no exception. The attempt to free society from the prudery of the past has brought an assumption that any shyness, any wish for privacy, any recognition that human relationships need time and sensitivity in order to flourish is a sign of sexual inhibition. This line of thought leads to a conception of sexuality that is dehumanized and dehumanizing. But the matter does not end there, and is more complicated.

The attitude which a particular society takes towards sexuality reflects its vision of man as a whole. The vision of our society is a technical one. It is not only that we increasingly rely on machinery of various kinds but that we increasingly conceive human nature in mechanical terms. Our ideal is 'science' as formulated by those who first brought order to the study of inanimate matter. The consequence is that people are nowadays subjected to quantitative psychological tests, reduced to inappropriate formulae, and their actions described in mechanistic terms. In the sphere of sexuality this means that the loving way in which two people meet each other physically is thought of as a technique rather than a spontaneous action; the significance of the experience as a human being is lost. In a rather disastrous way the revolt against prudery, taking the form of a 'short-cut' to human fellowship has, in contemporary society, met up with the short-cut approach of a technological age. It is the harmful consequences of this current distortion which David Holbrook explores in this book.

I am particularly pleased at having been asked to write this preface as I have long been an admirer of David Holbrook's writings on English for children. The present book shows a similar concern for the presentation of true reality to the young. Although written with passion there is no lack of considered thought or knowledge of the work of psychotherapists and philosophers relevant to his theme. One may disagree with some of his views and emphases—I personally feel that the dangers of censorship are greater than he implies and make it an unacceptable remedy to the problem—but his main thesis is, I think, irrefutable.

PETER LOMAS

Acknowledgements

𝔊𝔊𝔊

The completion of this book has been made possible by a grant to the author from the Arts Council of Great Britain, for which he is grateful. He is also grateful to the Elmgrant Trust for assistance.

Grateful thanks are also due to the following publishers for permission to quote from the works listed below:
William Heinemann Ltd for an extract from D. H. Lawrence's poem *Sex isn't Sin* taken from *The Complete Poems of D. H. Lawrence*; International Psycho-Analytical Library for extracts from Masud Khan's papers *The Function of Intimacy and Acting Out in Perversions* which appeared in *Sexual Behaviour and the Law*, and *Reparation to the Self as an Idolised Internal Object: A Contribution to the Theory of Perversion Formation* from *Dynamische Psychiatrie* No. 2, November 1968; Routledge & Kegan Paul Ltd for passages from *The Tacit Dimension* and *Personal Knowledge* by Michael Polanyi, and *The Phenomenology of Perception* by Maurice Merleau-Ponty; Souvenir Press Ltd for extracts from *Love and Will* by Rollo May, and *The Doctor and the Soul* by Viktor Frankl; Constable & Company Ltd for extracts from *An Analysis of Human Sexual Response* by Leslie Farber.

1
Introductory: on my 'attitude to sex'

My publisher has pointed out, with some justification, that, though
it might be possible to extract, from the essays below, an 'attitude
to sex', I don't in any of these essays make my own attitude
explicit. So, he suggests, I outline this in the first chapter. I attempt
to do so with some hesitation because I doubt whether I have
anything like a satisfactory, comprehensive and stateable attitude
to sex at all. What I believe I may have is a certainty that many
attitudes I encounter nowadays to this subject are absurd—which
is not at all the same thing of course, as having an attitude to sex.
But I can perhaps try to indicate how and why I came to write this
book.

The essays gathered here were each at first impelled by a sense
of outrage and astonishment, at finding so many intelligent people
today not only able and willing, but enthusiastically willing, to
believe absurdities about sex. Whether the matter under discussion
happens to be sexual behaviour or sex in symbolism, it seems to
make no difference. A certain kind of nonsense is taken today to be
a new kind of 'realism'. Often, to me, it seems not only nonsense,
but sinister nonsense, too.

Moreover, as I see it, the 'sex' nonsense that is talked and believed today belongs to a complex of certain false assumptions
about man in our intellectual and cultural life which are leading us
towards dehumanization. What I mean by 'false' should appear as
my argument proceeds. The prevalent attitudes to sex of the
'enlightened' simply cannot be reconciled with human truth as we
know it from our own experience, or with such truths as seem to be
established by what I shall call 'philosophical anthropology'—that
is, the collocation of insights from the subjective disciplines of
psychoanalysis, phenomenology, and those philosophies which
reject Cartesian dualism, and put the 'ghost' firmly back in the
'machine'.

Some absurdities about sex which dominate our popular thought
emanate from a science 'imprisoned', as Michael Polanyi argues, 'in

physicalism'. Some may be traced to certain claims made for 'scientific' disciplines in a realm where they have no validity and deserve no authority. Others come from that kind of psychology which, because it clings to 'objectivity', cannot find man's inner life, nor really, his consciousness—the kind of psychology called by some, such as Charles Taylor the philosopher of behaviour, non-psychological psychology. It is impossible to consider the depersonalization of sex in our culture without examining the whole tendency of our intellectual ethos to objectify—a tendency which menaces our whole society and its approach to man. As Michael Polanyi says—

The great movement for independent thought instilled in the modern mind a desperate refusal of all knowledge that is not absolutely impersonal, and this implied in its turn a mechanical conception of man.

Personal Knowledge, page 214*

Moreover, this objectivity has lent itself to what Polanyi calls 'fanatical immoralism'. My concern arises thus out of a concern with culture and education, an intellectual concern with the truth of human nature, and a social concern. The individual concerned with English as an educational subject inevitably becomes concerned with such ethical and social issues, and I conclude by writing as an educationist.

Perhaps, however, it is worth asserting that my concern is not a moralizing concern with other people's behaviour. Their behaviour is their business and individuals must be free to find their own meaning in life. I believe that increased tolerance has brought many benefits here. What I am concerned with is the way in which everybody's experience and behaviour is being influenced by certain cultural pressures and ways of thinking. I believe we must trust human nature, when it comes to 'ethical living'. But I am not so naive as to be unaware of the capacity in man to falsify ethical issues. The gravest problems are raised by the existence of a minority who have the capacity for passionate moral inversion and a destructiveness which, as I have tried to demonstrate in earlier works,† they are quite capable of communicating through culture, and indeed are sometimes motivated to do so by an intense if perverted idealism. I am therefore sure that we must accept the necessity of discrimination—and of some degree of coercion, to defend ourselves from those who would exploit us.

---

* Full details of all works quoted in this book are in the bibliography, see pages 218–221.

† See my *Human Hope and the Death Instinct* and *The Masks of Hate* (Pergamon 1971).

So, as far as the *personal* life of sex is concerned, I believe that the essential path to sexual knowledge is the individual's discovery of the realm himself. We must rely on each individual's moral dynamic, his own capacity for 'ethical living'. But since this capacity largely depends upon the intercourse between ourselves and our culture, I am concerned as an educationist and critic with cultural symbolism and intellectual attitudes and the ways in which these influence individuals in their attempts to discover a meaningful sexual life for themselves. Some present-day cultural influences, as will be seen below, I consider disastrous. I believe they belong to an 'anti-culture' that threatens much that our civilization has created, and not least those values to which, as Viktor Frankl says, love is the gateway.*

Of course, I suppose, if I find prevalent 'enlightened' attitudes so absurd, then I must have some assurance about what is 'true' about sex. So perhaps my publisher is right in asking me to try to make this clear. Let me begin then, in trying to satisfy his requirements, by saying that all I know about sex is that my experience of it is inseparable from a whole life experience with its normal pains and perplexities, joys and satisfactions. As D. H. Lawrence says, 'Sex is *you*': it is an expression of the whole self in the realm of the 'I-Thou'. My experience of literature, and other sources of information about human experience, including what others have told me, and what I have read, seem to me to confirm my impression that our sexual experience is no larger than life, and is not to be separated from the whole 'being-in-the-world' whose primary need is relationship. This is perhaps the most emphatic thing I would wish to say about the subject 'sex'. It takes its place among all our other confused and groping explorations towards a sense of meaning in existence, and only suffers if, as in too much of our culture, it is separated from everything else that belongs to being human.

So if I wished to explore 'sexual experience' with a 'humanities' class, I might well study the novels of Jane Austen or the poetry of W. B. Yeats. Having put those two cards on the table, I can imagine a heated response from the 'progressive' reader—from the representative of the ethos of 'enlightenment' and the 'sexual revolution'. Surely, such a one might reply, if you want to explore sexual experience, then you should turn to the novels of John Updike, or to a 'group grope' at the Living Theatre, or to the latest 'erotic' film, or to some of the new manifestations of extreme sexual preoccupation in *avant-garde* art? These surely offer us a new

---

* See his chapter 'On the Meaning of Love' in *The Doctor and the Soul* (Souvenir Press 1969).

expansion or enlargement of the sexual realm? He might well assert that there is nothing about sex in the novels of Jane Austen or the poetry of Yeats except perhaps the latter's lines protesting that—

> Love has pitched his mansion in
> The place of excrement . . .

Those disturbing lines would, I believe, give me an opening for a reply. I would argue that they indicate very clearly in their physical symbolism the whole relational problem. I would invoke what I would call the 'schizoid diagnosis'—a way of looking at human problems based on insights into problems of identity derived from recent psychoanalytical theory.*

From this point of view, we may assert that, at the deepest level, our sexual problems have to do with our sense of inner substantiality, and so with our innermost sense of meaning. A physical confrontation or 'meeting' with another being arouses in us all the schizoid problems of a fear of loss of 'inner contents', or of being threatened by 'bad inner contents' or 'emptiness': by our fear of love and our need to love. From this point of view, what is primary in the matter, 'sex' or whatever you like to call it, is the problem of relationship and the degree to which we can find meaning in relationship to establish an inward sense of form and content sufficient to offset our deepest fears of a *horror vacui* within.

How can we discover deep within ourselves what it is we need in the realm of the 'most intimate dialogue'? How do we know when we have the opportunity to fulfil this need through touch with another and how do we find and respect their needs? It is this which Jane Austen's novels are about; and so they are about 'sexual experience' in its deepest sense.

The 'enlightened' reader may gesture towards his copies of *Playboy*, or the latter's triumphant publication *The Sexual Revolution*, or the nudes pinned on his study wall (with obscene slogans painted on them attacking censorship), or his collection of books on sexual technique. Or he may offer me the explicitness of films, novels and stage shows today—and our 'frankness' at large. But I can only see these as manifestations which belong to that strange modern phenomenon which has separated sex in an unreal and dangerous way from human wholeness. Moreover, some of the trends of which he approves also seem to be moving in an anti-human rather than a human direction, and are likely to *limit* our capacities for the erotic.

---

* See H. Guntrip, *Schizoid Phenomena, Object-relations, and the Self* (Hogarth Press 1968).

In our present situation, in which dehumanized sex dominates the symbolism of our culture, it seems hopeless for the imaginative writer to offer, say, a love poem, or even a poetic statement of his attitude to love (such as my own poem 'Eros to Maidens' in *Imaginings*) as representing his 'point of view' on sex. It won't do to point to a passage in a novel in which one has tried to record the actuality—the admixture of love, uncertainty and joy mingled in any real sexual experience. It will not serve to quote a child's first gropings towards sexuality in symbolism, relying on the reader to note its essential tenderness and naivety—

> As the horses both approached
> The willow near the stream,
> A mare near them
> Which looked so feminine,
> Gave their blood full steam.
> When the stallion came quite near,
> She had a shiver ear to ear . . .
>
> by a 13-year-old girl, Melbourne, Australia

While the richness, depth and meaning to be found in love puts it on an altogether higher plane than eroticism or mere sexuality, at the same time love cannot be separated from an essential innocence, as part of our gropings, of our weaknesses, our fear of dependence and of the realm of 'being'. To campaign on behalf of love turns it into something too much like the activity of the sex emancipationist. I discuss this problem of how, in opposing those who would reduce sexual love to sex, one is easily defeated by joining them, in Chapter 8.

It was thus in self-defence that I turned at first, in my study of human nature, to psychoanalytical writers, because it did not seem enough to say of literature or one's own work, 'This is the record of genuine experience', and expect to be heard. One could be too easily laughed out of court by those who seemed to offer some larger-than-life 'freedom' and 'enlightenment', in an ethos in which falsification was arrogantly (and glossily) sustained, 'masculine protest' predominant, and while coarse bright voices asserted loudly, 'We will have no weakness . . .'.

How could one equal the fanaticism of the opposition? How could one talk of the sensitivities of a normal love relationship while journals like the *New Statesman* were dominated by voices which were coarse, loud and assured in their enlightened 'frankness' and 'realism'?

Their tone itself makes debate almost impossible. We may take as an example a mere phrase from an article in such a paper: 'nowadays, when so many men are *having it off* at parties for nothing . . .'* (my italics). The tone is that of a new freedom; the phrase 'having it off' here seems to mean 'getting rid of libidinal urges in an impersonal way'. Such a way of talking seems to offer us a truly tough 'sophistication' in the sexual sphere. But sex here is, significantly, reduced to 'it', while in the language itself there is an implicit reduction of man. 'Having it off' in fact, originates in criminal cant, where it means 'to thieve or rob successfully, to pull off a coup' (see Robert Roberts' *Imprisoned Tongues*). The kind of 'freedom' Kingsley Amis describes is achieved only by reducing sex to an act of hate, an 'itch' to be got rid of, and man to a hydraulic system: this he achieves by a suave, unfeeling and cynical tone. This explains the appeal that the reduction of sex in his novels to a ridiculous and banal function has for those whose education has taught them to think of themselves in this way, as if a 'taking' attitude to sex (*Take a Girl Like You*) was the only reality. And in a sense such a writer belongs to this world, in which man has become reduced to a mere organism, almost a machine, in our very thought-patterns and attitudes to ourselves.

The tone and manner exemplified in such writing are often a kind of verbal sleight of hand which seeks to persuade us that there is, or need not be, any problem of hate in sex. Guilt, fear, concern about harm, in this area, are all 'unnecessary', and can be swept away either by adopting a boldly 'amoral' position, or by anarchic reforms in society, so that what has been called 'immoral' up to now need no longer be considered so.

The implication that everything is 'new' and simple today should make one suspicious at once of yet another version of the destructive fallacy of human perfectibility.

One of the most absurd tendencies in modern popular thought is the evident desire to believe that, in some way, there are now completely different features in human nature—the pill, or 'openness', or mental knowledge, have somehow 'freed' us. This is a most dangerous tendency and it now seems necessary in the face of it to assert, with the author of *Ecclesiastes*, that—

What has happened will happen again, and what has been done will be done again, and there is nothing new under the sun. Is there anything of which one can say, 'Look, this is new?' No, it has already existed, long ago before our time.†

The essential sexual problems remain what they ever were, however much we approach them in different terms. Because we have some new devices and insights, we may be able perhaps to

---

* Kingsley Amis: *New Statesman*, 11th June 1965.
† The *New English Bible* translation.

avoid some of the old anxieties, but many problems have been merely driven underground. For instance, it is highly significant that technological advances in contraception have not done away with the problem of the 'unwanted' pregnancy, which can, in the opinion of psychotherapists, be the expression of an urgent desire to have a child to love—and so be a demand for passion (see page 35). Instead of love the woman gets a pill or an abortion. The essential problem remains that of accepting our humanness. The 'enlightened' view can even be a powerful threat to our new insights and new medical advances, not least to the new possibilities of intelligent reform, because it tends to shrink from the 'complexities of mire and blood', as Yeats called them, inevitably bound up with sex, and inescapable.

Predominant in my point of view obviously is the insistence that the primary need we are concerned with, when we discuss the problem of sex, is that of *meaningful relationship*. Dehumanization must inevitably follow if we attempt to divide whatever we mean by 'sex' from this, and from its whole complex, which is the problem of existence itself. To say as much merely confirms what we know from literature anyway: this essential aspect of the sexual life is expressed in *The Song of Songs*—

> Night after night on my bed
> I have sought my true love;
> I have sought him but not found him,
> I have called him but he has not answered.
> I said, 'I will rise and go the rounds of the city,
> through the streets and the squares,
> seeking my true love.'*

There could be no more forcible expression than the body of the great tradition of English love poetry of the truth that what is primary in all human beings is the creative proclivity to find the 'significant other'. As Donne says—

> Twice or thrice had I loved thee
> Before I knew thy face or name . . .

As soon as one begins to take into account such poetic statements of the truth of human relational needs, one becomes aware of other reasons for turning to the psychotherapist and those insights emerging from his grave discipline which are contributing so much to the emerging integrated view of man of philosophical anthropology.

Recent psychoanalytical thinking and philosophical biology have not only come to find relational needs as primary; they are

* The *New English Bible* translation.

also coming to the conclusion that the basis of our effective living, and of our very dealings with the world, lies in the sense of meaning we find in love. By implication, as we shall see, not only do 'hydraulic', mechanistic, and reductionist attitudes to sex tend to lower our human stature, but they actually tend to promote psychic impotence and loss of creative power in our dealings with reality. The prevalent cult of dissociated sex is thus a threat to the *imagination*, and this is why an individual such as myself is so deeply concerned about it. As C. H. Waddington said in the Alpbach seminar (reported in *Encounter*, November 1965, book version ed. Koestler and Smithies, Hutchinson 1970), it would even seem that our present society may be 'repressing the search for meaning'. Other thinkers like May and Frankl see dissociated sex as contributing to a deepening sense of existential emptiness. Where 'emancipationists' reduce love to mere sexuality they threaten one major source of a sense of value in life. The psychoanalyst can arrive at such conclusions because he knows from his experience of the psychotherapeutic relationship itself that this is a form of love from which a possible sense of meaning emerges.

This sense of possible meaning in life, such as emerges from adequate relationships of all kinds, as well as from the psychotherapeutic encounter, Rollo May links with the concept of 'intentionality'. This concept from the nineteenth-century philosopher Husserl expresses man's capacity to create his own meaningful world, throwing himself by imagination into the future. In the sexual realm, it is this intentionality that has suffered most from the prevalent reductionism. Again we may invoke Donne: 'Let us possess our world, each hath one, and is one . . .'

Emerging from clinical observations, and 'philosophical anthropology' are evident ethical implications, of which writers like May are becoming aware. These involve the whole question of our capacity for effective living, and the way this is bound up with relationship.

Decision, in our sense, creates out of the two previous dimensions a pattern of acting and living which is empowered and enriched by wishes, asserted by will, and is responsive to and responsible for the significant other—persons who are important to one's self in the realising of long-term goals. If the point were not self-evident, it could be demonstrated along the lines of Sullivan's interpersonal theory of psychiatry, Buber's philosophy, and other viewpoints. They all point out that wish, will and decision occur within a nexus of relationships upon which the individual depends not only for his fulfillment but for his very existence.

This sounds like an ethical statement and is.

Love and Will, page 268 (my italics)

It is the intention of the present writer to take this ethical statement, and introduce it into the debate at large about sex and
sexual depiction.

If our very existence depends upon significant relationships,
then the rejection of this fundamental truth in depersonalized
sexuality and its glamourization in our society must be regarded
with foreboding. According to psychoanalysis, our capacity to find
the 'significant other' is drawn out in us first of all by the mother,
and when this happens satisfactorily and creatively, then we are
able to enter into all those other relationships in which we may
find meaning—not least the adult sexual relationship, and a significant relationship with the world as a whole. If we accept this as
human truth, there can be no real or relevant discussion of sex
without taking the whole nexus of 'being in the world' into account;
while any separation of the sexual problem from these needs and
aspects of the whole being is liable not only to lead to dehumanization, but also to the reduction of our creative power to make our
world and to find answers to such questions as 'What is it to be
human?' and 'What is the point of life?'.

One of the most important findings of psychotherapists from my
point of view is that expressed by Rollo May when he writes—

My experience as a therapist suggests that the human being has to make
the creature with whom he has sexual relations in some way personal,
even if only in fantasy, or else suffer depersonalisation himself.

Love and Will, page 211

To suffer depersonalization is to suffer the sort of deep disturbance
which is characteristic of schizoid illnesses—a loss of a sense of
autonomy and wholeness. In so far as depersonalized sex is thrust
at us through culture, we suffer the threat of becoming involved in
schizoid illness, or at least driven from our natural impulse to
personalize. Thus we need to consider carefully those forms of
'cultural pollution' that are likely to affect our psychic health in
such ways.*

This problem has been hidden by the 'carefully contrived perspectives' of the 'enlightened' propagandist. He has managed to
hide the dangers of depersonalization by clinging to 'objective'
theories, in which the uniqueness of the individual being is
implicitly denied. From the point of view of serious studies of man's
inwardness we may accuse him of ignoring a whole area of responsible concern with human truth. For besides the bodies of thought

---

* See the *Final Report* on the *Intergovernmental Conference on Institutional,
Administrative and Financial Aspects of Cultural Policies*, UNESCO, Venice,
August–September 1970.

mentioned by Dr. May there is also plenty in the work of Ian D. Suttie, W. R. D. Fairbairn, Melanie Klein, D. W. Winnicott, Michael Balint, Harry Guntrip, Marion Milner, Leslie Farber, Viktor Frankl and others and in philosophical biology (Buytendijk, Straus) which bears out the same 'ethical statement'.

Turning back to the realm of experience rather than my intellectual convictions, I have continually struggled with the perplexity that, though I knew that marriage was the kind of committed relationship I needed—committed in the sense of two people 'contributing in' to a pledged togetherness, and to trying to shape a future—it also brought a closeness of 'meeting' of which I was afraid, and a degree of responsibility which I am still learning to accept. The satisfactions of love do, as Frankl says, 'Cast a spell upon the world . . . envelop the world in added worth'. Here, indeed, we 'know better than we can tell', to take another phrase from Polanyi. While I have tried to express something of what I 'know' in this realm in my poetry, it also seems to me at times that the way in which my life is bound up with my marriage only becomes evident at a distance, when I can look at my existence from the outside, in a particular place in space and time, as on the deck of an ocean liner, or alone in the night in a strange place.

From such vantage points, I can see how much 'an inner enrichment that goes beyond the Thou', as Frankl says, 'opens the gates to a whole universe of values'. Yet there have been many moments of torment and anguish, and my sexual life has been one in which the satisfactions which now grow richer year by year have had to be won in the face of many deep and stubborn psychic ghosts. Now I can see even the worst moments in my relational life as desperate attempts to find meaning when everything seemed threatened with meaninglessness because of depression or anxiety. To hang on, through bad moments, was to hang on to meaning, and this only lost its point if one merely thought of it in 'sexual' terms—for sexual difficulties turned out in the end to be bound up with problems of meaning, such as one's capacities to accept one's own female element, and to cherish and respect the essential femaleness of one's woman.

I recognize, however, that for many people marriage can never be the true solution, and my discriminations should by no means be taken to imply that other solutions in life are to be morally castigated or deplored. Some individuals will choose to be celibate; others may try to satisfy their relational needs by a series of love affairs into which they do not enter too deeply. These may be what Frankl calls 'sexually disposed persons'. Some may form homosexual relationships which may be inactive, or active sexually.

Some may find other 'strategies of survival' in the relational sphere. Recently, in Australia, talking with students, I heard of a man who has a 'steady' mistress in the week but 'sleeps around' every weekend. He is surprised that his woman does not follow the same pattern. My informant supposed that this individual was 'balanced': it seems to me unlikely that any relationship he has can be anything but shallow, and that this man's promiscuity was probably a guarantee against depth. Yet this is his chosen pattern. We are only concerned with it as an example: does it represent the most human way of realizing sexual potentialities? And, of course, we are concerned with the ethical implications—of the degree of possible suffering he may cause.

Some individuals are only capable of such 'split' behaviour, in which only certain aspects of themselves can be attached to one kind of relationship, while other aspects will be attached to another. Or they will relieve the exigent demands of marriage (which they are too immature to accept) by episodes of adultery, or a series of broken marriages, moving on to new expectations as each relationship becomes too real. Others may only be capable of eroticism, and they are not too concerned about the exclusiveness of their partners. By contrast, those who know love know that replacement of the beloved is unthinkable.

Though many 'unorthodox' manifestations have their own 'heroism' and seem often the only possible solution for the individuals concerned, there is, if we are to believe the philosophical anthropologists, a sense in which there are varying levels of sexual activity. Some of these are false (even if heroic) solutions to primary relational needs, and are 'aim-inhibited', or strategies of compensation for those who have never found in themselves the capacity for mature love.

Such observations might seem smug and even cruel if it were not that they are based on *what such individuals themselves tell the therapist, when all their efforts to find satisfaction for their needs in this sphere have failed.* For this is what we learn from those, such as Masud Khan, who have worked with perverted patients over many years in psychotherapy (see Chapter 6).

Among such human facts as have been established by these encounters, the worst aspect of our 'enlightened' intellectual dogma is that it tends to endorse false solutions in the realm of sex, and to deny that norms and values can exist. This is the effect of the 'daring' pronouncements of many fashionable 'free-thinking' commentators—such as Alex Comfort's remark that 'adultery has saved many a marriage'.

As the reader will realize, I am using terms which imply an ethical basis—such as 'false self' and 'false solutions'. Moreover, I have quoted Rollo May's insistence that there is an implicit ethical statement in psychoanalytical findings.

It is too commonly believed that the ethical view of psycho-analysis is 'tout comprendre, c'est tout pardonner'. Psychoanalysis seeks to understand the meaning of human acts of consciousness, in a phenomenological way. But it also seems to have established that there is a fundamental ethical problem, which is that some individuals, even in their search for meaning, must try to live at the expense of others. These are the 'wicked'. But yet there is also wickedness in all of us. Thus, when we encounter wickedness, we tend to treat it as we do the latent wickedness in ourselves.Since this latent wickedness in ourselves is an expression of our own lack of a sense of meaning, of which we are afraid, and on which we turn our own rejection, when we encounter wickedness abroad we project our own evil over it, and turn our hate on it. Christ was thus expressing a valuable insight when he said, 'Let him who is without sin cast the first stone'. This expressed a recognition that when we wish to punish someone, we are seeking to punish some-thing that is in ourselves. Once we see this, we need to remember the other maxim, 'Judge not that ye be not judged'. One's impulse to reject the sins of others gains energy in proportion to the extent that one has failed to acknowledge such sins in oneself. This realization, however, does not mean that there can be no rejection of wickedness, and no punishment. It means that even where social coercion is necessary, it gains from developing insight into the meaning of the wickedness that must be dealt with in any society. But there is a definite need for conscience, and for effective values in all human spheres, backed up by sanctions and coercion, as Polanyi argues.

One of the insights of psychoanalysis is that some individuals need to come up against the disapproval or restraining influences of others, in order to feel real, and in order to develop their own sense of identity. But psychoanalysis also indicates that there can be ethical values which are as 'near absolute as maybe', without any need to invoke a transcendental reality to sanction them. It points to the source of ethical values in: (*a*) *concern*, that is a natural concomitant of the growth of identity in each normal person, (*b*) the 'formative principle' at work in the 'True Self' of each individual, and (*c*) the cultural embodiment of values created by these energies in each individual, by the exchange and colloca-tion of 'naturalistic ethical descriptions'. These ethical implications of psychoanalytical thought will be discussed below. They offer a humanist challenge to the hypomanic (or hate- and guilt-denying) over-simplifications of 'enlightenment' with its absurd stance of 'amorality' and to the nihilism of Sartre's brand of existentialism.

To challenge this absurd abrogation of conscience and the present cult of 'fanatical immoralism' is especially urgent in the sphere of censorship and cultural tolerance. While debate on such topics is conducted (as in, say, *The Author*) in terms of inept arguments, malignant phenomena are now developing fast in the sphere of culture which it may prove very difficult for us to deal with without forfeiting some of our genuine gains in freedom, when at last we come to see that protection is necessary.

In the light of insights from Viktor Frankl, for instance, it seems that people can be educated in what he calls a 'thoroughly decadent sensualism', while for young people to be pressed into too-early sexuality can mean that their mental horizons can become limited, and their sexual capacities restricted. The 'sexual revolution' can be said, in the light of the work of Rollo May, Frankl, and Leslie Farber, to be placing limits on individual development, and taking the meaning out of sex, and life itself. Moreover, the demand for 'total permissiveness' in the realm of culture, and 'liberating' developments which have already taken place, are leaving this area open to the fanatical immoralist who is now threatening us with a schizoid inversion of values. From Erwin Straus's point of view, to affront shame too much could obstruct the possibilities of creative love.

As I shall try to indicate, our culture is now startlingly full of hate, perversion, and a menacing dehumanization. There are, I believe, serious social and political dangers in this—the promotion of irrationalism, the debasement of man's concepts of himself, an increasing predeliction for 'false solutions', and a growing sense of loss of meaning, even in our very perceptions of our world.

It falls to the poet, educationist, and literary critic to insist that in this sphere, despite all the new insights to which we now have access, the problems remain the same age-old problems of existence, and always will, and that our ethical and social values must needs be sought in the same age-old struggle to cherish and defend human meaning in life.

Culturally, our belief that we are moving forward or gaining in this sphere is misled. Looked at in the light of such truths as we may find in traditional literature and philosophical anthropology, many modern 'sex' books and theories appear absurd. Some even ignore, disparage, or dismiss the inwardness of the sexual life which is a major source of our sense of significance. Compare them with a great novel, and their ineptness is exposed. For instance, consider all the anguish that Jane Austen records, in young people who are trying to find themselves 'what it is they really want' in terms of a partner—what it is the 'true self' wants, beneath those false solutions to which one may allow oneself to give assent. Captain

Wentworth in *Persuasion* only finds out, despite his conscious persuasions, and despite his angry revengeful determination, that he cannot escape from the inward intention, manifest in some daimon within himself, some tacit dynamic in his true self, which has chosen the heroine for his 'significant other'. For both Anne and himself, fulfilling their own inward 'intentionality' is an anguished pilgrimage: in the end they discover the truth expressed in Dr. May's 'ethical statement' quoted above.

How strange it is to turn from such a novel, to a modern book of fiction or non-fiction in which sex is treated with cold detachment in language of triviality. (Over a girl's shoulder in a Melbourne tram I read, 'stop farting around and undress me'.) In these, often, sexual activity is treated as if it 'doesn't matter' to one's inward selfhood and may be dissociated from the problem of life.* Many modern 'non-fiction' books on sex give instructions for performance as if one were a machine, together with a few hints on etiquette and superficial self-questioning. People seem even able to believe that sex on the stage, utterly separated from love and the personal, and exposed to the objectifying effects of scopophilia, is a 'liberation'. What travesties of human truth one finds in such cultural artefacts and their absurd acclaim—popular and widespread as they are! Often, where attitudes are pretending to be 'scientific' they are most irrational and falsely subjective, full of hate and the impulse to debase man, not least by making him into an object. How much better a guide to the deepest sexual problems, in the widest sense, are novels such as those of Jane Austen or E. M. Forster, or the poetry of Donne, Marvell, Yeats, Wyatt or Chaucer.

It has been a great relief to the present writer to find that so many psychotherapists endorse the kind of truth we find in great literature. Indeed, these endorse one's attention to the best creative literature as one most valuable source of awareness of our existential needs, not least because it conveys those complexities of wholeness, of inner psychic reality, with which we must live, in our sexual life as in any other aspect of our being.

The implications of the work of many schools of thought in philosophical anthropology thus confirm what, as a 'literary' man one had always believed. They also confirm one's aims as a teacher. In education, we have been trying to foster in children that kind of creative imagination which can have vision sufficient enough to conceive of a world they wish to create and to find meaning in their world as they perceive it. One would hope that, as they become youths and adults, they would develop the capacity to inform their

---

* See my analysis of an Iris Murdoch novel in *The Masks of Hate* (Pergamon 1971).

own personal relationships with meaning in this way, as the deepest source of 'ethical living' in their sexual lives, as in all other living.

Yet one knows that children inevitably encounter a world and a culture (not least a 'pop' culture) which threatens this realm of creative intentionality, especially by dehumanizing sex. One only has to witness the delight in a new sense of value which a backward child derives from creative effort, to see the power of culture for good in our lives. What is the effect on the same child, become a youth, or an adult, of the 'teaching' of pornography, the obscene 'pop' lyric, or the 'sex' film, book or television play? I hope this chapter explains why, as a poet and educationist, I am concerned about the subject of this book.

The stages of my argument will develop as follows. First of all I shall try to alarm my reader about what is happening. Next I want to try to show that the present deterioration in our thinking about sex has its origins in the limitations of Cartesian-Newtonian concepts of the nature of knowledge. That is, its origins are in a science which tends to see man in terms of 'nothing but' an agglomeration of organic functions and material processes. This approach leaves out of account his consciousness, and the realities of 'sign' and meaning. It also separates off, in an absurd way, the functioning organism from man's culture and 'spirituality'—spirituality here being used in no religious sense, but in terms of the 'specifically human dimension', as Frankl puts it.

Because this 'objective' view of man is so simple-minded, and because it leaves out of account what Marjorie Grene calls 'the category of life', it places severe limits on our awareness of man's creativity. Implicitly it has come to limit his view of his sexual potentialities, and in the consequences of this naturalism and physicalism in our attitudes to sex the 'sexual revolution' tends, I believe, to narrow our sense of human possibilities, rather than open up new perspectives.

If, however, we accept consciousness and try to approach man's existence, including his sexual existence, in a 'whole' way, the question arises of what we can take to be 'truth' or 'fact' in human life. Here I turn to 'philosophical anthropology' and try to indicate what it has to tell us about sex and existence. This includes psychoanalysis since it ceased as a discipline to give total assent to the naturalistic reductionism of Freudian instinct theory, and philosophical biology as it becomes phenomenological, and takes into account consciousness, meaning and inwardness.

Some of the most recent explorations of psychoanalytical thought have been of the deepest problems of human identity at the core—where the capacity to 'be' is established by the mother's 'creative reflection' Where this drawing out of humanness has not been accomplished successfully there is a 'schizoid problem'. The diagnosis of the schizoid problem is one of the most significant areas of recent psychoanalytical thought, and this will be found to be tremendously relevant to the present topic. For the crucial question of the schizoid problem is the need for some individuals to base their sense of identity on hate rather than love, and to try to live by desperate and tragic moral inversions. These individuals have a special interest in culture and thought—and many of them become reformers and revolutionaries. Yet in their thinking there are two predominant false strands. They cannot easily find 'what it is to be human', and they are prone to seek a logical stability in complete moral inversion. This in its turn leads to a fanatical immoralism—and it is this, I believe, which bedevils our attitudes to sex today. The whole tendency to separate sex from the whole fabric of existence, which I am discussing here, arises from this schizoid tendency in an active minority, and in our own minds.

This threat of moral inversion, and dehumanization, coming from the schizoid minority, must be linked with yet another source of insights coming from psychoanalysis. The most recent insights of D. W. Winnicott and others, into schizoid problems, have been employed in the study of perversion. Masud Khan, a disciple of Winnicott, has made a special study of perversion, not least by analysing a number of perverts himself over the last twenty years. His theories of perversion have startling implications for culture and thought at large.

The pervert often has schizoid characteristics, and, as Kahn concludes, his perversion is a flight from madness. Thus, his approach to reality has an urgent quality and involves him in all kinds of activities designed to create a certain atmosphere, and a certain 'dream', in which others become involved. It will be argued that many prevalent attitudes to sex in our culture belong to the dream-like factifications of the pervert. These are found in many areas of our culture and thought and are tremendously powerful—but in the light of philosophical anthropology they appear as false, and even malignant. We know them to be so, in the light of what the pervert himself tells his analyst, when all his false solutions based on them have broken down, and he confesses in a genuine rather than in a false way.

From this examination of some of the sources of truth about human needs and nature in the sexual life, I shall go on to look at the ethical questions raised. From what I believe to be a position on which it is possible to base discrimination, I shall go on—with some dismay—to examine some of the manifestations in our culture which deal with the sexual. This will involve a look at the 'scientific' approach to sex in sexology; and then a look at some problems of sex in culture and prevalent attitudes to it. In the end, however, fortunately, I believe I find that, from those who are dealing in their daily work with individuals in deep sexual distress, there emerges a hopefulness, and a sense of how it might be possible for man to recover his decency and to rediscover, in this realm, as in others, a new sense of his creativity and spiritual potency.

However, when we turn to problems of the political and social regulation of culture, it is obvious that 'total permissiveness' cannot be the answer, but that in this sphere of human experience our essential freedom demands a degree of coercion. This is necessary to restrain the fanatical immoralist whose aim is the destruction of meaning, and the destruction of that love which he feels he can never know.

It is also necessary to assert our right to freedom from being objectified by the pressures of dehumanization. The educational effect of the propaganda of certain zealots in the sphere of sex threatens to divide our sexual lives from our whole existence. People can be divided from their consciences, and such protective devices as shame and modesty can be undermined—as they have been by what has appeared on television, stage and screen in recent years. Yet such manifestations have, as Merleau-Ponty has said, a 'metaphysical significance'. When individuals exhibit themselves in gross obscenity in public shows, and when children have forced on them images or accounts of sex which are banal and devoid of emotion or joy, the whole realm of unique meaning and significance in sexual love suffers, in everyone. To maintain our humanness, we must protect ourselves from those who, having failed to find their own humanness, seek to attack and diminish ours—and who have a special inclination, it seems, to make this reductive attack on children.

2

What is happening: the sadist revolution

𝔊𝔊

Our first problem is to open up the question at all. 'Dogmatic enlightenment', as Rollo May calls it, is not always as anxious to look at the facts as it appears. It is neither over-willing to look at the 'inward' factors involved, nor to examine the carefully contrived perspectives of certain 'progressive' arguments. First of all, what are the facts? The Scandinavian countries are generally believed by the 'progressive' to be the most advanced countries in terms of sexual and other forms of personal freedom. Do developments there support the assumptions of what D. H. Lawrence called 'the social idea'? A correspondent in *The Spectator* pointed out in March 1962 that in Sweden there were certain manifestations that should disturb the complacency of the 'progressive' thinker—

A falling birth rate which has meant the import of 108,000 workers from abroad. A falling marriage rate and an increased rate of legal separation (divorces and separations now amount annually to a third of the marriages); a steep, continuing rise in the incidence of drunkenness (as shown by police statistics), especially in the three weakest sections of the population—the old, the women and the teenagers, whose drunkenness increased by 140 per cent, 122 per cent and 143 per cent respectively in the period 1954-9, 1954 being a base year because of the new drink laws; a continuing increase of rape, of crimes of violence and—despite the slot-machines for contraceptives—of unmarried teenage mothers; a burgeoning of pornographic magazines and the trebling of their circulation during the past decade; an increase in illegal abortions (read Dr. Axel Westman's report to the International Conference on Planned Parenthood in Tokyo, 1955) despite the legalization of abortion and the intensive propaganda for contraception; the serious and continuing spread of veneral disease among children . . . a doubling of the number of teenage criminals in the eleven years preceding 1960; a constant increase (in the world's richest country!) in the number of children and of old people committed to public institutions; a steeply rising rate of alcoholism (especially of late, among women and old people); increasing incidence of clinical neurosis, i.e. breakdown of

reason . . . (All these statements are verifiable from Swedish sources . . .
The Spectator, 9th March 1962

Yet despite these disturbing facts, says this correspondent (Mr. Desmond Fennell) we have to suffer the—

personal arrogance of Swedes towards their Scandinavian neighbours and the general Swedish assumption of moral superiority towards the world at large. Towards the end of 1960, Sven Aurén, a Swede living in Paris, wrote an article in *Svenska Dagbladet* which was significantly entitled 'The Swedish Loneliness'. I quote—

> 'A Swede living abroad asks himself constantly why we feel ourselves obliged to behave as World Conscience, distributing loud-voiced ad-monitions and reproaches to foreign countries and governments, while at the same time displaying an almost comic prickliness when-ever we become the object of the least outside criticism . . . It is a curious fact that our irresistible need to sing out what we think about the state of the world has no parallel in any country' . . .
>
> ibid., loc. cit.

A parallel arrogance is becoming increasingly familiar among 'sex emancipationists', as they steadfastly deny the implications of certain evident facts in our society.

If these were looked at more realistically, the facts might suggest that prevalent social ideas about sex are inadequate because they take man's inward or psychic life too little into account, and so are bound to lead to such disasters.

We hear much for instance about the beneficial effects of the tolerance of pornography in Denmark. But as *Le Monde* said recently—

there are plenty of sceptics . . . How is it, they note, that in outlying districts in Copenhagen—where tourists never venture—automatic vending machines for pornographic literature do such a brisk business? And how explain the sudden rise of a Danish language daily newspaper that has broken all circulation records since it started running oddly worded classified advertisements and articles, photographs and drawings in very dubious taste?

As for statistics, they may not bear closer examination either. There has indeed been a drop in less serious crimes such as exhibitionism, but rape and sadistic offences continue on the same scale. Certain other figures which might be more revealing are unfortunately not officially available. Thus it is unclear whether the availability of pornography has cut down on suicide, psychiatric internment and divorce, in all of which sexual maladjustment is often a factor . . .

Le Monde, 19th August 1970

Pornographic magazines and eight and sixteen millimetre films are still selling well in Denmark and a new form of prostitution has grown up.

Impresarios who vie with one another to bring out the crudest shows have no trouble finding actors and models in every sector of the population . . .   ibid., loc. cit.

Yet the (conservative) Minister for Justice, Knud Thestrup—

seems relatively unconcerned by the growth of this new form of prostitution. At the same time he sternly refuses to legalize the oldest profession . . .

'The state', he explained in a recent interview, 'has no obligation to control what its adult citizens read or see; they are absolutely free to do what they want with their private life. But those who indulge in normal prostitution generally belong to the category of the mentally deficient. For that reason, we have a duty to protect them against others and themselves.'   ibid., loc. cit.

The illogicality of this view is surely indicated by the fact that—

A young Danish woman has made a name for herself and a great deal of money appearing with stallions and dogs . . . Lately, the Society for the Prevention of Cruelty to Animals petitioned the courts to prohibit the use of four-footed animals in live or filmed sex scenes with humans . . .   ibid., loc. cit.

If animals need such protection, so too, surely do those human beings who are either prepared to perform group sex or bestiality in public, or to watch these perverted activities—performing or watching being, from the point of view of psychotherapy, perverted activities possibly more mentally sick than prostitution?

If we look at the facts of what is happening in Denmark we are unlikely, if we are concerned with *meaning*, to be satisfied with the kind of 'research' which is only interested in whether 'sex crimes' have gone down in numbers. For, in the light of existentialist psychotherapy, it could be argued that the whole manifestation of liberated pornography has a symbolic meaning which is itself reductive of man. The *toleration* of perversion can have its own meaning, and can communicate abroad the implication that pscyhopathological 'solutions' are socially acceptable. (Of course, we have the same thing in war, which is, or was, a socially acceptable psychopathological solution to the problem of national identity.)

In Denmark, for instance, there are slot machines in which pornography is displayed night and day, and is available to children. At the Sex Fairs naked models were masturbating on the stands with automatic vibrators, to the amplified noise of orgasmic breathing, while it was possible to watch acts of group sex in a demonstration room.

From the point of view of the enlightened liberal such things apparently represent a new 'freedom', and it is a 'mature' society which can tolerate them. From my point of view they are psycho-pathological and perverted—and the toleration of them seems itself a dangerous form of dissociation. It was dissociation that enabled people to calmly work as usual while fixing the gas pipes and ovens in concentration camps: such disasters of dissociation begin in the minds of men. That usherettes can calmly sell ice-cream and programmes in the theatre when couples are simulating intercourse on the stage, as in London, or that people can sit drinking lager at tables while a man has intercourse with two women at once on a stage, as in Denmark, are manifestations of the same kind of dissociation. The 'coolness' manifests a mad splitting of normal reactions—of love, passion, shame, envy, modesty and meaning—from a perverted voyeuristic attention to meaningless activity. This, in its turn, brings a disastrous separation of values and ethical considerations from true erotic development, and perception and action in life, in general.

To look at such facts as the 'progressive' looks at them is to look from a point of view 'imprisoned in physicalism', according to which man is merely a bundle of functions. This 'objective' view has now become a dominant way of looking at life, dissociated from feeling and values which now appear unreal and irrelevant. If we look at them phenomenologically, in the light of philosophical anthropology, in terms of their inwardness and taking account of the elements of consciousness, imagination, symbolism and mean-ing involved, they appear perilously nihilistic, since they deny everything that we are.

So, when I read (June 1970) of a 'rock' gathering of youth in America, at which naked couples had sexual intercourse publicly on rafts in the swimming pools, I feel that values, meaning, and sanity are menaced. I am more concerned because such develop-ments are often happening not under the influence of theoretical principles (not even evil ones such as Nazism) or moral fanaticism, but as the consequence of the needs and character of an entertain-ment industry which shows it is all too willing to sacrifice human-ness to its profits and its continuing activity. Following the same phenomena at Woodstock, films and magazine accounts prompted imitations elsewhere. In such cultural media we have powerful forms of education which among other things implicitly seek to persuade millions of young people that depersonalized sex in public is 'love', and is the acceptable mode of behaviour. This is only one naive example: there are (increasingly) many others.

To me such propaganda is a form of teaching, and its inevitable effects seem to threaten everything I have tried to achieve as an educationist. For such manifestations seem, from the 'inward' perspective, not only to manifest a failure of love and creativity in a form of perversion, but to be aggressively directed at reducing the capacities of others to love and to be creative, by involving them in scopophilia and other perversions which, in Straus's words, manifest a 'disturbance in man's communication with the world' (see his analysis of voyeurism discussed below, pages 167 ff.).

Some of the more extreme activities of sexual emancipation are to me no 'breakthrough' into 'liberation', but rather seem to belong to such extreme dehumanization that we can only speak of an incipient fascism. Yet of course, the echo of these is already with us, with the arrival of the 'Sex Super Market'. To me it is significant that those attending the Danish Fairs were largely German men brought up under the Nazis, (i.e. men born about 1940 to 1945). It is possible that this phenomenon is but the tail end of Nazism and the Nazi destruction of values.

From my point of view, some of the younger generation have been disastrously involved in such sexual nihilism. Reporting from West Germany, Charles Whiting wrote of how—

In recent months, for instance, radical students have distributed leaflets in Hamburg's grammar schools which give the pupils the 'facts' in a decidedly direct and crude manner, and urge them to get rid of their virginity 'because it's old-fashioned and we're against old-fashioned things.' In a West Berlin holiday camp for teenagers, the supposedly shocked press discovered that the boys and girls were sleeping together with the express approval of their youngish camp leaders.

Two months ago a group of radical teenagers made love publicly in a stadium in front of many thousand spectators in order to 'shock' them . . .   *The Times Educational Supplement*, January 1970

Here surely we have dehumanization manifesting itself as 'radical', and in such a way as to remind one horrifyingly of the depersonalization of sex under Hitler.

My remarks, however, must appear naive to individuals who are continually in contact with commercial and *avant-garde* art of all kinds. Preparing a work on the mass media and feeling that my attitudes were perhaps uninformed I looked up various magazines in the library. The experience I found deeply disturbing, not because the material was 'aggressive', but because in so many artefacts the obsession with sexuality was so compulsive and bizarre. Almost every issue of the journal *Films and Filming*, for instance, contained a picture or pictures of naked couples in sexual intercourse, or undressing one another. Virtually every film seemed to have offered this particular kind of still for magazine use. Not content with this, the voyeuristic element was often deliberately exaggerated ('her husband watches through the keyhole'). By contrast with ordinary life there was an exceptional preoccupation with perverted sex—groups of naked people lying together, individuals torturing others (*De Sade*, February 1970), or photographing others while they copulated (*Danish Blue*, March 1970). There were photographs of a prone nude woman with a face between her legs, 'trying a sexual experiment', of girls in leather bikinis with long whips in their hands, and a man with a top hat hanging on his erect penis. Indeed, there were, throughout the magazine, photographs of every conceivable sexual perversion, some of which were so bizarre that it must have required extraordinarily unbalanced minds to have conceived and planned their performance on film.

Never before in the history of man can there have been such a cultural manifestation which concentrated so exclusively, and with such devotion, on deviant sex 'from the outside'—offering its audience such a continual stream of dehumanized sexual images. Yet even the most extraordinary of these films were offered by the magazine with a note of glad triumph, if the films had 'managed to get a licence'.

What is even more alarming, however, is the blandness with which all this is greeted. As the exploitation of symbols based on perversion is increased for commercial reasons, so more and more absurd vindications are written by apologists, and the tone, even of provincial film reviewers, is increasingly acquiescent. For instance, your normal film-goer may be shocked by the elements of cannibalism in Godard's *Weekend*, or perhaps the shot in another film by the same director in which a fish is inserted into a girl's vagina before she is killed to eat. But not so the reviewer of the film in the local press, who heads his piece, 'Inhuman idea? Remember Swift' and writes—

The film is Swiftean in conception and its disgust of life. It would be as ridiculous to accuse Godard of inhumanity as to suppose that Swift really advocated child eating as the answer to famine. It really is intensely moral and real.   The *Cambridge News*, 24th November 1970

I have tried to analyse such developments in *The Masks of Hate*. Here it will be necessary to trace the origins of schizoid moral inversion again. Of course Godard's film is 'moral'—but in the service of a total reversal of values so that evil becomes good and good, evil. It belongs to fanatical dehumanization: but fashionable criticism has managed to get this accepted as 'liberating'.

The naturalistic view of man has left us with no grounds from which to take alarm at such developments in our culture: if it is natural for man to be aggressive and sexually rapacious, then the emergence of brute force is only to be expected and accepted. The emergence and celebration of the inhuman is only to be expected, too. There seems to be no 'real' position from which to object.

We have a tremendous problem of shifting perspectives here. An educated person, moreover, may have no essential humanistic values by which to reject the reduction of man to a mere organism at the mercy of impersonal forces, or the cult of nihilism that endorses hate. So, even in the programme of the Cambridge University Film Society we find films given an endorsement which exclaims that such and such a story of perversion is 'not marred by twentieth-century psychological interpretation' (which means that values and human truth are not invoked) or that another represents 'Britain's first Sadist film'—as though these were signs of cultural advance. In the implicit rejection of 'philosophical anthropology', and of the truths upheld by philosophical biology, there emerges an anti-intellectual impulse, and an irrationalism which do not trouble the student as they should. He is even untroubled by the nihilism of the 'underground' press and its anti-human destructiveness (a student told me 'what we need is more meaninglessness').

Where such reductionism takes hold of educated minds, I believe we have grave cause to be worried. In our time one important source of meaning, love, is being reduced to mere sexuality by influences which have great prestige. All our students are exposed to pornography, and 'underground' films, all of which are enthusiastically applauded by *avant-garde* criticism. Behind these manifestations are philosophies with intensely destructive aims. Viktor Frankl, the existentialist psychotherapist who survived Auschwitz, says that he is 'absolutely convinced the gas chambers of Auschwitz, Treblinka and Maidenek were ultimately prepared not in some Ministry or other in Berlin, but rather at the desks and in the lecture halls of nihilistic scientists and philosophers'. Polanyi sees the fanatical immoralism of our time as the inevitable outcome of naturalistic theories of human make-up. What catastrophe are the sexologists and 'free-thinkers' of our time, in the realm of sex, who deny man's spiritual qualities, values, and creativity, preparing for us? The young are certainly being rapidly and profoundly influenced.

Though it is perhaps not quite exact to speak of fascism, there are many aspects of the present scene which seem likely to generate a situation in which fascism could breed. Fascism, as Polanyi shows, arose out of inverted moral fanaticism, and psychoanalysis has been able to show that this kind of inversion is based upon the substitution of hate for love, by the schizoid minority, to whom such immoralism is a matter of life and death. To substitute hate for love has what Polanyi calls 'the logical appeal of the apparent stability of the total inversion of values'. Below, as we shall see, there are now valuable insights into this problem coming from the 'schizoid diagnosis'.

All this can be seen to belong to desperate attempts to find something 'real' in a society where things have gone meaningless. But yet it seems to have taken a 'black' and widdershins direction to which one can only give the name 'fascist'.

About the time the concept of 'sexual fascism' came to mind, I was relieved to find the terms already being used in American comment. The existentialist psychotherapist who sees the schizoid elements in our society is also deeply alarmed by some of the more extreme forms of sexual dehumanization. Rollo May for instance questions many of the prevalent attitudes of 'enlightenment'. Discussing *Playboy*, for instance, he quotes Harvey Cox, from a symposium at Michigan State University in 1961, who said: '*Playboy* is the latest and slickest episode in man's continuing refusal to be human . . .'

May also quotes Calvin Herton, a poet and sociologist, who in discussing *Playboy* and the fashion and entertainment world, speaks of the 'new sexual fascism'. Of *Playboy* itself, May says—

The illusion is air-tight, ministering as it does to men fearful of their potency, and capitalising on this anxiety . . .   *Love and Will*, page 59

The 'air-tightness' is that of a cultural manifestation which nowhere touches life as we know it—indeed, for those who seek to create this dissociation, it must not be allowed to. *Playboy*'s triumphant special issue called *The Sexual Revolution* is fanatical propaganda which is concerned to shout down any insights into the objectification which Hefner's organization is spreading. This syndrome manifests that schizoid separation of passion from activity, of love from will, which Rollo May diagnoses at the root of our psychic impotence in the modern world. The 'schizoid diagnosis' reveals our obsession with sex as a manifestation of our fear of love—a mark of dissociation from our own deeper needs. Vivid epitomes of this breakdown in the sexual sphere are the *kitsch* and *ersatz* pictures of nude models in 'sex' magazines. May finds in their dead-pan faces the same blankness of expression as is found in gravely ill schizoid patients. The same blankness may be studied on the faces of participants in certain activities in the American *avant-garde* theatre: for instance, in one of the illustrations of the recent edition of the *Journal* of the drama department of New York University, a group of devotees are watching simulated sexual intercourse between characters with exactly this blank expressionless look, expressing neither shame nor joy. The same blankness of face is now a feature of our cultural demoralization: people are 'not worried' where they should be.

These schizoid elements permeate the whole phenomenon of 'sex' in our culture. We need, I believe, to see the symbolism of the prevalent cult of 'sex' as being something quite apart from the meaning of sexual reality in life; though of course, it has its influence on our actual experience of the sexual.

The schizoid element here has a social significance, because to the schizoid individual the 'other' is regarded as less than human, and he wants to objectify him. One cannot, therefore, have a free society in which individuals are regarded as equal, if schizoid attitudes to human nature predominate. To be able to recognize the equality of the 'other' in sex means that one must be able to accept one's need for the other, but be able, too, to allow the other person to exist in his or her own right. To do that, means one must accept one's own dependence, and this means facing one's own weaknesses —and this can be painful. The appeal of 'schizoid' sex is powerful, because it has the immediate effect of making us feel 'strong' in terms of the identity, by separating sex functions from love and 'weak' feeling. It fends off weakness by 'masculine protest', in the denial of 'female element being'. These terms will be developed below, and when we turn to culture we shall examine the exploitation of sex as a form of 'bad thinking' such as is found in patients under psychoanalysis. As Harry Guntrip reports, some schizoid patients with feelings of emptiness need continually to sustain 'bad thinking' in order to hold a self together. In the background is the 'taboo on weakness' which Guntrip speaks of as underlying what Ian D. Suttie called the 'taboo on tenderness' in our society.

In its extreme forms, such 'bad thinking' and such 'hate' solutions can become a form of collective psychopathology. As Winnicott says, it is because of their unconscious fear of woman that men put themselves under a dictator. In so doing they act out of a nameless fear of the 'imago' woman who emerges from our primitive fears of the 'castrating mother', and of annihilation. This woman symbolizes men's own feminine vulnerability, and so any collective 'masculine protest' manifests a fear of humanness and the sensitive emotional life. Flying from the complexities and dangers of love, men may fly into false solutions based on the purity of 'pseudo-male doing', and hate. So, they give allegiance to a trend which seems to offer magical and pure solutions to the old problems of weakness and complexity.

This 'masculine protest' of collective fascism would seem to me exactly parallelled today in such an event as the Danish Fairs, or the Kronhausens' exhibitions of Erotic Art. All such phenomena involve putting oneself in submission to a larger-than-life manifestation which encourages one to suppress one's own more sensitive and vulnerable daimon, one's 'little feelings', in favour of something outward and portentous—as at the Nazi rally. What ambivalent, normal, striving private personal relationship between two human beings, full of anxiety and timidity, can assert itself against a public 'sex fair' in which views of sexual intercourse are projected on huge cinema screens, 'complete with sound-effects', with an export industry in the background running into millions? From my point of view what we have here is the ultimate reduction of humanness to pragmatic utilitarianism and commercial homunculism. The same fascist elevation of 'masculine protest' sex in *Playboy*'s *The Sexual Revolution* is not accompanied by a balance sheet of Hugh Hefner's vast, and cynically acquired, fortune. Yet the liberal is supposed to endorse all these horrifying trends as a new 'freedom'!

Such dehumanization is nowadays openly endorsed by such public figures as the former Bishop of Woolwich, John Robinson, who recently, in an interview in *Playboy*, praised some photographs of a nude dancer, complete with pubic hair and all. Such comment no doubt seems to some to be made in the name of 'freedom', 'openness' and 'candour'.

Yet surely from a serious point of view concerned with human phenomena, the 'girlie' magazine is a form of scopophile perversion, if only a mild one. It has certain side-effects, which we need to examine from a concern with what Frankl calls 'psychological hygiene'. 'The psychological dangers', he says, of 'materialist eroticism', which reduces the partner to a possession and the sex act to a commodity, are that these 'take sex to be a mere means to the end of pleasure' in meaningless sensuality.

Below we shall try to analyse the origins of propaganda for perversion, in the need of the pervert to make others 'a sort of thing in his dream'. This insight I believe we need to apply to many propagandists for dehumanized sex.

To seek to vindicate their continual pursuit of false solutions in mere sexuality or superficial eroticism, such individuals must strive to convince us that aberrant behaviour is not a manifestation of weakness, but rather of strength. The result has been a disastrous confusion of attitudes.

Some of this confusion is caused in the name of 'objective' approaches to the nature of man and society, which, when examined, are not very objective. For instance, in *Eros Denied* Wayland Young compares 'non-orgy' societies with 'orgy' societies, in relation to problems of identity. He says—

Take a husband and wife. If they live in a non-orgy society, their sense of identity is continually buttressed by their monogamy; they both know who they are and are reminded of it by the fact that they are married to each other.   *Eros Denied*, page 122

What is interesting is the astonishing change of tone when he turns to the 'orgy' society—

If our husband and wife live in an orgy society, things will work rather differently. Once or twice a year they will go out and eat and dance and get drunk and fuck absolutely anybody, without even knowing who they are. *The whole point of an orgy is not to know who one's partner is.*

Otherwise, presumably, one starts thinking, 'Do I love this person? If I do, would I not rather be alone with them? If I don't, what the hell am I doing here?'

At an orgy, their own identity as individuals gets no buttressing from the identity of the unknown other. . . . *when one is fucking an unknown person* there is no reflection, no confirmation, and the identity of each one runs out to meet the identity of each other in a common pool . . .
op. cit., page 122 (my italics)

The first quotation might be accepted as having a tone appropriate to anthropology. The second is different. Not only does it misrepresent anthropological evidence. (As J. D. Unwin says, 'So far as we can tell, complete sexual opportunity has been denied to every human being, for in every human society known to us there were always some women to whom a man could not have access and some men who were denied to every woman'.*) There was never any society in which it was permissible to 'fuck absolutely anybody'. But why is the passage so enthusiastically written, as if it were a personal confession ('When one is fucking an unknown person . . .'), as if the reader were being invited to identify with someone at an orgy?

A genuine anthropologist would surely feel that to take on such a tone might have a bad effect on his readers. It might make them feel somehow unsophisticated or unfashionable, or even perhaps not 'objective' in their approach to human sex, if they weren't prepared to see the problem in such a 'value-free' way. Or it might persuade them that values were so relative in this field that perhaps they should try a sex orgy, to see what happened to their identities. That is, the tone adopted has the effect of 'breaking down the barriers of shame', and inducing, by a kind of propaganda for 'collective' sex, people's normal and natural feelings which are that such group sex is a manifestation of flight from emotional surrender and from the creative secrecy necessary for love.

By considerable emotional bias in the writing, that is, Wayland Young seeks to make the orgy seem an acceptable mode of behaviour for *us*—despite all the indications to be found in

* *Sexual Regulations and Human Behaviour* (Williams and Norgate 1933).

psychoanalytical writing and even anthropology that might make one doubtful. Most significant are his references to 'reflection', in the light of Rollo May's passage on the 'ethical statement' quoted above (p. 8), involved in the relationship between our need for 'confirmation' from the object of our love, and our capacity to perceive the world. Implicitly Wayland Young is seeking to deny this ethical statement. Yet the study of sexual behaviour in primitive peoples and in history made by Dr. J. D. Unwin in *Sex and Culture** would seem to confirm it. Unwin indicates that it is impossible for human beings to enter our 'rationalistic' stage of society unless 'the mothers of a future generation spend their early years in a tradition in which sexual opportunity has been reduced to a minimum by such regulations as compel both the male and female to confine themselves to one another for the whole of their mortal lives'. Roughly speaking, this scientific view established that marriage and object-constancy are the basis of a rational and complex society—and you cannot have one without the other.

But Young's persuasive, personal tone has the effect of making it seem that orgiastic behaviour is perfectly acceptable in our kind of society too. It has the effect of making us feel that if only we look at the phenomenon 'realistically' and reject the value-systems of Christendom, there is nothing wrong with such perverted behaviour or with the rejection of responsibility in sex. As Frankl says, the sexual partner who is 'replaceable' cannot burden a man with responsibility. She has no value as a person, and the man simply 'has' her. Such sexuality has become detached from the whole human person and his deepest needs, and from meaning. The body is reduced to a functioning machine, and the woman degraded to the status of object. As the work of Erwin Straus, Rollo May, Masud Khan, and Viktor Frankl indicates, it is the aim of the pervert to make the 'other' into an object, in whom personal value and complexity are reduced to a minimum. This ambition is driven by a basic dread of 'emotional surrender'. The effect of Wayland Young's enthusiasm for collective sex in the passage quoted has the effect of denying such truths, and endorsing false solutions to sexual problems.

Such a division of sexual activity from emotional commitment and meaning is a manifestation of the schizoid dissociation in our society which Rollo May analyses in *Love and Will*. It cannot be accepted without entering into dissociation from the created values of our civilization, and from our own 'healthy moral sense'. A critic of my point of view says that 'Wayland Young is merely

---

* *Sex and Culture*, O.U.P., 1934, the full study from which the quotation above was taken.

stating a fact': but his tone here is hardly factual! He is using a selection of facts from history and anthropology to endorse a powerfully emotional argument in favour of what psychotherapy would see as aberrant behaviour.

We should, I believe, regard such enlightened persuasions with grave doubt, because they are likely to promote dissociation. Dissociation is something we recognize in a soldier who simply 'carries out his duty' and shoots civilians. Or we recognize dissociation when a racist who is otherwise law-abiding and decent turns his venom on a Jew or a negro. We are disturbed when we read of how a large number of people sat at their windows around Central Park in New York and watched a murderer stalk and kill his victim, while doing nothing about it. But in the realm of sex we are, in some strange way, prepared to be blind to dissociation. Yet Wayland Young's strange paragraphs on the orgy are almost as dissociated as the words of Susan Atkins at the Manson trial: 'Remorse? What I did was right for me!' That is, Young appears to be trying to persuade us to accept a moral code, or an amoral code, in which it would be possible for us to permit ourselves to do things which would otherwise, without his persuasions, be recognized by us to be immoral. And not only immoral for, as his passage indicates, what is involved is no less than the forfeiture of our 'ego-boundaries'. The significance of this will become obvious when we turn to Masud Khan's analysis of the persuasive talents of the pervert.

By such 'enlightened' arguments, I believe, what is being spread abroad, even with the best intentions, is a form of schizoid dissociation in the realm of sex that has its roots in our 'physicalist' or 'naturalist' approach to man. The escape from being human and from human values is combined with the appeal of possibly becoming a Big and Bad Sinner—and so 'someone' rather than an insignificant 'nobody'—which is, as Guntrip points out, the appeal of schizoid (or 'hate') inversion, in an age troubled by the 'taboo on weakness'.

Here we have much to learn from Leslie H. Farber's account of the occupational hazards of treating schizophrenics.* Our culture (as Rollo May suggests) is rapidly becoming dominated by schizoid influences and may be compared in some respects with the atmosphere encountered by the doctor who treats schizophrenics. As Farber says, one effect of this ethos is that the doctor who becomes influenced by schizophrenics cannot offer them his normal satisfactions because they mean nothing to such patients: so his ordinary everyday life and its satisfactions come to seem to him

---

* See *The Ways of the Will* (Constable 1966).

'artificial and pallid', and he does not mention them. Although schizoid modes essentially arise from *failures* of communication, and are 'crippled', they also have a desperate larger-than-life quality, to which the psychotherapist as desperately yearns to respond, even at the expense of his normal perspectives.

This seems to me to explain much in our culture. Because our attempts to find 'humanness' are desperate if futile, such things as the kind of sexual 'happening' prompted by the American *avant-garde*, depersonalized forms of sex (such as the orgy), pornographic magazines and obscene stage shows can come to seem more significant, *because they are schizoid*, than any record of normal relationship. They certainly seem to the world more significant than the sexual love between two lovers or married people in secret, of which there are no witnesses, and to which the world at large gives no excited attention. Though such schizoid modes are really as much marks of failure of human communication as the brothel, they can come to daunt our everyday real relationships, not least because of their seething vividness. They have all the appeal of large postures of hate, of 'giving oneself up to the joys of hating', because love is too human, too weak, to be faced.

Mere sexuality, which can be entered into (it seems) at will, and in which any partner will do, is an attempt to defeat time and mortality. So it seems to offer an escape from the anxieties involved in the normal processes of a real relationship, in which one has to wait for the electricity of love to 'happen', and in which one defeats time only by waiting for time to bring a valid moment of love. Committed passion in a marriage relationship may yield to those involved in it deep satisfactions which may not only fulfill relational needs but also generate a meaning that is 'stronger than death'. Yet the very possibility of achieving such satisfactions and meaning is something the *avant-gardist* or 'liberated' individual must fanatically deny, just as the psychotherapist treating a schizophrenic patient comes to avoid ever mentioning his own normal existence and its satisfactions.

Unfortunately, today, those who seek the truth in this sphere, are driven to be more explicit than they would want to be, because of the cunning, slickness and fanaticism of the opposition. They have to work hard to find norms by which to resist the intensity of the moral inversions which are being thrust at us from every direction, despite their (on reflection) fallacious and absurd grounds. Yet we can never claim to have anything larger than life to offer, only evanescent love, with all its normal anxieties and frustrations, as a defence against one's own 'nothingness'. Inevitably, those who speak of truth in the sphere of sex are much less likely to get a hearing than those who falsify. In this work I have tried to cope with the laborious task of obtaining a hearing for the truth about human sexual experience.

But certainly we may challenge the self-confidence of the opposition—for time very quickly exposes the drabness and emptiness of what they offer. As Frankl says, mere sexuality merely exposes an individual to time and mortality even more. Love 'can only be experienced *sub specie aeternitatis*'. Mere sex is exhausted by the discharge of tension and detumescence, and leaves one exposed to nothingness again. Yet the 'sexual revolutionary' is hell-bent to try to reduce everyone's love to mere sexuality, with restless fanaticism, and so exposes us even more to the awareness of death and time, and exacerbates the problem of meaning. This kind of revolutionary accuses his opponents of 'puritanism', and so implies 'Good be thou my evil'. His opponents are often protesting, like Frankl, that man's deepest satisfactions are bound up with person-to-person uniqueness, and values. This arouses his most fanatical spleen, and the word 'love' makes him 'puke'. His intensity of reaction indicates his fear.

In this sphere indeed today 'the best lack all conviction' while 'the worst are full of passionate intensity'. As Rollo May indicates, there is a tremendous energy behind the 'new puritanism', and its moralizing insistence that to be 'good' (or healthy) one *must* be sexually active all the time, one *must* use the 'frank' sexual language, and one *must not* be in any way ashamed, modest, reticent, delicate or private in this sphere. But he sees that this fanatical energy is itself schizoid and concerned to hold off love and passion because these cannot be tolerated. It must be vigilant, and is often intolerant, when faced with criticism—because basically it is a defence *against* sexual passion.

The sexual revolutionaries must—out of fear—seek to give the sexual life the dimension which they have chosen for it, because it is the only dimension by which they can tolerate sex. *Playboy*'s *The Sexual Revolution* proclaims that the *Playboy* movement has swept away puritanism: but *Playboy*'s depersonalized sex itself manifests a fear of love and 'being' as fanatical as that of the puritan, however much its inversion. As *Le Monde* said reviewing *Oh! Calcutta!*

people who make fun of sex in such a smutty way . . . must either be puritans in their heart of hearts, despise physical love, or be ignorant of it . . .

One would almost think that these self-styled 'liberators' were aiming only to give the man in the street a distaste for the sexual act . . .

Le Monde, Summer 1970

Rollo May, pointing out the difference of the new puritanism from Puritanism as a historical manifestation, defines the contemporary phenomenon thus—

I define this puritanism as consisting of three elements. First, *a state of alienation from the body*. Second, *the separation of emotion from reason*. And Third, *the use of the body as a machine*.

In our new puritanism, bad health is equated with sin. Sin used to mean giving in to one's sexual desires; it now means not having full sexual expression. Our contemporary puritan holds that it is immoral not to express your libido . . .   *Love and Will*, page 45

As May points out, at the heart of the 'sexual revolution' is the impulse to separate sexual activity as a machine activity (the body being a 'Machina Ultima') from the emotional life—

People not only have to learn to perform sexually but have to make sure, at the same time, that they can do so without letting themselves go in passion or unseemly commitment—the latter of which may be interpreted as exerting an unhealthy demand upon the partner. The Victorian person sought to have love without falling into sex: the modern person seeks to have sex without falling into love . . .

op. cit., page 46

Both, says May, are complementary forms of that puritanism which 'came down via our Victorian grandparents and became allied with industrialisation and emotional and moral compartmentalisation'.

Flying from 'nineteenth century puritanism' people are thus flying into a twentieth-century puritanism which simply seeks to drive love out of the window by different means. This is disguised by strange uses of terms, so that it is almost impossible now even to use the word 'love'. An actress writing about being in *Oh! Calcutta!* speaks of how, when black audiences came, the theatre was 'filled with love'. Yet how can such perverted antics as the simulated enactment of group sex, masturbation, and sexual intercourse, the handling of one anothers' genitals on the public stage, lewd calls about menstruation, and shouts of 'Prick!' and 'Fuck!' be called 'Love'?

Whereas, once, one felt that it was the authoritarian and the reactionary whose attitude to the sexual life was to be suspected, today a psychopathological tone is often to be found in popular newspapers such as the *Sun*, student and underground newspapers, and documents of the left wing. Here, for example, is a quotation from a leaflet given out at an anti-war demonstration in Melbourne, Australia, on behalf of 'Women's Liberation'. The heading is 'Women Demand the Right to Control Their Own Bodies', and the text ran as follows—

We should all get our priorities straight and organise round our own injustices, our own condition. There are a lot of people here who feel strongly about the Vietnam war. But how many of you, who can see so clearly the suffering in Vietnam, how many of you, who can see at the end of your piggy noses the women who can't get abortions, how many of you would get off your fat piggy arses and protest against the killing and victimisation of women in your own country? Go check the figures, how many Australian men have died in Vietnam, and how many women have died from backyard abortions. Yes, that's cool, they're only women, and you'll perhaps worry if your chickie gets pregnant . . . and I say to every woman that every time you're put down . . . or fucked over, every time they kick you cunningly in the teeth, go stand on the street corner and tell every man that walks by, every one of them a male chauvinist by virtue of HIS birthright, tell them all to go suck their own cocks. And when they laugh, tell them that they're getting bloody defensive, and you know what size weapon to buy to kill the bodies that you've unfortunately laid under often enough. ALL POWER TO WOMEN.

The amount of hate that leaps out from such material is disturbing. But not only do we find such psychopathological energy today in such extremist material. We also find it in the general run of commercial periodicals, too, not least from those we used to call the 'serious' weeklies, as well as in such slick sources as *Playboy*, *Mayfair* and *Nova*. Because of the tone these have adopted and because of the orthodoxy they have created, it is almost impossible to argue seriously a totally different point of view. The actual vehicles of dialogue and expression in which debate can take place have thus themselves been corrupted, and the problem is almost 'beyond the access of ethical debate'.

'Enlightenment' would seem to be hiding something, just as it turns a blind eye to the alarming implications of certain social facts. Rollo May asks—

May there not be a gigantic and extensive repression underlying all this? A repression not of sex, but of something underlying body chemistry, some psychic needs more vital, deeper, and more comprehensive than sex? A repression that is socially sanctioned, to be sure—but just for that reason harder to discern and more effective in its results?

Love and Will, page 66

May makes it plain that he does not want to go back on the development of such scientific advantages as contraception, nor does he wish to retreat from open discussion of sexual problems, into more rigid *mores*. It is not for this one challenges 'enlightenment'. But there are problems we must face and which are glaring enough, though 'enlightenment' blandly ignores them—

We pick up the morning paper and read that there are a million illegal

abortions in enlightened America each year ... We are confronted by
the curious situation *of the more birth control, the more illegitimate
pregnancies*. As the reader hastens to cry that what is necessary is to
change barbaric abortion laws and give more sex education, I would not
disagree; but I could, and should raise a caveat. *The blanket advising of
sex education can act as a reassurance by means of which we escape having
to ask ourselves the more frightening questions*. May not the real issue be
not on the level of conscious, rational intentions at all?

op. cit., page 67 (my italics)

Such fallacies and dangers are those we fall into, if we refuse to
take into account, in considering sexual problems, the fact that the
most important aspects of this realm of intimacy are 'not on the
level of conscious, rational intentions at all'. To behave and
theorize as if they were is to promote social disaster and to
contribute to dehumanization.

May goes on to discuss pregnancy as a symbolic act, as he knows
it from patients in his clinical work. The 'unwanted' pregnancy is
often desperately wanted.

We could conclude [he says of a patient, from a home in which, obviously
contraceptives and sex knowledge were never more available] that
she became pregnant (1) to establish her own self-esteem by proving
somebody wants her—as her husband did not (2) to compensate for her
feelings of emotional poverty—which pregnancy does quite literally
fill ... (3) to express her aggression against her mother and father ...

op. cit., page 69

But besides these more obvious unconscious factors, there is
still another which Dr. May detects—the pregnancy may itself be
a 'return of the repressed', a manifestation of a desire for eros and
passion, for *love* of which the dissociation of sex has robbed her.
In a world of explicitness, of self-consciousness, of dissociation
between sexual activity and love, the 'unwanted pregnancy' may
itself be a protest of a primitive kind against the deep anxiety
which freedom itself brings—

a return of eros which will not be denied no matter how much it is
bribed on all sides by sex; a return of the repressed in a primitive way
precisely designed to mock our withdrawal of feelings.

op. cit., page 70

What is believed to be sexual emancipation, May suggests, may
not be an expression of 'eros' at all, but a willed and intellectual
way of *avoiding* the deeper daimonic needs for passion and committed relationship which he calls eros—

The error into which we have fallen obviously consists not of our
scientific advances and enlightenment as such, but of using these for a
blanket allaying of all anxiety about sex and love ... The passion

which is one element of the denied eros then comes back from its repression to upset the person's whole existence.   op. cit., page 72

The personal disasters with which a therapist deals often emerge as a protest from the primary impulses in those human beings who have been misled by 'enlightened' theories—not least over the problem of *meaning*. We need, therefore, to concern ourselves more, where ethical and social problems of sex are concerned, with meaning.

From my point of view, as an educationist and student of symbolism we need to examine the meaning of cultural artefacts where these include 'sex'. Those who are willing to exhibit themselves in sexual intercourse or in a depersonalized sexual way, may be acting under an unconscious impulse to dehumanize themselves symbolically, or in an 'acting out' way—as may be those who are compelled to watch them. The proclivity for such psychopathological behaviour would seem to be latent in us all. We need have no doubt that such tendencies can be brought out in us. Parallel forms of mental illness are brought out by bearbaiting, public hangings and fanatical political rallies. Those who go to such shows out of curiosity (and we are all curious*) are fascinated by the dehumanization as much as by anything else, but, inevitably, it is impossible to join in without becoming involved in the psychopathology.

Many inconsistencies arise because a naturalistic 'scientific' approach, while it may see the problem of mental illness and corruption in physical sex, is not willing to recognize these problems in symbolism. We have seen how the Danish Minister of Justice speaks of the need to 'protect' prostitutes who are 'mentally deficient' against 'others and themselves'. There would seem to be no indication in psychoanalysis that prostitutes are *mentally deficient*. (Such a statement would be, in fact, capable of reasonably objective analysis, and statistical examination, and is most unlikely to be confirmed). So, we must suppose that by this statement the Danish Minister really meant something by his words like 'psychically inadequate', or 'mentally ill'. That is, he was making a statement that allows truths which could only be recognized by subjective disciplines. The implication of his statement is that those whose sexual behaviour is a symptom of psychopathological states require protection from the law from exploitation, by themselves or others. But why should this not apply to pornography——to scopophilia, which is also an illness?

Viktor Frankl makes it plain that the commercial exploitation of sex has dangers. He is speaking of prostitution; but since he is

---

* A sex magazine I saw recently on sale is called *Curious*.

concerned with psychic health we may extend what he says to cover cultural perversion—

A materialist eroticism not only makes the partner a possession, but the sex act itself a commodity. This emerges most plainly in prostitution. As a psychological problem, prostitution is as much the affair of the prostitutes as of the 'clients'. What we have said earlier in another connection is relevant here also: that economic necessity would not force a psychological and morally normal woman to prostitution. On the contrary, it is amazing how frequently women resist the temptation to prostitution in spite of economic necessity. That solution for economic distress simply is out of the question for them, and their resistance seems as natural to them as soliciting seems to the typical prostitute.

As for the prostitute's client: he is seeking precisely the sort of impersonal and non-binding form of love which the relationship to a commodity will give him. From the standpoint of psychological hygiene, prostitution is as dangerous as it is from the point of view of bodily hygiene. *The psychological dangers, however, are less easily guarded against.* The chief peril is that it nurtures precisely the attitude towards sex which wise sex education tries to prevent. This is the attitude that takes sex to be a mere means to the end of a pleasure—a thoroughly decadent sensualism. Sexuality, which should be the means of expression for love, is made subservient to the pleasure principle, and the gratification of the instincts, sexual pleasure, becomes an end in itself.   *The Doctor and the Soul*, page 156 (my italics)

When pornographers claim 'freedom' we should reply, I believe, that nothing forces them to be pornographers *except the need to prostitute*. This in itself is a clue to their motives. And as with the prostitute the effects of their prostitution, too, are less easily guarded against than the physical dangers of prostitution (in which, after all, individuals find a degree of personalization and friendship).

The inconsistencies in such a view as that of the Danish Minister of Justice, however, do not seem to trouble the 'enlightened' modern mind. Many comments on this subject in newspapers and magazines today are nonsensical to a staggering degree—and, indeed, sometimes completely invert the facts and truth of our experience.

For instance, let us take an article on 'What has Happened to Sexual Privacy?' in the American magazine *Look*. The author was the Senior Editor of this glossy journal, which had a huge world-wide circulation. The subject was privacy in a technological age.

One might expect technology to make it more possible for us to have sexual privacy, so that one could cry out in ecstasy in one's flat without being heard next door. Enough slag wool would surely do it? However, the writer claims, 'technology' is making privacy impossible, and therefore we must give it up. We must simply go with the tendency of the homunculist Frankenstein—

As technology increasingly depersonalises and dehumanises our lives, it is spawning in us a need to reassert that which is most basic and vital in us, our instincts. However, technology is sweeping us into an epoch when privacy is becoming quite literally impossible. It will become impossible, on the one hand because of sheer population density, and, on the other, because of rapidly advancing technical means of surveillance in a civilisation whose societies obviously intend to keep all individuals under constant watch.   *Look*, 20th October 1970

The arguments are inept: is it really likely that the world must become so crowded that lovers cannot find a secluded spot? I haven't noticed, even on a crowded liner, a technological environment if there ever was one, a lack of privacy. I quote the passage merely to show the kind of absurd powerful propaganda which is put out to persuade us to forfeit our values in favour of some new 'liberation', from a point of view which reveals, when examined, a fundamental contempt for human beings. The latter is evident when such a writer claims that what is 'basic' about us is our 'instincts'—

One paramount need thus is dawning: the need to dwell, more or less as human beings, in a society in which privacy is out of the question. Our answer apparently is going to be to adopt a mode of life in which privacy is no longer considered necessary. So I suspect that public sex should be seen as the wave of our future just as it must be seen as the tide of our innocent past.   ibid., loc. cit.

This specious argument is backed up again by a view of human nature which reduces man to a bundle of functions. (What, by the way, does the writer mean by 'more or less as human beings' in the passage above?)

Our brain started out as a rudimentary apparatus, a mechanism that responded to sensory perceptions and sensations by triggering the psychological reactions appropriate to fear, rage, hunger, and the sex drive . . .   ibid., loc. cit.

Again, we have man reduced to a model which expresses contempt for him and divests him of all those primary needs by which he achieves his dignity—his needs to symbolize, to love, to find meaning, which arise out of his capacity to question his existence.

Perhaps most people simply shrug their shoulders after reading such nonsense. But the development of the dissociated modes of behaviour which such propaganda is meant to vindicate—in this case public sex—goes on apace, and such modes are now increasingly found socially acceptable by people who would once have been shocked and who would have protested. Yet as they become demoralized they are in consequence losing the very gains of civilization itself as well as significant human rights, such as the right to privacy and the right to be protected against objectification by the 'public'. Sexual privacy has been a great gain, and it was achieved through the growth of the sense of human dignity and value that grew with the Renaissance. It belongs to those values which are found in the idealism of Science itself, and in the growth of our rich Western culture. One only has to study architecture historically to see how man came to value privacy. Moreover, there is a kind of depth of experience which is *only* possible in privacy—the open coition of Tahitian girls with Captain Cook's sailors seems simple and superficial compared with the world two lovers can create in the post-Renaissance world—as when Donne addresses the sun and tells him—

'This bed thy centre is, these walls thy sphere . . .

The value of privacy belongs to 'being', and technology must serve this human realm. Human beings *make* technology, and they should demand of it that it *serve privacy*. If technology devises means of 'surveillance', then laws must be devised to restrict these. The magazine *Look* itself, of course, belonged eminently to the age of technology.

Inevitably, the Editor of such a paper, since he has to supply a certain commercial product based on sensationalism and kodak voyeurism, has to try to vindicate his position. But in this article what was astonishing was not only the bland (or 'sophisticated') inversion of moral values but the equally 'cool' vindication of this inversion as a form of 'protest' *against dehumanization*. Here we have the problem of the corruption and misuse of the very terms we use. Even as I write a book called *Sex and Dehumanization*, I find the latter term being used to defend dehumanization itself. As so often, a subtle American demoralization corrupts language, modes of thought, and attitudes to experience all over the world.

The *Look* editor's 'philosophy' is, of course, nonsense, and no scientist would write as he does. But he takes his impulse to reduce man to a mere organism from 'objective' scientific thought, and takes over his essential pessimism from our intellectual ethos. People used to feel that sexual privacy was a human right: now that advertisers, film-makers and magazine publishers need to restore flagging markets by exploiting nudity and sex further, the value of privacy must be destroyed. How long before an advertisement appears showing a couple in coition? The Penguin Books advertisement for John Updike's *Couples* came as near as maybe to it in 1969, and now (1971) such pictures are an everyday feature of such magazines as *Man and Woman* on public sale, of not a few film posters, and also of 'pop' ads in *Oz*.

There are, of course, sincere people who believe that such 'forthrightness' is a mark of liberation and progress. Wayland Young, for instance, argues in his *Eros Denied* that—

Around the thought and act of sex there hangs a confusion and a danger, a tension and a fear which far exceed those hanging over any other normal and useful part of our life in our culture ... many, perhaps even most, people spend their lives in hesitation and confusion about sex and love. They hesitate and are confused because they are not free ...   *Eros Denied*, page 13

In our society, Young says, the full use of our freedom is denied 'by staining, by flawing, by cutting off, demarcating, labelling with a notice "this is a special corner" the area where physical desire and fulfilment have their function'. Wayland Young wants this area *not* to be 'special', and so we may take him as a typical emancipationist.

There is, he believes, a 'new class of people', because of 'technology', to whose lives the old restrictions and traditional morality need no longer apply. He believes that 'exclusion' is the trouble with sex—if excluded 'it becomes strangulated or gangrenous, like a limb beyond a tourniquet'.

His solution is the 'inclusion' of everything. He dismisses suggestions that anything will corrupt or deprave us—

We do not know people are 'corrupted' by reading 'obscene' books because we do not know what corruption is ... But perhaps we should adopt the canon of judgement by states of mind. We should then first have to decide by what means states of mind at any given moment are to be determined ... this approach is ridiculous.   op. cit., page 45

The only data he will allow is the record of such activities as masturbation, as a consequence of erotic depiction, since this is one action that could be outwardly seen! Only by such objective facts could the effects of pornography be measured in a way that could satisfy a Professor Eysenck.

Only if a statistically valid and psychologically thorough investigation of this work ('through interviews conducted by psychologists and analysed by statisticians') had been carried out could we begin to think about an obscenity law that might actually do what we want it to do ... whatever that is ... all the present law does, he says, is to express our mistrust and fear of erotic images.   op. cit., page 46

Because the effects of 'corruption' defy objective investigation, Wayland Young takes this to mean that there is no value in investigating such problems by subjective disciplines. Obviously, such a position is absurd, as Young would no doubt admit if we were discussing the cultural problem of racial propaganda, education, or the value of Hawksmoor Churches. Innumerable laws and social values which we uphold by legislation are based on assumptions that the inner life of one person can be violated by another, and improved or harmed by forms of influence. A man who exhibits his penis, touches strange women in public, or peers through their blinds is restrained. How do we come to the conclusion that 'indecent exposure' or 'indecent assault' are harmful? We decide by the collocation of subjective insights. We recognize the act of the molester as a form of mentally ill behaviour in an individual who needs others to respond in a shocked way. We may understand that *he* needs a reaction, so that he can feel real. But we also recognize that making use of others in such a way is likely to reduce their living capacities, and thus offends a universal ethical principle. Sexual exhibitionism is to be condemned because it has the effect of violating the intimate sensibility of others to whom the bodily exhibition, depersonalized and de-emotionalized, unredeemed by vision, love and imagination, is shocking *because it is meaningless*, and has a negative, insulting meaning.

Of course, it has a meaning to the exhibitor. If his penis is seen and is reflected in the face of another, it must exist, and so must he. But the shocked observer has feelings aroused which are unpleasant and disturbing, and these objectify her and arouse strong feelings in her which are uncomfortable and destructive to her emotional life. The exhibitionist is acting out a primitive (or early infantile) phantasy, and demanding from the spectator an equally primitive response—but an inappropriate one, for the exhibitionist is not an infant, but a grown man, and the woman is not his mother. Because of the disturbed elements, the effect may be to make the spectator feel mad. This mentally ill element goes with a dehumanizing dissociation, for the act is dissociated from all personal meeting and meaning. So, it is a kind of rape—a psychopathological exploitation and invasion of another being. One individual is seeking to feel 'ego-strength' at the expense of the feelings and inner security of another.

We can see, in more serious sexual crimes, how desperate such 'hate-solutions' can be, and, as Masud Khan shows, such approaches to others by the pervert can have in them malignancy and destructiveness, with roots in psychotic energies. Something strange has happened to our attitudes so that in this sphere such dangers are today denied (so that psychopathological public exhibitionism on the stage is tolerated in consequence). While such propagandists for 'enlightenment' as Wayland Young would support restraint in such a sphere as racial hate, they are fanatically anxious to promote toleration and 'freedom' for hate in the sexual sphere, even if it is perverted and spreads madness. They involve for this purpose those theories derived from physical science which deny man's inward life altogether. (The phenomenology of a Straus contradicts them from science itself.)

His failure to find this realm of 'being' and love explains the depressing effect of Young's book, with its boring lists of sexual extravagances, and its continual preoccupation with act and orgasm. His sex is always 'other people's sex', an activity separated from the unique personal experience. His view endorses as an achievement the kind of sex discussed by Rollo May as a disease of our civilization—

a great deal of talk about sex, a great deal of sexual activity, practically no-one complaining of cultural prohibitions over going to bed as often or with as many partners as one wishes.

But what our patients do complain of is lack of feeling and passion. 'The curious thing about this ferment of discussion is how little anyone seems to be *enjoying* emancipation.' So much sex, and so little meaning or even fun in it . . .   *Love and Will*, page 40

To the 'progressive', *Eros Denied* appears to be a tract for freedom, advancing the campaign for greater tolerance and self-realization. He urges 'a true image' of common humanity which, even if it portrays lovers in coition, 'will not make us recoil'. He campaigns for the 'inclusion' of erotic art, even straightforward portrayals of sexual intercourse—

. . . forthright descriptions and depictions of people making love . . . a direct celebration of what people do to express the love they have for one another and to continue their kind. Images which do this, do it successfully, and do nothing else, are extremely rare in our culture.

Eros Denied, page 42

He wants 'perfect freedom' in sex—

Perfect freedom for everyone to live in the manner he has been conditioned to by change and society, or has chosen by introspection and will. A time when men can be faithful husbands, unfaithful husbands, Stakhanovites, orgiasts, homosexuals, whoremongers, kinkies or monks . . . exactly as they choose . . .   op. cit., page 250

Yet, as often with the 'sex emancipationist', if we look closer, we find an intense moral fervour in favour of complete 'objectivity' and 'freedom', mingled with highly emotive language and severe moral judgements whose self-contradictory implications suggest subjective needs behind the argument which are not recognized— a need for dehumanization, combined with a fear of being human.

Despite his rejection of discrimination in the realm of sex, for instance, it is strange to find severe value judgements expressed in Wayland Young's book against prostitutes. Compared with his tolerant view of the ponce, this seems to express something like fear and even disgust. Some of the aspects of prostitution which Young comments on would be seen by psychoanalysts as manifestations of identity problems—

They . . . suggest a temperament that is already in some way reduced, depleted, disabled, lacking . . .   op. cit., page 132

To be 'reduced' suggests a norm from which one may be reduced, while 'disabled' implies a contrasting state, as of ability. Here Young recognizes an 'able' state in which the prostitute 'ought' to be, if she had not become a prostitute: his comments imply an 'ethical statement', such as we find in psychoanalysis, despite his denial of levels of being in sex.*

For an angel of enlightenment his tone when discussing prostitutes seems strangely aggressive—

Others let the curse make no difference . . . they plug themselves up and bash right ahead, draining between clients.
. . . little recking that her flaccid flesh is still reeking from the forty or fifty slavering lechers who have been before him, enjoys her.
                                        op. cit., page 137

This seems hardly the voice of one who really believes in 'complete freedom', and who has achieved (as psychoanalysts often have) a deep and compassionate understanding of the meaning of sexual deviation.

Again, despite his ridicule earlier in the book of the words 'enjoy' and 'laid', Young himself uses them, as above and here, with aggressive force, as for instance in: 'He took her home and laid her so well . . .'. Such aggressive verbalizations of acts of sexual possession of the woman are common in his book—

She is perhaps held down by a couple of stable boys . . . partly if one woman is fun, two would be twice as much fun . . . the painters painted pictures of women they liked to fuck . . .
                                        op. cit., *passim*

Such a tone seems to reveal a strong unconscious hostility to woman—or, perhaps more accurately, to the 'female element' or 'anima' in oneself. There are some interesting notes on the symbolism of man's fear of the anima or female element in Carl Jung's *Man and His Symbols* (page 177 ff.). Significantly he says: 'The

---

* If a whore is 'reduced', ought anyone to have 'complete freedom' to be a whoremonger?

anima appears in crude, childish form in men's erotic fantasies—
which many men indulge through forms of pornography' (page
181). We may, I believe, often suspect that those who are enthusiastic for pornography want to see woman, as a symbol of our
humanness, humiliated and objectified.

Here it may be interesting to examine the prevalence of the view
that verbal 'directness' is good in itself, and to ask if there isn't a
good deal of aggressiveness in that. The freedom to use obscene
language is nowadays demanded as if this marks 'maturity', and a
new 'freedom'. If we look closer we may suspect that the fervour
with which this new purity of impurity is asserted in itself belongs
to some form of 'masculine protest' or false toughness, expressing
a hatred of weakness, and our more 'feminine' sensitive side.

The primitive aggression in obscene talk seems obvious if we
take the view of a psychoanalytical writer, Dr. Leo Stone, writing
on 'The Principal Obscene Word in the English Language', in *The
International Journal of Psycho-analysis*—

The oral receptive attitude of sucking may provide the conceptual and
linguistic *Anlage* that ultimately eventuates in basic words for sexual
intercourse in English and ... the evolution in roots shows a tendency
to correspondence with a putative psychic evolution through predominant oral aggression, towards ... the active phallic sexual attitude ...
The International Journal of Psycho-analysis, Vol. 45, Part 1, pages 30–56

Dr. Stone also mentions the anal-aggressive elements. The use of
'four-letter' words in our culture may be a mark of aggressiveness
belonging to the 'early oral stage', full of 'anal assertiveness', and
expressive of a desire to attack others. It is as if some individuals
need to impress others with a strength of identity based on a male
kind of assertiveness, to compensate for an over-dependent 'sucking' need. The word is linked by rhyme, as Dr. Stone points out,
with taking in from the breast (by sucking) and in this lies the clue
to what it conveys of a primitive oral-aggressive need for a 'part-
object'. The preoccupation with the word among the new puritans
of the 'enlightenment' suggests that their attitude to sex is the
aggressive attitude of what Guntrip calls 'the "sucking" impulse of
the adult neurotic'.

Rollo May has some interesting things to say about the new
puritanism which fervently implies that we must use four-letter
words.

the interesting thing is that the use of the once-forbidden word is now
made into an *ought*—a duty for the moral reason of honesty ... But it is
also dissimulation to use the term ... for the sexual experience when
what we seek is a relationship of personal intimacy which is more than
a release of sexual tension, a personal intimacy which will be remem-

bered tomorrow and many weeks after tomorrow . . . [this is] dissimulation in the service of alienation of the self, a defence of the self against
the anxiety of intimate relationship . . .   *Love and Will*, page 47

The use of the 'realistic' terms, says May, tends to limit the
concept of the sexual act itself—

If the therapist does not appreciate these different kinds of experience
(as implied by the different words for sexual intercourse) he will be
presiding at the shrinking and truncating of the patient's consciousness,
and will be confirming the narrowing of the patient's bodily awareness
as well as his or her capacity for relationship.   op. cit., page 48

We may conclude, I believe, that much 'frank' explicitness has the
effect of limiting consciousness in this way, while involving us in a
hatred of being human.*

For at the same time, they can indulge that kind of aggressiveness which implicitly expresses a hatred of the 'female element
being' in our intimate life and of passion, by using words with a
powerful charge of primitive oral sadism, which spreads abroad the
sense that sex is a crude 'taking' function. As May says—

It is not surprising that the new puritanism develops smouldering
hostility among the members of our society. And that hostility, in turn
comes out frequently in reference to the sexual act itself . . . [It is used
as] a term of contempt to show that the other side has no value whatever
beyond *being used and tossed aside*. The biological lust is here in its
reductio ad absurdum. Indeed, the word . . . is the most common
expletive in our contemporary language to express violent hostility. I
do not think that this is by accident . . .   op. cit., page 48

The hostility and the contempt involved in using this 'frank'
language, express a contempt for being human, and, like many
things in the 'sexual revolution', threaten to limit our experience
rather than enlarge it.

In the light of all this it is characteristic that Wayland Young
does not want sex to be 'mysterious'. He attacks—

the simpler feeling, arising straight out of the cultural taboo with which
this book is mainly concerned, that sex is 'mysterious' that the pleasure
of it depends on the mystery, and that in a word 'knowledge casteth
out love' . . .   *Eros Denied*, page 101

To Wayland Young the sense of mystery is an enemy! With what
delight one turns back to Donne after such a dismal and inhuman
functionalism!

---

* We may deduce from my above paragraphs that when the Literary
Adviser to our first National Theatre puts naked people shouting obscenities
on the stage he wants to shrink and truncate the consciousness of his
audience—and express hostility, by an anal-oral sadistic mode.

> Some that have deeper digg'd loves Myne than I
> Say, where his centrique happinesse doth lie:
> I have lov'd, and got, and told,
> But should I love, get, tell, till I were old,
> I should not finde that hidden mysterie . . .

Young attacks the 'mysterie' as if it were the source of a taboo. He
fervently denounces the attitude that love is something 'wild, free
and holy'. Yet, a scientist such as Michael Polanyi can say, 'an
unbridled lucidity is destructive of meaning', while pointing to a
dimension of knowing which Young denies.

So, I believe, we can be very suspicious of such propagandists for
'enlightenment'. Despite its gesture towards scholarship, *Eros
Denied* really amounts to little more than the excuse to utter a
great many rude words, often in what seems a quite schoolboyish
way, to quote obscene poems, to grub out a few minor works of art
for the sake of their 'forthright' qualities, and to assemble a hotch-
potch of graffiti from the lumber-rooms of pornography. And this,
again, is true of much of today's 'frankness': it expresses essentially the delinquency of the immature, and the desire to thrust
objectification into our secret life.

With his attempt to raise Aretino, the pornographer and black-
mailer, to a status level with Galileo and Michelangelo, Young's
attitude seems virtually an attempt to seek to reverse the whole
revelation of the inherent uniqueness and value of the individual
to which such a cultural manifestation as Renaissance painting has
contributed. As Dr. Gregory Zilboorg says of humanism—

This striving towards an ideal through the recognition of man as an
individual, as the greatest ethico-psychological force of human functioning, is the humanism which has come up time and again in the history
of mankind; occasionally it would appear to have been forgotten, then
it would appear with renewed assertion . . . the Renaissance let it be
known that you cannot submerge the individual and still attain
salvation.
The Psychology of the Criminal Act and Punishment, page 106

Through his faith in Behaviourism, his rejection of psychoanalysis,
and his devotion to culture as though it provides objects to devour
with ocular sensuality, Wayland Young seems to reveal an essential denial of the 'striving towards an ideal through the recognition
of man as an individual'. He says of a painting by Courbet—

This picture does not just put you in mind of sex in general, which is
what pornography does; it makes you want to fuck that particular
person, *whoever she was.*   *Eros Denied*, page 98 (my italics)

The effect of Wayland Young's attitude is to reduce the creative symbol of a person, in all their complexity, to a simple object of scopophile hunger—so that Botticelli's Venus might become a dish, and Michelangelo's David a tasty bit of crackling. It is a strange and dismal reductionism which his book exerts on us.

One strange, if incidental, aspect of such 'enlightened' commentators on sex is the way in which they are driven not only to assault the adult sensibility, but also the child's. This manifestation is strangely common in sexual 'enlightenment'. Is it that the enlightened individual so fears his own 'regressed libidinal ego', because of its infantilism, that he seeks to attack this focus of immaturity by projecting it over the immature and attacking it there? As Guntrip points out, the fear of the split-off, weak, female element in themselves impels some men patients to attack women and girls over whom they have projected it. It is possible that some 'enlightened' individuals project their own regressed ego over children and assault it in them, with fervent moral energy.

Driven, presumably, by his own unconscious curiosity about sex-as-eating and the Primal Scene, Young seeks to vindicate the exposure of children to sex at a time when, in the light of psychoanalysis, it might well be damaging. Here we see the dangers of hate in modern 'enlightenment' in its effect on the child, who is thus betrayed by the adult's immaturity: if we accepted Wayland Young's attitude here we could again be rejecting important ethical achievements of our civilization. Young quotes a stanza of Aretino's in which coition accompanies rocking the cradle. He points out that in Japanese erotic prints the children are present—

over and over again the child of the marriage looks on, sometimes with his tiny erection to show he's keeping up with father, sometimes watching the mechanics with awed delight. op. cit., page 56

He questions our prohibition on incest, and urges that we should break the taboo of fear and mystery of sex, in order that our children should be made 'aware of their origin'.

When we call sex a blind force we deny our children, casting them off from the chain of existence which justifies us and defines them, by denying their origins. op. cit., page 107

In this attack on modesty and reticence, where children are concerned, we seem to have an impulse which is most retrograde. It threatens the advances we have made in recognizing the sensitivity of children to sexual experience and those insights which suggest we should cherish sexual awareness delicately. This impulse to force explicit male knowingness on children is a disturbing feature of Wayland Young's writing, and reappears in more recent sex-propagandists such as the Kronhausens. To invoke Straus once

more, 'Youth keeps its secret still, while age has become knowing'
—and this is part of youth's sexual becoming. The 'emancipationist' wants to invade this secrecy destructively—in order to objectify the creative eroticism he fears.

In Wayland Young we find a strange combination—a 'biological'
naturalism which allows no ethical creativity in man, since he is
but a functioning organism, aligned with a belief in an 'original
innocence', the naturalism of Rousseau which asserts that, left to
himself, man would be pure and innocent. With Rousseau, Young
must blame 'society' for our faults, in order to avoid our responsibility for our own guilt and hate. As Money-Kyrle has said of
philosophers in the past—

Some have sought to evade [the problem of hate] by treating it as
solely external. Rousseau, for example, blamed society for all our faults
and tried to construct an ideal one in which we should all be good as
well as happy . . . (he) . . . substituted, as it were, a myth of primal
innocence for that of original sin. Thus his system was achieved at the
cost of leaving something out—namely the whole problem of the
individual's sense of guilt which is rooted in ambivalence . . .
Psychoanalysis and Contemporary Thought, page 111

An 'enlightenment' which fails to engage with the essential
problems of ambivalence—of our inevitable guilt, love and hate—
can never find the deeper questions of meaning in human life to
which Rollo May points. Young's kind of progressive fervour tends
to suffer still from Rousseau's faults: 'The shadowy figure behind
the scenes of *The Social Contract* . . . displayed a child-like, injured
innocence in the face of the discovery of evil and appeared to
derive extraordinary satisfactions [moral masochism] from dis-
cerning injustices . . .' (Robert W. Daly, reviewing Blanchard on
Rousseau, *Psychoanalytic Review* 1965, Vol. 56, Part 1). As another
biographer of Rousseau warns, there is always the problem that the
liberal reformer may become a tyrant. One may detect in much of
the propaganda of the 'sexual revolution' that air of what May
calls 'dogmatic enlightenment'—as in its tolerance and blindness
to other points of view—that could easily become tyrannical. Its
tyranny is already manifest in its assault on the shame that
protects our creativity.

We still need greater tolerance in society. But to tolerate perversion need not imply the acceptance of deviant behaviour as equal
or as healthy as the behaviour of integrated individuals. As Masud
Khan shows in the essays I discuss below, there *is* perversion
which must be regarded as 'aim-inhibited' and can be unethical.
Wayland Young wants us to accept aberrance, pre-marital sex,
orgiastic behaviour, and pornography as of equal validity in the
solution of life's problems, beyond the scope of ethical values,

sanctions, or even insights into human truth. He even declares, discussing Aretino, there is nothing essentially unethical about blackmail: even here too values can be relative.

There seems to be nothing in philosophical anthropology to justify Young's 'amoral' position which is that we no longer need to choose between love and hate, true and false, ethical and unethical in the sphere of sex. Below, as we shall see, Michael Polanyi traces the fanatical immoralism of our time both to its origins in naturalism, such as could see no objections to the moral inversions of a Marquis de Sade who destroyed all doubt that stood in the way of his pleasures. Young's language at times is strangely sadistic.

Christian and post-Christian and Communist culture is a eunuch; pornography is his severed balls; thermonuclear weapons are his staff of office. If there is anything more deadly than impotence it is murder.

Eros Denied, page 107

Young is fascinated by de Sade's remark—

'To attack the sun, to expunge it from the universe, or to use it to set the world ablaze—these would be crimes indeed.'   op. cit., page 243

'Freedom' for sex is now an integral part of 'protest' and 'revolution': yet the implications remain essentially pessimistic. Our fundamental drive, the implication is, is the pleasure principle, which must be released as much as possible from the restraints imposed upon it by 'society'. Yet in this attitude the 'sexual revolution' remains essentially a Sadist Revolution, because it requires the destruction of all scruples that stand in the way of pleasure. Yet, as Frankl says, mere pleasure is but a temporary condition: man's need is for joy, love and meaning which transcend all temporary states. The basis of man's nature is not the instinctive drive of the will to pleasure, but the will-to-meaning.

From the point of view of philosophical anthropology, moreover, the simple solution of the 'progressive' seems to contain within itself somewhere a fear of humanness rather than a conviction of its worth. His 'forthrightness' itself seems to belong to an impulse to attack the realm of being, rather than to respect and enhance it— consider, for instance, the sheer ugliness of pornography in the 'underground press', at Danish Sex Fairs, and in the sketches of *Oh! Calcutta!* The reduction of shame and modesty seems more like an attempt to escape from being human rather than a desire to be more human. As Money-Kyrle says, those who pretend to have no conscience pride themselves on being supernormal: in reality they have not begun to understand themselves. What is happening in this realm seems to be moving towards a new darkness rather than towards the light.

3

Philosophy, science and meaning

The implication of philosophical anthropology is that we should always try, in discussing human problems, to keep man in his totality, as a 'being-in-the-world', in view. Such an approach is evidently very different from the approach of more academic philosophers whose concentration is on intellectual structures, divorced as far as possible from the life of the body and being. No-one is more enthusiastic than a certain kind of philosopher in the denial of 'psychic' or 'inner' reality. His intellectual scheme of existence may quite leave out of account the fact that mind only exists in a body—a body which once had a mother, out of whose psychic matrix alone can emerge the human individual, as she draws his potentialities out of him by her 'creative reflection'.

It has been the concern of the existentialists to restore man's 'totality' to philosophy. Kierkegaard, Martin Buber says, 'was of all thinkers the one who most forcibly indicated that thought cannot authorize itself but is authorized only out of the existence of the thinking man'. This particularly applies to the problem of the sexual life, for it is absurd to approach sexual experience without taking into account the being in his whole existence, and our concern here with philosophy is to find an approach which seems most true to our life's experience. As Merleau-Ponty says—

the body expresses total existence, not because it is an external accompaniment to that existence, but because existence only comes into its own in the body . . .

'The Body in its Sexual Being', in *The Phenomenology of Perception*, page 166

This unity, in our approach to man, is being striven for by various disciplines: by the philosophy of Michael Polanyi, the scientist turned philosopher, and his interpreter Marjorie Grene, who is one of the chief opponents of Cartesian dualism in approaches to the mind-body problem. It is being sought by philosophical biologists like Buytendijk and Straus. It is also being striven for by psychoanalysis, chiefly in the 'existentialist' schools in America (Leslie H. Farber and Rollo May) and in Vienna (under the influence of Viktor Frankl, who is President of the Austrian Medical Society of Psychotherapy). This work, again, links up with the studies of those such as Ernst Cassirer and Suzanne Langer, who believe that symbolism is a primary need of man—so that in looking at his nature we should place sign and meaning, and culture, at the centre of our picture, and concern ourselves with these as primary.

The effect of all these approaches is to show that it is meaning-less to approach man unless one takes into account first and fore-most his consciousness and questions of his creative freedom. To quote Merleau-Ponty again—

There is no doubt that we must recognise in modesty, desire, and love in general a metaphysical significance, which means that they are incomprehensible if man is treated as a machine governed by natural laws, or even as a 'bundle of instincts'; and that they are relevant to man as a consciousness and a freedom.   op. cit., page 166

'Modesty' and 'love' are often completely ignored in many contem-porary approaches to sex—indeed, one often finds it implied that 'modesty' for instance, is perhaps better done away with, as though it were some relic of 'Victorian puritanism'. While such an 'en-lightened' approach has the appeal of reducing something which is very complex to oversimplification, so that it seems to offer a new 'freedom', the freedom which it offers can only be a freedom from being human, and a freedom from aspects of our existence which have a deep metaphysical meaning in our lives. (Metaphysical here, I believe, means something like 'symbolic' or 'that which transcends the physical' rather than a term which invokes any spiritual dimension.)

For instance, it is now accepted by the 'progressive' in England that nudity on the stage is a movement towards a new 'liberation'. Yet in fact the exposure of the 'private parts', and the simulation or enactment of sexual acts on the stage may in fact be infringing modesty—as a manifestation of 'being'—in a deeply damaging way. These manifestations, seemingly justified by the approach to man which assumes that he is a 'bundle of instincts', may, in the light of the philosophy of Merleau-Ponty and the biology of an Erwin Straus, be likely to cripple sensitive aspects of our con-sciousness and freedom. The following argument from his work may be studied in the shadow of the revue *Oh! Calcutta!*

Usually man does not show his body, says Merleau-Ponty, and, when he does, it is either nervously or with an intent to fascinate. 'He has the impression that the alien gaze which runs over his body is stealing it from him, or else, on the other hand, that the display of his body will deliver the other person up to him, defenceless, and that in this case the other will be reduced to servitude'. Shame and immodesty, then, take their place in a dialectic of the self and the other which is that of master and slave: 'in so far as I have a body, I may be reduced to the status of an object beneath the gaze of another person, and no longer count as a person for him, or else I may become his master and, in my turn, look at *him*'. But this mastery is 'self-defeating, since, precisely when my value is recognised through the other's desire, he is no longer the person by whom I wished to be recognised, but a being fascinated, deprived of his freedom, and who therefore counts no longer in my eyes'.

Recognizing I have a body is thus a way of saying that I can be seen as an object and that I try to be seen as a subject: shame and shamelessness express the dialetic of the plurality of consciousness, and have a metaphysical significance.

The same might be said of sexual desire: if it cannot accept the presence of a third party as witness, if it feels that too natural an attitude or over-casual remarks, on the part of the desired person, are signs of hostility, this is because it seeks to fascinate, and because the observing third party, or the person desired if he is too free in manner, escapes this fascination. What we try to possess, then, is not just a body, but a body brought to life by consciousness.

Phenomenology of Perception, page 166

As the title shows, *Oh! Calcutta!* is based upon an approach to the naked body which is all 'too free in manner' and expresses 'too natural an attitude'. The cast who write about their experience speak often of their sense of 'vulnerability' and also with some contempt of the audience. The sense of vulnerability expresses that 'nervousness' of which Merleau-Ponty writes, and the emotions expressed reveal that, in their nakedness, the actors are experiencing the conflict of feelings about slavery and servitude that are to be found in such exhibitionism.

Such exhibitionism as is overtaking us on stage, film and television, therefore, can be seen as no liberation at all, but rather as likely to bring us excruciating experiences of a sense of loss of freedom, and objectification, all of which are exploited for sensational purposes.

The effect of such a conflict is no 'liberation', indeed, but has the effect of 'reducing people to the status of an object which is being exploited'. At the same time, the obscene remarks made in *Oh! Calcutta!* by the naked cast (such as, 'I expect you're wondering what she does when she has her period') are an intensifying of the hostility to which Merleau-Ponty points, as a concomitant of our feelings of enslavement when naked and exposed. The effect is to increase the sense of the loss of power to fascinate, frustration of the impulse to achieve mastery, and feelings of fear of being reduced and exploited. More damaging are feelings of being subjected to contempt and of being reduced to a dehumanized object by the mere fact of being deprived of value as a person, and depriving others of their freedom, making them no longer count as persons.

In the light of such a philosophical approach as that of Merleau-Ponty, then, what seems to the mind trained by natural sciences as a bright 'liberation' can be seen from another point of view as a loss of freedom and values. Thus, the toleration of pornography, as in Denmark, could mean that, phenomenologically speaking, what has been released is a tide of assault on the meaning of modesty, the uniqueness of commitment in love, and on the significance of love and personal value. To a Straus, shame 'safeguards immediate becoming'—and makes creative eroticism possible.

We are, however, so imprisoned in physicalism and naturalism, that it will be very difficult to escape in order to see how false our position is. For, as Marjorie Grene says, what is involved is nothing less than a complete reconsideration of our ways of thinking—

Only, I believe, when a deep-lying conceptual reform in our view of knowledge has been assimilated, when we have overcome within ourselves our Cartesian fear of the category of life, and our Newtonian simplemindedness about the nature of the nature we strive to know, only then will we be able to open our minds to a new and richer ontology [i.e. a science of being]. Such an ontology, to be adequate to the facts of our cognitive experience, will have to include the recognition of the multiplicity of forms as an aspect of the multi-dimensionality of being.   *The Knower and the Known*, page 224

What such a thinker is concerned to reform is our whole rational study of man's existence. In the face of the arrogance and complacency of opinion at large about such complex problems as sex the task seems hopeless. Fortunately, we can always rely on the commonsense of people in general, and the 'tacit dimension' by which they themselves know the truth, and try to live by it. Yet, obviously, attitudes to human nature which reduce man's stature are powerful in their influence on our attitudes to ourselves. And, as Viktor Frankl continues to emphasize, there can be disasters in men's minds, in their attitudes to themselves, which continually overtake us and wreak havoc. Our prevalent attitudes to sex seem likely to bring about another such disaster, unless we can achieve the new and richer approach to the nature of being which Marjorie Grene seeks.

Perhaps the hardest problem here is how to overcome people's inclinations at large to accept attitudes to man which are reductive and pessimistic. We need hardly mention the vast popularity of the 'naked ape' approach promoted by such writers as Desmond Morris and Robert Ardrey. These arguments are based on fragments of scientific observation which are in themselves valid enough, but are no valid basis for the generalizations in the sphere of 'philosophical anthropology' which are made from them.* Significantly, the popular success of Desmond Morris's books has been promoted by highly suggestive covers showing nude men and women—an advertising gambit which conveys by symbolism the reductionist implications of the text. The implications of the text that we are nothing but the product of impersonal forces of sexuality and aggression is that we need not feel responsibility for these forces—they are, quite simply, the nature of the beast—and so any sense we have of modesty, ethical consideration, love, or meaning are all 'bunk'. Yet this pessimistic and devalued view of man is widely popular, not least because of its dehumanizing effects, which reduce our sense of responsibility for being human.

The appeal of such theories of man is, I believe, explained by some comments of Frankl's on the appeal of the 'chorus-girl type'—

The chorus-girl type is impersonal with whom a man need have no personal relationship, no obligations; a woman he can 'have' and therefore need not love. She is property without personal traits, without personal value . . . she cannot, in her impersonality, burden him with responsibility . . .   *The Doctor and the Soul*, pages 145–6

The attraction such a dehumanized 'object' has for us is that she does not burden us with responsibility, and does not involve us in the problems of respecting (her) personal value. Woman in such symbolism stands for an aspect of ourselves, and so the 'dolly girl' everywhere reduces us and releases us from the problem of obligations to our being. Yet if it is true, as Frankl says, that 'human existence is fundamentally grounded in responsibility', then to accept such models of ourselves is to accept being cut off from the roots of meaning in existence.

Our attempts to develop a better approach to the nature of being needs to begin with questioning some of the implications of popular thought, and to see their psychological undertones. There

---

* See my discussion in *Human Hope and the Death Instinct* (Pergamon 1971) and also *Naked Ape—or Homo Sapiens?* by Bernard Towers and John Lewis (Garnstone Press 1969).

is a great appeal in completely dehumanized models, such as Barbarella, a completely non-human 'space fiction' woman, in the erotic film made by Roger Vadim. In the Danish sex fairs it was even possible to buy a 'doll' with which to copulate—

an inflatable doll which a lonely man can bring into his house. The manufacturers have thought of everything, to the most intimate detail. They may not speak, but they have heads of hair and pubic hair too; ample, generously shaped doll, closing its eyes when it is touched. The breasts are usually large. Several models are displayed—Marilyn Monroe, Jayne Mansfield, Carrol Baker, Gina Lollobrigida . . .

The Danish Sex Fairs, page 44

Associated with these are vibromasseurs, some made to simulate exactly the shape and pressures of the female genitalia, fitted with two speeds. In these we may find symbolized the total reduction of sexual activity to an activity devoid of all complexities of human being. They are, of course, forms of perversion. But they are also an embodiment of the Cartesian *cogito*, and his dualism. As Merleau-Ponty says—

There is interfusion between sexuality and existence, which means that existence permeates sexuality and vice versa, so that it is impossible to determine, in a given decision or action, the proportion of sexual to other motivations, impossible to label a decision or act 'sexual' or 'non-sexual' . . . Sexuality therefore ought not, any more than the body in general, to be regarded as a fortuitous content of our experience. Existence has no fortuitous attributes, no content, which does not contribute towards giving it its form; it does not give admittance to any pure fact because it is the process by which facts are drawn up. It will perhaps be objected that the organization of our body is contingent, that we can 'conceive a man without hands, feet, head,' and, a fortiori, a sexless man, self-propagating by cutting or layering. But this is the case only if we take an abstract notion of man in general, into which only the *Cogitatio* is allowed to enter . . .

The Phenomenology of Perception, pages 169-70

Yet who can really aspire to sustain Merleau-Ponty's careful and complex insistence of the indivisibility of being human, in the face of the Danish Sex Fairs, arrogantly upheld as the ultimate 'liberation' of man, by the discoveries of science?

Our failure here, surely, is a failure of education and a failure of science itself. What protest do we hear about the excitement registered in a news item concerning reports in *Nature* about the ambition to 'make life in a test-tube'? In *The Times* of 24th February 1970, for instance, a headline spoke of 'Progress towards a Test-tube Baby'. In an article the writer spoke of the 'possibility of biological engineering'. It may indeed be possible to set off various processes of growth in cells, and to manipulate these. It may be possible to set off the growth of a human embryo in an environment outside the body. But this is to say no more than that tissue culture has reached a certain stage of technical efficiency. What would grow could only be something which, after a while, would not be able to exist and develop within the whole complex ecology of growth within the womb about which processes, as biologists admit, we know hardly anything.

Whatever shapeless lump of tissue grew, it could never, outside the womb of one specific woman in time, become a human person, or even a viable monster of some kind. For, as many studies seem to indicate, there is a psychic parturition as well as a physical one, and this begins at a very early stage, so that there is a response of the foetus as 'being' to a 'facilitating environment'. The popular notion of a 'test-tube baby' belongs to schizoid phantasy rather than to reality, and yet there is far too little understanding of the important philosophical need to reject such a concept, because of its implicit reductionist effect. This is true of many excitements in the realm of popular thought about what 'science' can do—from headlines such as 'ARTIFICIAL MAN VISUALIZED' to the title of Edward de Bono's book *The Mechanism of Mind*. As Viktor Frankl points out, there are many books to be found which approach man as—

nothing but a complex biochemical mechanism powered by a combustion system which energises computers with prodigious storage facilities for retaining encoded information.

Quoted in *Encounter*, November 1969, page 54

He speaks of man's 'nihilistic tendency to devalue and depreciate that which is human in man'. A similar reduction of man to a machine that merely functions according to steam-engine principles is found in many books on sex in which, as Rollo May says, the body is reduced to the 'machina ultima'. The 'sex technique' book makes similar assumptions about the realm of sexual experience.

One of the best-known sexual reformers in England today is a zoologist, Dr. Alex Comfort, who has called sex 'the most popular human sport'. Dr. Comfort approaches sexual problems as a scientist, and it is interesting to note that in one of his recent books he has reached a point at which he finds himself confronted by the reality of love—

the psychiatric evidence seems now, in many people's view, to point to the same force which, in socialized primates, made us able to live in families, and motivated our personal and social behaviour, namely sexual love—extended, through the peculiar role it has come to play in human economy, far outside its original context of the desire to copulate, and made more similar to the poet Schiller's idea of 'joy'; a sexual affection, carrying the same pleasurable intensity we find in man/woman relationship, even our relationship with things . . .

Nature and Human Nature* (reviewed in *The Times Literary Supplement*, 22nd January 1967)

As *The Times Literary Supplement* said of this, 'It will be interesting to see how Dr. Comfort develops this suggestion in subsequent works . . .' From the point of view of philosophical anthropology it still shows the scientist 'imprisoned in physicalism', and only grudgingly willing to admit to realities that belong to consciousness, meaning, and culture. His paragraph implies that we are only 'socialized primates', so the essential differences between ourselves and apes—which is our primary concern with meaning, symbol, and culture also our consciousness which belongs with these—is obscured. Our capacities to find 'joy' in sex derive from the effect upon us of 'economy', so that relationship becomes a product of 'social and economic forces' rather than something inherent in human nature, and an aspect of our being. Dr. Comfort's approach to the whole question is one rooted in quantitive analysis—as if there were only a certain amount of material or energy available which, at last, was able to 'spill over'. The implication of this is reductionist in that it implies that 'joy' and love are, as it were, unnecessary trimmings of biological existence not primary aspects of our existence at all, but perquisites we have fortunately managed to pick up by the chance of socialization.

To the thinking of psychoanalysis and phenomenology, love is the basis of the capacity to perceive, so that it is not simply a matter of love 'spilling over', but of there being no capacity to perceive the world by a specifically human consciousness without the experience of love-in-relationship in infancy, and without the sense of meaning that is found in love. This is recognized by the biology of Buytendijk.† But a scientific mind such as that of Dr. Comfort's cannot easily grasp this 'other' dimension—which means also that he cannot see the limitations of his own. Thus, he comes to edit a popular magazine called *Man and Woman* which is intended to enlighten people about sexual reality, and sticks almost exclusively to the 'naturalistic' approach. It contains a great many articles, illustrations and charts which look at sex from the 'outside', as the sexologist does, in a dimension in which the meaning of sex, which is what the reader seeks, can never be found. Yet it would be quite impossible to point out to Dr. Comfort what a delusion this was.

---

* Published by Weidenfeld & Nicholson, 1966.

† See *Approaches to a Philosophical Biology*, Marjorie Grene (Basic Books 1965).

In order to begin to unravel such absurdities we have to examine the assumptions behind 'science' when it turns to a subject such as sex. First of all, it assumes that there is such a 'subject' when, in truth, as my quotations from Merleau-Ponty make plain, there is no such subject. There is only the indivisible human being. This raises the whole question of what the 'facts' are in the realm of sexual experience.

In discussing the question of the tolerance of pornography, for instance, the progressive individual will tell us that 'scientific studies' show that there has been a reduction in Denmark of the number of sexual crimes. He will also claim that there is no 'hard fact' statistical evidence that pornography ever did anyone any harm. In the face of such an assertion the liberal feels that his only authentic conclusion can be to endorse total permissiveness. He believes that it would be 'unscientific' to believe otherwise, and he believes that it would be 'irrational' to endorse the continuance of censorship and regulation. This is the kind of thinking behind reports on the problem of pornography in Denmark and America, and reports by the Arts Council Working Party in Great Britain.

There are, however, many absurdities in this approach which seem no longer evident at large. For one thing, there is an implicit reduction of man to an 'input-output' mechanism, as if whatever were put in of a certain kind resulted in behaviour of a parallel of some kind. No educationist would ever support the view that, say, by teaching a certain thing such as a reasonable attitude to cigarette-smoking or the ethical attitudes of Machiavelli, every child, or even a significant proportion of children would, in the next few weeks, apply these in their own behaviour. This draws attention, of course, to the whole question of education and the assumptions of educationists: the teacher simply believes, perhaps not always strongly, though sometimes passionately, that what he teaches has an effect. He can never prove this, and it is not demonstrable except in examination results, which we regard anyway as not very satisfactory when it comes down to what we really are trying to do in education. Education depends upon a passionate belief in the value of such processes as instruction, learning and symbolization without there being any question of the effectiveness of education ever being wholly subject to quantitative scientific analysis.

Yet when it comes to pornography we invoke 'science' to construct for ourselves a carefully contrived perspective, so that we may equally well believe that in the depiction of sex there is no question of there being any educational effect at all.

The inconsistency is bound up with another philosophical

assumption lurking in the background. This is that where the sexual life is concerned the only thing that is 'scientifically valid' is the measurement of behaviour as *seen from the outside*. Here, indeed, we find ourselves imprisoned in physicalism in such a way as to lay open our whole world to the inherent nihilism in science itself.

Yet one can see how such absurdities arise. As Polanyi points out, for some people to entertain evident 'inward' facts of experience is itself a threat to their adherence to science. Their lives are bound up with belief in science, and since their science is based on reductionist and mechanistic monism, and is held by them to be the only tenable view of the world, it has no place for recognition of consciousness. The neurologist who cannot 'find' consciousness will jump up at a conference and cry, 'At least we know that ideas don't move muscles!' (a cry which Polanyi quotes). If such a scientist were to admit consciousness or love as realities, he would be forced to admit that his methodology could not 'see' such evident facts, and so the science which he regards as the one exclusive source of truth about the world would lose its validity. He would be forced to recognize the uncertainty, including the evident fact that there are other ways of knowing (as he admits tacitly when he lets his wife deal with his baby). He must either maintain an absurd split between the man who is conscious, does scientific experiments and loves, but cannot admit these facts in his descriptions: or else he must assert that 'scientifically' love and consciousness don't 'really' exist, or will be eventually explained away one day in terms of nerves and arteries and veins.

It is this absurd 'naturalism' which undermines in a most sinister way today our attitudes to ourselves, and what we believe to be real and meaningful. We have reached a situation in which the valuable passionate endorsement of reason and empiricism in our epoch has led to an equally passionate and absurd denial of all knowledge which is not 'objective'—even though we know (as Polanyi points out) that even in learning to ride a bicycle we depend upon 'other' modes of learning, and upon such tacit capacities that belong to being as 'in-dwelling', or 'attending from', that is, intuitive knowledge, bound up with imagination, and moving from the 'inside' of our experience.

In 'scientific' psychology this leads to much sleight of hand, so that 'inward' processes can be smuggled in without being admitted. As we shall see, the sexologist is prey to the self-deceptions which Michael Polanyi indicates, speaking of Behaviourism—

Behaviourism tries to make psychology into an exact science. It professes to observe—i.e. *look at* pieces of mental behaviour and to relate these pieces explicitly. But such pieces can be identified only within that tacit integration of behaviour which behaviourists reject as unscientific. Thus the behaviourist analysis is intelligible only because it para- phrases, however crudely, the tacit integration which it pretends to replace . . .

'The Logic of Tacit Inference', in *Knowing and Being*, page 153

Just as 'Behaviourist psychology depends upon covertly allud- ing to the mental states which it sets out to eliminate' so sexology depends upon covertly alluding to and depending upon the mental states which it eliminates from its researches—both in the subjects and the observer.

Because of this failure to take into account the 'tacit integration' of normal ways of exploring the problem of love, and because it concentrates on 'looking at' sexual behaviour and seeking to relate its 'pieces' explicitly, sexology is inevitably destructive of mean- ing.

As Polanyi says, in the same essay—

By concentrating his attention on his fingers a pianist can paralyse himself; the motions of his fingers no longer bear then on the music performed, they have lost their meaning.

. . . So long as you look *at* X, you are not attending *from* X to some- thing else, which would be its meaning. In order to attend *from* X to its meaning, you must cease to look *at* X, and *the moment you look at X you cease to see its meaning.* . . . to attend *from* a thing is to *interiorize* it, and . . . to look *at* the thing is to *exteriorize* or *alienate* it. We shall then say *that we endow a thing with meaning by interiorizing it and destroy its meaning by alienating it.*   op. cit., page 146 (my italics)

All our knowledge involves, as Polanyi shows, an orientation from within the body, and imaginative projection. As we 'attend from' a thing and know it inwardly or tacitly, we 'dwell in it'. Polanyi's book springs from the discovery by a scientist (based on observations by other scientists) that the conventional account of 'knowing' on which so much of our thinking is based, is inadequate to explain many common phenomena, such as our capacity to recognize a face. There is a whole 'tacit dimension' in knowing, upon which the relatively limited modes of 'scientific knowing' are essentially based: yet this is an imaginative projection into the 'inside' of things.

If this is so, then we need to reconsider with some urgency our assumptions about human 'fact', and what is 'real', not least when we assume we are being 'rational'. But Polanyi's work makes it clear that it is most unscientific not to see that these modes exist, are valid, and underlie whatever it is we call 'objectivity'. Here, of course, we enter into many problems, of 'being-in-the-world', of time,* and of human creativity and the uniqueness of individual experience. As Ian D. Suttie pointed out a long time ago, it would be impossible to devise a laboratory experiment to discover, describe or define 'love'. Yet love is evidently a human fact. Ours however is an age in which one sees everywhere a paperback on the bookstall with a salacious cover, and the title *The Love Laboratory*. In such a phenomena we experience the 'pathology' of science. Yet, as we shall see, the sexologists who are the subject of such a work disclaim all responsibility for the effect of their studies on moral attitudes. They are, in truth, having an effect on the very way in which we experience our world.

The predominant enlightened approach to sex, to which sexology belongs, is biased in favour of excluding everything except *that behaviour which is observable*, separated from the living dynamics and intentions of a whole 'being-in-the-world'. The consequent reduction of man, with all its unconscious appeal in the way it releases us from responsibility, tends to be nihilistic. It tends to fill us with a sense of futility and impotence in the face of what seem to be impersonal biological forces over which we can exert no creative will of our own.

This reductionism arises out of a confusion between the methodologies of science and the proper philosophical implications of empiricism. Science needs, for certain purposes, to regard the world and the universe as a series of mechanisms, in a cause-and-effect relationship. This is adequate as a deliberate technique if it is used for conducting certain observations and for making and testing certain hypotheses. But it is fallacious to elevate this methodological system to the status of the *only* way of accounting for all truth so that everything in the world is taken to be, wholly and exclusively, explicable in terms of that kind of 'model'.

As Professor W. H. Thorpe has said—

There is a widespread tendency among ordinary people, and indeed among some scientists, to assume that the method of science based on the assumption that a significant understanding of natural events can be reached primarily—if not entirely—by regarding the world as an interlocking series of mechanisms can be a basis of a general philosophy. Scientists make these assumptions as a working hypothesis; deliberately,

---

* 'We *are* the upsurge of time, and creative imagination, which moulds the present and even the vision of the past and of futurity, out of its projection of what we long to be—creative imagination through which we shape the time that we are: this is our most essential gift . . .' Marjorie Grene, *The Knower and the Known*, page 143. See also *The Primary World of Senses* by Erwin Straus (Collier-Macmillan 1963) on the conceptual and epistemological confusions of behaviourism, and on the observation of life in time and space.

for practical purposes, leaving out of the picture the mind, the perceptions and the personal devotion of the scientist making the study. This approach can be called 'mechanistic monism'.

The Times, 25th January 1969

The scientific view, this biologist writes, is a 'partial view'—a deliberate restriction to certain areas of our total experience—a 'technique for understanding certain parts of that experience'. Mechanical monism, like reductionism, is of course, an essential tool for science—

but as a general philosophy it can have no validity whatever.

ibid., loc. cit. (my italics)

Yet fallacious extensions of this theoretical tool which have no philosophical validity tend to dominate our thinking today about man, not least in the realm of the relational life and sex.

It should be added that by no means all scientists fall into these fallacies. There is no call to regard the 'objective' approach to sex, for instance, as the characteristic view of 'the scientist'. As Professor Thorpe says of attitudes in science in general—

I recently heard one of the most distinguished theoretical chemists in this country state that his own scientific drive was based upon two fundamental attitudes: 'a conviction of my own responsibility' and 'an awe at the beauty and harmony of nature'. It is these attitudes which are and have always been the mainspring of the scientific enterprise—and these are essentially subjective preoccupations.   ibid., loc. cit.

The reductionist pronouncements of those who wish to substitute 'mechanism' for 'mystery' have not only had a profoundly destructive effect upon our attitudes to ourselves, but also on the prestige of science. As Professor Thorpe says—

may it not be that the present trend of young people away from science is a reflection of this misunderstanding and a feeling, perhaps inarticulate but nevertheless compelling, that, because so many scientists and technologists do indeed show a lack of responsibility, this is characteristic of science itself?   ibid., loc. cit.

One consequence of such feelings about the human irresponsibility of science and its apparent discovery of our impotence in the face of blind 'impersonal forces' makes it difficult for many to sustain a sense of meaning. This consequence surely arises from the nature of 'physicalist' science itself, which is at last being shown as philosophically inadequate. Nineteenth-century natural science was based on Newtonian-Cartesian modes of thought, and the habits of mind which have predominated in the 'science of man' belong to the 'study of dead objects'. In consequence it has been impossible for the study of man to escape from habitual assumptions that what was being observed was an organism which was to all intents and purposes inert on a bench, divorced from the living dynamics and intentions of a conscious being.

It is this which has led to the dehumanization inherent in science —tendencies which belong to what Viktor Frankl calls 'homunculism'—that is, the reduction of man, in our thinking and attitudes, to an over-simplified, mechanistic, and dehumanized model or hominid, lacking in all those creative and inward dynamics in which alone we can find a sense of meaning. For it is in raising the question of the meaning of his own existence that man is distinguished from the beasts.

Frankl decided he survived Auschwitz because of his love for those dear to him whom he never expected to see again. He is now a therapist concerned with what he calls 'logotherapy', that is, a form of 'creative reflection' in treatment which is concerned to help the patient to find meaning in his life.* He says—

Such an undertaking is more important than ever in a time such as ours, when man is threatened by existential frustration, by frustration of his will to meaning, by his unfulfilled claim to a meaning for his existence, by his existential vacuum, by his 'living nihilism' . . .

From Death Camp to Existentialism, page 109

Many of our attitudes to sex and current modes of sexual behaviour and symbolism seem to me to belong to this 'living nihilism'. In one sense public sexual activity is a protest against the existential vacuum of our age: but this sex has also been separated as a function from the realm of meaning, both in actual relationship and in culture and symbolism. Frankl's remarks about nihilism can apply as well to 'sex' in our time as to anything else—

For nihilism is not a philosophy which contends that there is only nothing and therefore no being: nihilism says that being has no meaning; a nihilist is a man who considers being (and, above all, his own existence) meaningless. But apart from this academic and theoretical nihilism there is also a practical, as it were, 'living' nihilism; there are people who consider their own lives meaningless, who can see no meaning in their personal existence and therefore think it valueless.

op. cit., page 298–9

This 'living nihilism' has obviously overtaken many in our age of what Leslie Farber calls 'the disordered will', or what Rollo May calls a schizoid society faced with 'emptiness'. Moreover, schizoid tendencies in culture, in the reduction of human meaning there, find their fanatical advocates.

---

* See 'On the Meaning of Life' in *The Doctor and the Soul*, page 26 ff.

As May points out, Marshall McLuhan and George Leonard say that 'sex as we now think of it may soon be dead ... the foldout playmate in *Playboy* magazine ... signals the death throes of a departing age'. As May says, their reassurance that life will 'be more erotic than now seems possible', are based on amazing confusions and a disastrous failure to recognize human truth. Their picture of the human being is one from which all human being has been removed.

In likening Twiggy to an X-ray as against Sophia Loren to a Rubens, they ask, 'and what does an X-ray of a woman reveal? Not a realistic picture, but a deep, involving image. Not a specialised female, but a *human being.*' Well! an X-ray actually reveals, not a human being at all but a depersonalised fragmentised segment of bone or tissue which can be read only by a highly specialised technician and from which we can never in a thousand years recognise a human being or any man or woman we know, let alone one we love. Such a 'reassuring' view of the future is frightening and depressing in the extreme.

Love and Will, page 62

Such a view is also horrifyingly anti-human. Yet in the enthusiastic acceptance by such individuals of schizoid dissociation we have a complete betrayal of intelligence to a new forfeiture of sanity in the sphere of the erotic—in the guise of being 'scientific'.

As Frankl says of those involved in the 'living nihilism' of attitudes to man as a kind of machine, this emerges from our intellectual ethos and education—

Nihilism has held a distorting mirror with a distorted image in front of eyes, according to which they seemed to be either an automaton of reflexes, a bundle of drives, a psychic mechanism, a plaything of external circumstances or internal conditions, or simply a product of economic environment. I call this sort of nihilism *'homunculism'*, for it misinterprets and misunderstands man as a mere product. No one should be surprised today that young people so often behave as if they did not know anything about responsibility, option, choice, sacrifice, self-devotion, dedication to a higher goal in life and the like. Parents and teachers, scientists and philosophers, have taught them all too long a time that man is 'nothing but' the resultant of a parallelogram of inner drives and outer forces ... man becomes more and more like the image of the man he has been taught about ...

From Death Camp to Existentialism, page 109

This intellectual homunculism has actually become a barrier to our discovery of our best potentialities, not least of our daimonic richness, our creativity and psychic potency, bound up as those are with the sexual in the fullest sense.

In discussing the problem of 'sex' therefore, we inevitably encounter some of the deepest problems of knowledge, and of the uses to which knowledge is put in our world. Here it is important to invoke Marjorie Grene in the rejection of our assurances about 'objectivity'. There is never anything other than ourselves trying to make sense of our lives.

As we have seen, too much in our thinking about sex today tends towards the implicit assumption that we can now, or should be able to, because of enlightenment or 'frankness' and the existence of a body of 'objective fact', be released from all the old problems of 'sex'. As Rollo May indicates, all this means is that we are misled into believing that the essential problems may be merely avoided in a new way. As Leslie Farber suggests, here is a new version of the perfectibility of man and a new subjection of living truth to the arrogant will. The danger here is that the divinization of science has led to a new kind of magic, which is bound up with the reduction of man to an automaton as far removed from the human as possible—and so, tractable, as the living being is not.

The inner impulse to dehumanize oneself out of fear, and the philosophical rationalization of this fear, have gone together in history. Science itself has been the most effective kind of knowledge in the history of mankind, and from this fact has grown an increasing divinization of the power of science. But, as Professor John MacMurray has pointed out, this can give rise to a new obscurantism which seeks to make science all-powerful, not least in areas to which its terms of reference cannot apply by any philosophical justification. The effectiveness of science in dealing with the outer world has been quite fallaciously extended into a belief that it can eventually be equally effective in dealing with the inner psychic world of which we are so afraid because it is the sphere of our existential weakness. It is not difficult to see how this fallacy arose, especially in the sphere of medicine, where the rapid success of science in dealing with physical ills was unthinkingly transferred to the psychic dimension and led to the development of physical treatments for mental ills and the belief that these arose from the inhibition of physical processes. Of course, some physical treatments are effective in affording relief: but it is becoming increasingly recognized that many psychic ills need to be looked at in terms of the failure to find meaning—in work, in love, in life itself. In the realm of the sexual life it is too easily assumed that sexology or education in 'sex technique' will bring success in treating sexual disorders that arise from failures of love, the capacity for relationship, and meaning.

Where science is extended into realms beyond its scope we often have a powerful irrational element, which can be seen as the expression of a powerful subjective need to deny our human weaknesses—to deny our ambivalence and our essential dependence on others. That is, it marks, a denial of primary needs—not least that we owe everything to the mother, who drew out the identity as a potentiality in our 'psychic tissue'. One of the most uncomfortable facts of our existence is that we are, at the moment of the formation of our identity, of our very mind and being, totally dependent for our phylogenic history, psychically and organically, on a woman, on an imperfect mother, who draws out our creative form by intuition and imagination (if she can) in a sphere in which intellect and action are no substitute for love. So, in biological history, *being human* depends upon what has developed and become self-conscious and aware during many millions of years, and on the miraculous processes of primary nurture by innumerable creative processes—and innumerable mothers—over immense areas of biological time. In so far as we have humanness, there can be no substitute for that long energy of parental care, as the basis of our identity. The human soul is the product of aeons of love.

How can we 'know' such things? Fortunately scientists who have turned philosophers, like Michael Polanyi, have demonstrated that science itself depends upon 'faith'—its whole confidence depends upon our giving endorsement to a group of persons, and accepting that their disciplines are authentic. In any case, their experiments and deductions would not be possible, were it not for the 'tacit dimension' of human capacities for knowing—subjective elements which enable us to exert our imagination, to foresee results as yet unknown, and to make sense of what has at first no meaning. If science denies the right of other disciplines to approach other truths (such as 'inward' truths of experience) by using the same methods of employing 'the tacit dimension', it is merely denying the roots of its own disciplines.

In psychotherapy, just as a general practitioner relies upon the 'tacit dimension' in diagnosis, and improves his skill in recognizing the physiognomy of disease by continual experience and use of his creative imagination, so a therapist who is in continual relationship with patients, can employ his 'tacit dimension' to give coherent accounts of certain universal elements in human life whose patterns he sees. He 'dwells in' his patients, and by projective identification discovers not only the nature of their present experience, but, because of 'transference' becomes something like a parent to them, and thus discovers a great deal about their infancy, and their experience of their parents. He is thus able to explore more deeply the meaning of their attitudes, phantasies, and symbolic thoughts and actions in the here and now, and to examine how they perceive, how they put their world together, and how they know themselves.

In exploring the origins of identity he finds elements of the primary state of mother and neonate which have yet to be explained, and which are especially discomforting to the scientist. For example, there is the telepathic element between mother and baby from before birth and immediately after their physical separation, and also the inexplicable 'couvade' role of the father in 'backing' the mother in her forfeiture of her self-interest for the infant.*

Obviously, it can seem a threat to 'objective' science to have to recognize that one of the primary facts of existence—love—is beyond its scope, for love can never be 'found' as a fact by empiricism. Of course, this only seems a threat as long as one adheres to the belief that 'objective' truth is the *only* truth, rather than simply the product of one way to one kind of truth. Once one grasps that all truth, in any case, depends upon the indefinable and intangible 'tacit dimension', the way is open to the scientific discovery of those truths of living experience which are only to be found by 'indwelling'.

If we re-examine our assumptions in this way about knowledge, science, and the nature of man, a new dimension of human and social reality confronts us. 'Objective' knowledge is revealed as only one limited kind of knowledge. That kind of knowing can only do partial things for us. Moreover, the whole question of the relationship between man and society has to be reconsidered, because neither knowing, nor the knowledgeable tolerance of society can save us from such problems as guilt.

To be sure, there are important positive results of the new enlightenment, chiefly in increased freedom for the individual. Most external problems are eased . . . sexual knowledge can be bought . . . contraception is available everywhere except in Boston . . . Couples can, without guilt . . . discuss their sexual relationship and undertake to make it more mutually gratifying and meaningful. Let these gains not be underestimated. External social anxiety and guilt have lessened: dull would be the man who did not rejoice in this.   *Love and Will*, page 40

'Enlightenment', however, has not solved the sexual problems of our culture—

But internal anxiety and guilt have increased. And in some ways these are more morbid, harder to handle, and impose a heavier burden upon the individual than external anxiety and guilt . . . In past decades you could blame society's strict mores and preserve your own self-esteem by

---

* See Winnicott on 'Primary Maternal Preoccupation' in *Collected Papers* (Tavistock Press, 1958), Guntrip's discussion in his two major books, listed in the bibliography on page 219, and mine in *Human Hope and the Death Instinct*. See also Marjorie Grene on Buytendijk, *Approaches to a Philosophical Biology*, pages 162–78.

telling yourself what you did or didn't do was society's fault and not yours. And this would give you some time in which to decide what you want to do, or simply to let yourself grow to a decision . . . (now) your own sense of adequacy and self-esteem is called immediately into question . . .   op. cit., page 41

Dr. May's comments here on problems of sexual freedom are a kind of sociology. But his approach is based on what he knows of human beings through the face-to-face contact of psychotherapy, and by tacit inference.

So, his 'sociology' belongs to subjective disciplines, and it is his kind of inward human and social fact of which we urgently need to take account, in the realm under discussion. But yet the prevalent 'enlightened' attitudes to sexual reality and to obscenity and pornography remain encapsulated in the 'objective' approach. They conceive of 'evidence' and 'fact' in 'objective' terms, so that this objectivity itself defines the way in which the subject is approached. The effect is to objectify us and our 'sex' in a disastrous way.

To find our way to a more adequate approach to sex, therefore, we must first re-examine the nature of science itself.

As Marjorie Grene says—

Knowledge can never be wholly impersonal. Even the publicly confirmed and reconfirmed statements of science are rooted in the consensus of professional opinion, in the accepted conceptual framework of a given generation of those considered competent to judge . . . the knowing mind is always a whole person . . .   *The Knower and the Known*, page 57

Science is 'something scientists are doing', and there is 'no such thing as a mind by itself'. There is no body of 'objective fact' which exists anywhere apart from persons holding beliefs about 'facts' and 'laws'. Of course, in truth, there is a reality to which scientific descriptions accord, and in which they have proved effective. But scientific facts are always essentially 'contingent', and, where man is concerned, only a very partial view of the picture.

Failure to take these problems into account can mean that a 'scientific' approach can do enormous damage, of a dehumanizing kind. For instance, into a world already suffering from existential frustration, comes a Kinsey who is to reveal to us our 'sexual reality' in an 'objective' way. He looks at the 'facts' or 'outside' of sexual behaviour and presents us with statistics of behaviour which seem to show a conflict between what we believe to be our experience, and what we take to be our ideals and ethical values, and how we actually behave in 'fact'. Apart from misleading us about 'what is real' in 'sex', the effect of his value-free approach is to make it seem that our emotional needs, and our ideals and values bound up with meaning are 'bunk'. The effect of his work is thus to make it less possible for us to hear the voice of the true self expressing our deeper needs. Rather than draw attention to the 'meaning' of wickedness, he merely presents it as equal to goodness.

Despite Kinsey's idealism, the effect is to make us perhaps feel even less human than before, since now all seems meaningless.This new 'realism' may threaten even that imagination, that visionary quality, that 'intentionality' we previously threw into our sexual gropings. It certainly threatens love. Its 'value-free' approval, exceeding the valid limitations of science, may bring us to feel that all our concern with meaning is 'relative', 'subjective' and invalid.

What is primary in sex, Kinsey implies, by an invalid and fallacious 'scientific' methodology, is not the search for meaning and fulfilment through meeting the 'significant other' in love, or even the attempt to find meaning by wickedness, but the hydraulic 'release' of pleasure-seeking impulses in an organism conceived in homunculist terms. Thus from his work arises an inevitable symbolism with reductive effects, having behind it a basic fallacy by which a mechanistic model is built up to the status of a general philosophy of man from which the will-to-meaning is excluded.

Kinsey substitutes for our most agonizing problems of love and relationship questions of technique, of orgasm, of sexual performance, of our place in the tables of statistics of frequency of act. On his scale of human prowess, are we a one-orgasm-a-fortnight man, or a four-orgasms-a-day man? Are we a woman who is capable of 'achieving orgasm' or not? Can we 'satisfy' our partners? Thus, all the anxieties which previously attached themselves to the whole problem of being-in-the-world, the conflict with the external morality of society, and to relationship, now become attached to an activity—along with car-mending-and-driving activity, commodity accumulations, weekend-suburban group-sex activity, and other forms of 'doing', and quantitative approaches to identity.*

It attaches sex to that pleasure-seeking which (as May says) will never be satisfied because of the very way in which it is diverted from true aims. Sex, consequently, has come to belong to all the other forms of that 'bustle' which 'distracts us from confronting

---

* In some offices men have 'league tables' showing the number of members of the women staff they have 'laid'; in America wife-swapping is felt by some people to be necessary if they are to be 'up-to-date'; a psychiatrist in Leeds reports that youth feel it is 'chicken' not to have premarital sex; in *The Times Educational Supplement* a breakdown of sex by numbers by schoolboys was reported. All these belong to the age of Kinsey, and the reduction of love to meaningless sexuality conceived as an 'activity' to be estimated in quantitative terms.

the problem of existence', as Buber puts it; and it has also become part of what R. D. Laing has called the 'hell of frenetic activity' to which the modern world is devoted. Instead of enjoying the 'significant other', at many levels of 'meeting' and finding satisfaction in a larger human meaning, instead of realizing love in the family and community, married couples and lovers keep diaries in which they record their frequency of intercourse. They scan these statistics in search of some absolute objective and trustworthy indication, on Kinsey principles, as to whether love is growing cold, or whether their sexual lives are breaking down or not. Having attached their sense of meaning to potency and performance, they have attached it to a realm in which no positive sense of meaning is to be found.

Love is also 'tested' in the laboratory. If Popper is correct, in this testing there is only the possibility of error.* There is only a *negative* possibility as in the empirical experiment—and since sex has been transferred to the laboratory bench, the 'laboratory' (Yes-No) situation now influences each individual's attitude to love. That is, the sexologist attaches the problem of existence not to creative possibilities, but to a test-bench situation in which we can only know *when we are wrong,* and when there is 'failure'. Intentionality is eliminated from love and the major concern is rather with the fear of impotence than with what can be created and endowed with meaning by imagination.

The philosophical issues here that I have tried to raise in this chapter I believe to be crucial, not least because, unless we solve them, we cannot find grounds to resist the fanatical 'moral inversion' of the immoralists in this sphere. They will be discussed later. On this problem, however, it is worth noting that Polanyi points out that it is our system of thought itself which is denying reality to *values—*

It is dangerous to rely on it that men will continue indefinitely to pursue their moral ideas within a system of thought which denies reality to them. Not because they might lose their ideals—which is rare and usually without serious public consequences—but because they might slip into the logically stabler state of complete moral inversion.

Personal Knowledge, page 234

This question becomes most important when the existence of 'scientific facts' is used, as in psychology or sociology, to make declarations on human problems, without the philosophical assumptions involved being examined, and without the methodology

---

* See Karl Popper, 'On the Source of Knowledge and Ignorance', *Proceedings of the British Academy* XLVL (1960), and Marjorie Grene's discussion in *The Knower and the Known* (Faber 1966).

being put to a philosophical test. Yet ethical values may be undermined all the same. Here sociology is one science which has had a
bearing on sex in our time, as the influence of Kinsey shows.

In sociology there are areas in which the proper 'data' are inner
aspects of experience. Yet sociology has sometimes tried to claim
for itself that it is 'value-free', though in fact, by implication, it
often deprecates any other form of investigation than its own, and
so implicitly evaluates non-sociological investigation. As Paul
Roubiczek says—

A sociologist who emphasizes that the scope of sociology is limited . . .
nevertheless feels entitled to assert: 'It is impossible to exist with full
awareness in the modern world without realizing that moral, political
and philosophical commitments are relative,' because 'one's own
culture, *including its basic values*, is relative.' . . . He wants to leave
room for other approaches, but actually deprecates any non-sociological
investigation of values and precludes any ethical, existential or religious
approach which judges on the basis of their intrinsic merits . . .
Ethical Values in the Age of Science, page 48 (my italics)

Such an approach shows, says Roubiczek, not so much the attempt
to make sociology 'value-free', but disregard for the vigorous
demands of science. While this is fallacious as 'science', it also
means that there is often in sociology, a *tendency working against
morality*. Such sociology invites our assent, yet—

a scientific apparatus is often used to support arguments against the
belief in an absolute morality, and thus sociology encroaches—illegiti-
mately and unjustifiably—upon the sphere of ethics. The whole man is
lost sight of because sociology itself is used to determine a moral
position . . .   op. cit., page 49

As Roubiczek asserts, there is no authentic 'scientific' reason for
doubting the existence of values, or for disposing of them as
'relative'. Nor is 'science' able by its terms of reference, to pronounce on the question of ethics, or the ethical basis of law. It is
true that scientific data may help us to judge whether or not to act
or legislate in this way or that, but such data cannot be the whole
basis for such legislation. Many pernicious laws and traditional
customs have been 'unmasked' in our time, by sociology and other
investigations. But—

only on the basis of *ethics* are we able to decide which beliefs should be
dismissed, which freed from abuses, and which judged on other grounds
or upheld against society.   op. cit., page 49 (my italics)

A belief in mere 'relativity' in place of such ethical concern could
lead to the 'destruction of the validity of all values and beliefs'.

Ethical considerations in the realm of culture are not disposed of by 'science', and though the conclusions of such disciplines as psychology, sociology or even sexology may be found relevant, they cannot in themselves be made properly the basis of ethical conclusions. Yet the whole trend of our 'enlightened' opinion fallaciously supposes that they can, as in discussions of the question of toleration. At the same time, those disciplines which deal with man as 'being-in-the-world', are declared by the 'enlightened' to be 'merely subjective' or 'speculative'.

Often the most profound question of all, which is the essential concept we hold of ourselves as beings, is missing from the debate. For where conduct and morality are concerned, what is most significant are the concepts we hold of 'what it is to be human', and these are developed in the dynamic between our inward quest for the true self, and the inherited tradition of culture. This I believe brings us to the crucial problem of human evil, or wickedness, and its origins. Here perhaps we may find a clue to the rejection of other sources of ethical concern which are not 'objective': original sin and the Devil are no longer acceptable as explanations. It seems more acceptable to believe that wickedness is to be attributed to social causes, or to 'animal instincts' or other forces outside ourselves. This of course fits the 'homunculist' model of man. But here again, philosophical anthropology is throwing up an even more satisfactory explanation of the *meaning* of wickedness—which seems more human.

When we turn to study the meaning of human phenomena, we can see even the worst aspects of such manifestations of a desperate quest for something to believe in, for something real. The worst manifestations here are thus manifestations of the lack of a sense of meaning. As Viktor Frankl says 'Where existential frustration is acute, sexual libido becomes rampant'. When an individual is threatened by a deep lack of the feeling of being real and alive, he may take recourse to frenetic sexual activity or sex-thinking, as a desperate but false solution to his deeper psychic needs. As we shall see, such activity may even be a defence against psychosis— and this seems true of much of our cultural obsession with sex. But such an obsession with 'sex' remains a defence because the only possible solution to our existential anguish lies in finding meaning, and in the sphere of sex meaning can only be found through love. This again draws our attention to the essential indivisibility of human experience which philosophical anthropology emphasizes. To quote Merleau-Ponty once more—

when we say that sexuality has an existential significance or that it expresses existence, this is not to be understood as meaning that the sexual drama is in the last analysis *only* a manifestation or a symptom of an existential drama. The same reason that prevents us from 'reducing' existence to the body or to sexuality, prevents us also from 'reducing' sexuality to existence: the fact is that existence is not a set of facts (like 'psychic facts') capable of being reduced to others . . . but the ambiguous setting of their inter-communication, the point at which their boundaries run into each other, or again their woven fabric.

The Phenomenology of Perception, page 166

As an editorial in *The Human World* has said—

Our experience of sex—the events bodily and social, the dreams, the memories, the talk, the thought—if it *is* our experience, occurs in our lives . . . the significance is expressed in the man's life, the woman's life as a whole. . . Any value that belongs to any experience of sex comes, inexplicably and as a gift of grace, into the individual life . . .

The Human World, No. 3, May 1971, page 5

So—

any judgement of pornography involves questions about values. For, even if pornography could be caught causing events . . . what is and what is not depravity depends not upon events but upon a scheme of values . . .

op. cit., page 4

It is this that those who cling to a 'scientific' approach forget: the ultimate judgement here is one which involves our possession of values—and our idea of man, with a philosophy of biology in the background, by which we interpret both events and meanings. There can be no 'objective' conclusions, unless we deny that man is more than an object, which is absurd. But such doubts do not trouble scientists who appear in court to defend obscene publications, with no sense of the absurdity of their position.

4
Psychoanalysis and sex
ᏮᏮ

Throughout this book I have been constantly referring to psycho-analytical insights, and perhaps this is the point at which to give a brief summary of the implications of psychoanalysis, in particular of the object-relations and existentialist forms of psychoanalysis, about sex.

According to the philosophical anthropology emerging from psychoanalytical theory and elsewhere (as from the philosophy of Martin Buber and the philosophical biology of Buytendijk), the human identity begins with a mutal relationship of love. This is expressed physically by the sucking of the child at the breast, and the way in which their mother 'presents' the breast—letting the child make use of it psychically as well as physically, as a means to become himself. On her part the mother helps to 'put the child together' by her tender caresses, and her imaginative response. The essential experiences here, which we do not yet have the language to speak about, yet which create every new human being, belong to the dimension and realm of what Winnicott has called 'female element being'—to the intuitive, the emotional, the creative, and to bodily existence. These insights take us to the very beginning of human identity, and to its core.

The adult sexual relationship is also a mutual relationship of love, and we can enter into it successfully to the degree that our capacity *to be* and *to love* have been created in that first relationship with the mother. This adult mutual relationship is expressed physically in ways which we learn at first from the mother—kissing which re-enacts sucking at the breast, body caresses which re-enact the mother's care for her child, and the sexual act itself which is, as it common name implies, a form of mutual sucking. The same terms are used for sexual desire as for hunger, and just as the baby yearns to feel confirmed existentially by being cared for and handled at the breast, so the lover finds himself confirmed in his existence by making love. Our capacities for bodily mutual-ity are therefore created in the first place by the primary soul-and-body relationship between mother and male child and mother and female child. In the background of every sexual relationship, as Freud saw, there are four antecedents—two fathers and two mothers, and so male and female elements in the husband and male and female elements in the wife. Sex is the area in which 'doing' and 'being' are both involved, and here we have a most complex aspect of our whole 'being-in-the-world'.

Since psychoanalysis has come to reject the Freudian hydraulic picture of a 'mighty sexual instinct' which 'may well absorb all the energies of a human being,' it has come to see human sexual problems in terms of problems of identity and the search for meaning by 'finding' the 'significant other'. These problems are very much bound up with the realm of 'female element being', in which love seems to be fundamental, for strength or weakness. As Guntrip says—

it is always the female element that we find dissociated, in both men and women, and . . . the fundamental dissociation is of the female element . . .
Schizoid Phenomena, Object-relations, and the Self, page 253

Where there are sexual problems the fundamental source is in the 'psychic tissue' at such depth. It is absurd from this point of view to try to solve such problems by explicit or 'outward' means, as if they could be tackled merely by the male attributes of 'analytical thinking' and activity.

This poses severe problems for our kind of civilization, in which the female element capacities in men and women are undervalued, while the sense of identity has been to be attached predominantly to 'male element' doing and 'thinking', not least by our education. It is thus inevitable that we should tend, as we do, to subject the sexual life, which is bound up with 'female element being', to 'activity' and intellectual analysis, which belong to 'male element doing'. In the light of the insights of psychoanalysts such as Harry Guntrip and Rollo May such approaches would seem to have something schizoid in them. They resemble the phantasies of the schizoid patient who is suffering dehumanization. They can be seen as forms of 'masculine protest' against the more feminine, vulnerable aspect of one's self.

Such forms of protest against one's humanness must inevitably fail because they are denials of the deeper needs of love and being. As we shall see in Chapter 5 when we take into account the work of W. R. D. Fairbairn on schizoid characteristics, the energy of those who must deny love and base their dealings on hate leads them to seek to invert moral values with fanatical nihilism. In the realm of culture they seek to persuade us to base our sense of identity on hate and on 'false male' solutions.

This 'schizoid diagnosis' of the origins of the 'pathological morality' of our time seems a better explanation of what has happened to sensibility in the realm under discussion than that offered by D. H. Lawrence, though Lawrence came very near seeing the problem, as is evident from the poem printed as a motto to this book. In his contrast between the characters Gerald and Birkin in *Women in Love* he also gives us many insights into the differences between 'pseudo-male doing' and 'the disordered will' on the one hand and the true quest for 'being' on the other. However, at this point I must admit, as a pupil and admirer of F. R. Leavis, that I cannot endorse the latter's insistence that Lawrence represents 'sanity' in his dealings as artist or commentator on the realm of the sexual life. As a literary man and an admirer of Lawrence my own struggle to find a right attitude to sex has been much bound up with his work. Lawrence, it is true, saw that in the realm of sex, 'mental consciousness' could become a blight. As G. H. Bantock points out, he followed Nietzsche in this. Nietzsche, as Bantock says, 'projected back into Greek times, the tensions he felt to be characteristic of his own era'—

and these, by implication, he interpreted in terms of the confrontation of the spirit of Dionysos (the god of wine and therefore of primitive instinct) by the great exemplar of theoretical man, Socrates. What Nietzsche implied by this confrontation was the conquest of instinctual, spontaneous life by science and knowledge and conscious intelligence. Translated into Lawrence's idiom it involved the perversion of direct sensual awareness of mind-knowledge and 'ideas': 'because if you think of it, everything which is provoked or originated *by an idea* works automatically or mechanically.' (*Fantasia of the Unconscious.*) Men were becoming over-self-conscious and hence too inhibited . . .
Culture, Industrialisation and Education, page 20

Nietzsche and Lawrence both saw the confrontation as being between 'instinct' and 'conscious intelligence'. As Guntrip points out, this is the same traditional interpretation of the duality of 'mind' and 'body' made by thinkers from Plato and St. Paul to Freud himself. Guntrip regards this as a chimera to hide the true problem, which is fear of weakness and meaninglessness. If we consider these two opposing poles of knowledge and experience in the terms used by Winnicott and Guntrip, then we can perhaps see that what preoccupied Lawrence was the possibility that 'pseudo-male doing' and 'thinking' could take over as false solutions to the problem of finding a sense of identity. Lawrence could see that the sense of meaning in life had to be achieved in the realm of 'female element being'. But Lawrence's attitude seems at times to have moved towards irrationality: philosophical anthropology has enabled us to become able to see the problem in terms not of 'reason' versus 'instinct', but from the point of view of the 'schizoid diagnosis' as a struggle to feel existentially secure—against emptiness and 'ontological insecurity'.

The effect of Lawrence's work and theories has been in our time to contribute to the widespread belief that we shall be happier if we release our 'instincts'. This has led to the bold voyeurism of the film *Women in Love,* which contains love scenes so explicit that an individual who showed them in Perugia was imprisoned. Those who campaigned for *Lady Chatterley's Lover* to be freely on sale believe implicitly in the benefits of 'openness' about sex. The compulsive attention to sexual activity in that book has now become an obsessive feature of our culture.

Below we shall have to examine the problem of ethics. But here it is necessary to say that there is nothing in recent psychoanalytical work that endorses, as the one solution to our sexual problems, the mere increased 'release' of libido. Neither is there any endorsement of the enthusiasm for the 'new amoral society we have created' (the *Guardian*) and there is certainly no fanatical immoralism, or obsession with sexual activity. Indeed, some psychoanalysts, Masud Khan for one, are talking of the 'over-permissive' society.

Perhaps the most valuable effect of psychoanalytical insights is they not only vindicate 'ethical living', but make the human ethical problem seem more hopeful. The attitude of recent psychoanalytical theories is positive and optimistic. It suggests that most individuals become aware of their humanness in a real and creative way and want to be 'good', as this enhances their sense of personal value. For most 'normal' people, there is both a personal moral sense, and also there are values which are absolute 'as near as may be', arising from love and human 'encounter'.

The 'ethical living' of normal people is based upon *concern,* the 'formative principle' inherent in the true self, and the acquisition of the values of their culture. Concern emerges from the first awareness of the distinction between the 'me' and the 'not-me'. For as the self becomes aware at first of the not-me, it also becomes aware that the self is dependent upon the not-me, which is at first almost entirely the mother. At the same time the infant is entirely at the mercy of an incorporative urge, which is here the expression of both its physical and deep psychic hunger. At the same time, the infant is not aware very clearly of the distinction between phantasy and reality. So, he feels, his phantasies may have the effect of 'swallowing up' the 'other', and thus destroying his world. This fear of incorporating the object and destroying one's world remains in sexual appetite, and underlies many sexual problems. But it also explains why we find such satisfaction in making 'reparation', as Melanie Klein called it: all acts of giving, love and 'meeting' tend to help overcome this fear of one's incorporative power, by 'filling in' the 'other', and putting a body of riches 'in' the emptiness we feel we may have caused. Thus, it is natural, where development has gone normally, for human beings to be good, and society itself depends on this.

Winnicott and Marion Milner both believe that within human beings, even the 'wicked', there is a formative principle and a 'healthy moral sense'. This cannot be argued at length here, but perhaps a quotation from Marion Milner will suffice—

Increasingly in my clinical work I had found myself needing to find what verbal concept in psycho-analytic thinking corresponded with what L. L. Whyte has called the formative principle.

Patients seemed to be aware, dimly or increasingly, of a force in them to do with growth towards their own shape, also as something that seemed to be sensed as driving them to break down false inner organizations which do not really belong to them—something which can also be deeply feared, as a kind of creative fury that will not let them rest content with a merely compliant adaptation; and also feared because of the temporary chaos it must cause when the integrations on a false basis are in the process of being broken down in order that a better one may emerge.   *In the Hands of the Living God*, pages 384–5

This inner principle has a ruthlessness that seeks to realize an inherent identity, and, as Winnicott indicates, this 'true self' can be so uncompromisingly moral as to prefer death to insult.

Later we shall examine the implications of all this for ethics. Here it is important to note that ethical capacities are drawn out at first by mother love—

The mother says, 'How would *you* like it', i.e. 'How much is your complaisance due to the fact that it's you who are pulling the cat's tail and not vice versa?' And in this she is *not* merely putting something into the child but *bringing out* the uneasiness which lurks in *him* just as it did when biting her breast he laid waste his world and with it himself.
                    John Wisdom, Review of Waddington's book *Science and Ethics* in *Philosophy and Psychoanalysis*, pages 102–11

Thus, psychoanalysis sees the ethical problem as a complex one, involving the creation of an adequate capacity for 'ethical living' which is brought out in the child, and developed by his culture and growing pattern of relationships (involving, for instance, identification with 'good figures'), the capacity to be in touch with one's 'true self', and one's most inward needs, anyone's relationship with the created meanings and values in one's civilization. This is a much more complex view of ethics than is found among most 'enlightened' commentators today, especially those who are simplistic and reductionist.

One of the complexities may be indicated by a sentence from Guntrip: 'Only the strong can love: it is the weak who hate.' This may seem like a religious text. It is, in fact, rather a conclusion derived from the personal experience of many desperately ill people, some of whom say to their therapist, in various ways, 'If you can only love the baby in me . . .' True solutions involve the acceptance of weakness of those areas of one's psychic tissue which remain least grown, most infantile and vulnerable. Accepting this means suffering—because of the fear involved—the pain of recognizing one's dependence on others, and one's own essential ambivalence.

For many, however, who cannot accept dependence, or for whom such hope is simply not available, the only solution may be the false, if heroic one, of turning to hate in order to hide the weakness and to escape intolerable suffering of feelings of loss of identity.

While we may have compassion for the individual in this predicament, and should try to understand him, we must obviously, as we have seen, see that where his solutions involve turning against his own true nature, they are 'false' and may be unethical or destructive.

Here I believe there are many valuable insights in recent psychoanalytical papers which move towards the very centre of human problems of identity. Especially valuable are insights in those papers which deal with male and female elements in the personality, for this is particularly relevant to the discussion on sex, which after all is the meeting point of male 'doing' and female 'being'. As Guntrip says—

A man and woman expressing together their mutual love in sexual relationship will both alternate in reacting on the basis of both female and male elements. A man and woman making love passionately together are both reacting with their maleness, actively 'doing'. A man and woman lying quietly and restfully in each other's arms, simply aware of mutual well-being and security are both reacting from their female element, simply experiencing their secure existence each in themselves but in the medium of their being securely together; so much so that they can afford without danger to their separate individualities, to forget their separateness, and experience identity and oneness, as they may also do at the height of mutual sexual orgasm. This relives on the adult level the primary identification each of them had as infants with mother if all went well. Furthermore, one may be male, actively doing, while the other is female, quietly and receptively 'being', each in turn.   *Schizoid Phenomena, Object-relations and the Self*, page 258

This duality runs through all human relationships, not least marriage, in which both partners, for instance, relate to each other and their children in both a 'female being' and 'male doing' way, while the children take both male and female elements from each parent into their personalities by identification.

The capacity for 'being' is, however, the fundamental female and maternal element—a truth which seems evident from Winnicott's work, and from the philosophy of Martin Buber. The relation of the child to the mother is fundamental in a way in which that of the father is not: and so, Guntrip concludes, where things have not gone well there, the consequence is a weakness in the capacity 'to be'. This can lead, in the adult, to a *fear of being*, and so to some of the most perplexing ways in which man can be his own worst enemy.

5

The dangers of moral inversion

I have said that psychoanalysis has enabled us to be more optimistic about human potentialities for moral goodness. This is true, and it indicates how it is that 'permissiveness' works—it works because most people are 'good', and gain great satisfaction from being moral and faithful to their 'formative principle' and the needs of the 'true self'.

Psychoanalysis, however, also indicates that there is a minority to whom such concepts have no meaning: or they may need to invert them. Moreover, because they are suffering, essentially, a problem of the fear of weakness that we all have within us, they can enlist us and draw us into their 'false solutions'. They can draw us into forms of collective psychopathology. Hence arises the perplexing problem of *moral inversion*.

In his most important paper on *Male and Female Elements** Winnicott suggests that where there has been a failure of integration and of 'being', the individual male splits off his female element with a consequent loss of touch with potentialities.

Guntrip discusses this very complex phenomenon in a patient of Winnicott's thus—

some constitutional potentiality that has been left out at the beginning of the process of growth, something apart, unevoked, blocked off from the start, never integrated or given a chance to develop. In this case the constitutional male and female elements in the psyche will have failed to become associated together in the early stages of development so that an incomplete self comes about. Winnicott regards the 'dissociated' as something in the patient's make-up that he himself cannot know; it is outside the range of his ego-experience, conscious or unconscious. It is something the analyst must discern for the patient . . .
Schizoid Phenomena, Object-relations and the Self, page 253

This undiscerned element Guntrip relates to the 'true self in cold storage', and generalizing from this case-history Guntrip says—

---

* Published in *Playing and Reality*, Tavistock 1971.

If 'being' exists, doing will follow naturally from it. If it is not there but dissociated, then a forced kind of 'doing' will have to do duty for both, but where the capacity for 'doing' fails completely, it must be because the sense of 'being' is totally absent . . .   op. cit., page 253

Where the mother does not have the capacity to create the sense of 'being' by *being for* her child, in what Winnicott calls 'primary maternal preoccupation', she may try to make up for this by a bustling kind of activity which belongs to 'male modes rather than female'. Guntrip quotes a male patient as saying—

'I always think of a real mother as not a bustling busy, organizing woman who 'runs' the household, but as a quiet, serene, warm deep character whose very presence makes the family feel secure.' Such a woman is quite capable of 'doing' but is likely to get things done with little fuss and without seeming over-busy.   op. cit., page 259

On the other hand, the kind of mother who cannot 'be' for her child is likely to deal with him in such a bustling 'male' way that her care is felt as an *impingement*—and even, as Winnicott suggests, as *hate*. Such a woman is acting from what Winnicott and Guntrip call 'false male doing' in lieu of true female being, and the effect of her heroic attempt to overcome her disability is to implant in her child a deep fear of woman, of dependence, and of the female element in itself—which merges with the deficiency of a secure sense of being. He himself afterwards may only be able to hold himself together by hate. Here is the source of 'masculine protest' and a desperate 'doing' activity based on hate and 'bad thinking' to keep a self together. Much of the depersonalized sex of our culture is an expression of just this 'false male doing' in lieu of being. The consequent agony in the attempt to feel real may be studied in such an individual as the poetess Sylvia Plath.*

Such an individual's world can only be held together by what he or she has learned from the mother—which is a 'doing' activity that has little or no 'being' content, and consists of acting and impinging, on a pseudo-male basis, and often of 'hate'. Guntrip also sees *thinking*—intellectual ratiocination—as a version of *doing*, while reflection and meditation, as it were, belong rather to being. Thus the individual who has to deal with his world by 'pseudo male doing' will also tend to deal with it, in terms of *pseudo male thinking as a form of activity*. Implicit in this will be a fear of woman, of 'being' itself, and of all that belongs to the female element modes. *It is this kind of false male doing, to which depersonalized sex and pornography belong.* And because of the implicit fear of the sensitive, female area of being which is half the

---

* See *The Colossus*, especially the last poems; also *Ariel* and *The Bell Jar*.

nature of sex, this 'half' will be denied and attacked by this pseudo-male preoccupation with 'activity': it has in it, thus, aspects of a denial of being human—a denial of dependence and of primary emotional needs. Thus mere sexuality and pornography always express a hatred of our essential and most vulnerable humanness, and can convey this hatred abroad.

Guntrip quotes a patient, on his own 'false male doing'—

I feel now that my physique is weak and girlish, but I felt I was becoming masculine when I got a motor-bike. Now I have a car but I still fantasy myself as a ton-up youth taking a shadowy girl on the pillion. She never has any real personality but is only there to admire me. When I feel anxious I still put on my leather jacket and tight belt round my waist and look at myself in the glass and feel tough and masculine.   *Schizoid Phenomena, Object-relations and the Self*, page 256

Here we have the epitome of that pseudo male doing, which can develop into sadism and conveys a complementary idea of woman as the weaker sex. We find this pseudo-male doing in the sexual symbolism exploited by the advertiser, and in commercial culture at large. Here is the very basis of the arrogance of *Playboy*'s depersonalized image of sex, and its sexual fascism. The same pseudo-masculinity takes an intellectual form in 'permissive' writers. We may often find that for them women seem essentially shadowy figures whose function is but 'to admire them'. Pseudo male too is the analytical and external concern with 'doing' of the sexologist and propagandist for sexual 'freedom'.

The connexion between the fear of one's female element, and one's fear of the 'baby within us', the unborn self or regressed libidinal ego, is obvious. One's inability to find security in the realm of being is obviously related to not having been sufficiently mothered, or to having been mothered in terms which seemed threatening: so, one has this unborn baby in oneself, which the female element never brought to psychic birth through together-ness. Just as we hate our regressed ego baby self, so we may hate our female element. As Guntrip says—

The female element may be defined as the need to be emotionally susceptible, the capacity for sensitiveness to what others are feeling. By contrast, the male element, seen as the need to be able to take practical action in an often difficult and dangerous world, and if necessary to harden the heart and do what is unavoidable, had to fall to the lot of the father who could not afford to be sensitive . . . the female element is the emotionally sensitive self that can be more easily hurt, and then can be felt as a weakness to be resisted, resented and hidden behind a tough exterior. Patients who have not been able to develop the tough superficial defence but have remained too vulnerable and sensitive, may generate an intense unconscious hate of their female element in human nature, and if projected may be either desired as the one thing needful or hated as a weakness to be destroyed in some female person, as often as not a girl child.   *Schizoid Phenomena, Object-relations and the Self*, page 264

This raises considerable cultural problems. The philosophical anthropology of object-relations psychology asserts that even the most desperate crimes have a positive symbolism, in the attempt to feel *guilty*. Behind this, psychoanalysis reveals, there is an even more terrible problem, of needing to feel *real* enough to feel guilty (for one can only feel guilty in so far as one is aware of *me* and *not-me*). This reveals that there exists a group of individuals who must base their whole lives on hate, because they cannot feel real in any other way. Moreover, such individuals tend to have a particular preoccupation with cultural expression. This most valuable insight comes from W. R. D. Fairbairn, and the insights are given in an essay 'Schizoid Factors in the Personality' (1940) in *Psychoanalytical Studies of the Personality* (Tavistock 1952). This essay points out that 'intellectual pursuits as such, whether literary, artistic, scientific, or otherwise, appear to exercise a special attraction for individuals possessing schizoid characteristics to one degree or another'. Because such individuals have never been given sufficient security of identity in themselves, by love in infancy, they feel, because they are so hungry for love, that love is harmful: their own inner love seems to threaten all their objects. They therefore tend to invert morality, by substituting hate for love. This may be done for two motives both of which have a profound (and sometimes tragic) effect on their life. The schizoid individual feels that love is destructive, and so he becomes impelled to hate and be hated: yet all the time he wants, deep down, to love and be loved.

This is a tragic predicament, and it leads to very serious moral problems—

There are two further motives ... by which an individual with a schizoid tendency may be actuated in substituting hating for loving—curiously enough one an immoral, and the other a moral motive; ... the immoral motive is determined by the consideration that, since the joy of loving seems hopelessly barred to him, he may as well deliver himself up to the joys of hating and obtain what satisfaction he can out of that. He thus makes a pact with the Devil and says, 'Evil be thou my good.' The moral motive is determined by the consideration that, if loving is overtly destructive and bad, it is better to destroy by hate, than to destroy by love, which is by rights creative and good. When these two motives come into play, therefore, we are confronted with an amazing reversal of moral values. It becomes a case, not only of 'Evil be thou my good' but also of 'Good be thou my evil.'

Psychoanalytical Studies of the Personality, page 26

These observations, of course, belong to a psychology which has rid itself of the absurdities of physicalism and Freudian naturalism, and which takes cognizance of the inner ethical energies of each human being, and the dynamics of meaning in a being-in-the-world. It demonstrates that an individual can be motivated by *an intense moral impulse to be immoral.* This explains the logical inconsistency to which Polanyi refers, in *Knowing and Being,* as an aspect of the fanatical nihilism abroad in the modern world, and it reveals the source of the 'pathological morality' of which he speaks, and its appeal in terms of its simplicity, and its 'logically stable state'.

Obviously, such a pathological morality, with its inversion of ethical values, because it is based on hate, must inevitably come into conflict with society—not least with all the best that has been created in society. To say that it 'inverts' morality of course implies that there is a normal morality based upon love. Thus values, in the light of this psychoanalytical approach, are not merely relative, they are the expression of the healthy moral sense of the majority who have known love, and who have thus sufficient security of being to be able to base their ethical living on love. Love implies concern for others—caring for others. Hate is inevitably the impulse to live at the expense of others—thrusting harm into them, emptying them, disturbing their inward dynamics, arousing anxieties in them, all in the service of the schizoid individual's need to protect himself by keeping their love turned away from him.

He mobilizes the resources of his hate, and directs his aggression against others—and more particularly against his libidinal objects. Thus he may quarrel with people, be objectionable, be rude. In so doing, he not only substitutes hate for love in his relationships with his objects, but also induces them to hate, instead of loving him: and he does all this in order to keep his libidinal objects at a distance.

Psychoanalytical Studies of the Personality, page 26

It should be noted that the motive of the schizoid individual is not only to hold others at a distance, and to alienate them, but also to *destroy* them, or what he can of them. As R. D. Laing points out, the schizoid individual can be so afraid of the 'implosion' of his inner emptiness by the impact of another person on him, that he will try to attack the other individual first—to petrify him, or incapacitate him in some way, before this happens. *He is impelled to destroy the other out of fear.* Obviously, not only is this unethical, but it must be taken cognizance of by the legal systems of society, which are the product of centuries of effort directed at minimizing the effects of hate.

All these manifestations can take place in the realm of culture.

There the 'destruction' can take place at a distance, so that the conflict between needing to alienate and yet, deep down, desiring to be loved, can be reconciled: eventually it may be possible for the schizoid individual who expresses hate to become loved and respected (as with Genet). But in the process his *hate* and 'pure' moral inversion may come to be loved and accepted, too.

Here we have implications for culture of great importance. Where women and children are killed in strange 'hippie' rituals, or in murders such as those of Ian Brady, we may diagnose that it is the female element in human nature which is being attacked, by such processes of projection and acting out in a mood of schizoid moral inversion. This explains the pathological morality by which such murders are done with a profound sense of moral righteousness, as among the followers of Charles Manson. What is being destroyed in such cases is the need for sensitivity itself, that human need for love, that seems to threaten the pervert's world. (In a recent murder, done under the influence of LSD, the murderer ate his victim's heart—the symbolism of which is obvious.*)

But such terrible murders, with all their fanatical nihilism, have their cultural counterparts—and, indeed, as we know, they are often backed up with cultural justification: Brady was a reader of the Marquis de Sade, whom Simone de Beauvoir regards as a moral hero, and Charles Manson is a hero of underground culture. At root we may find in such manifestations a fanatical *denial of being human* which in some individuals is acted out in murder.

In our culture at large, both in its thought, and in much of its symbolism, we find arid and powerful manifestations of all these anti-human tendencies of the schizoid individual, not least in the sphere of sex. The very need for sensitivity itself, for sympathy, to be feeling and human, *to be*, is often projected over a woman-symbol—and then attacked or humiliated. The motive behind the attack is to destroy a weakness in oneself, a weakness in humanity itself. This, of course, in terms of collective psychopathology, makes it parallel to the attempt by the Nazis to destroy human 'impurity' by projecting this over the Jews and destroying them wholesale. Sexual fascism belongs to the same syndrome. Yet because of its moral fervour such a schizoid development can disguise itself as rational and 'enlightened'. So, even the impulse to destroy the most human germ in our innermost selves, can be acclaimed because it is attempted, even in the realm of the most intimate dialogue, under the banner 'Good be thou my evil'.

---

* LSD now seems to produce in some a delayed psychosis, of which acting out primitive phantasies is a characteristic. See *The Lancet*, 10th October 1970.

As we shall see, this kind of schizoid inversion can be accepted by a pathological morality—as with the Sartres's acclaim for the Marquis de Sade as a moral hero. Sartre's theory is a patently schizoid one—we find our freedom in 'endless hostility'. As Roubiczek points out, Sartre's arguments could be used not only to make saints of Genet and de Sade, but also to endorse the worst Nazi atrocities. Where inverted morality comes to be embodied in structural organization, as Polanyi says, 'once they are immanent, moral motives no longer speak in their own voice and are no longer accessible to moral arguments; such is the structure of modern nihilistic fanaticism'. Something of the same kind is happening in our culture, in that the media and even the stage and the printed word are being so largely dominated by those who have given assent to fanatical immoralism. Political movements like the 'underground' have been captured for schizoid moral inversion, so that one is confronted with the absurd spectacle of students, selling pornography when they are supposedly fervently seeking a new world in which 'love' shall be possible!

One of Polanyi's most illuminating philosophical essays here is one called 'The Two Cultures' in *Knowing and Being*. This discusses the influence of scientific ideas on culture at large. Polanyi is concerned with the 'disregard of truth in favour of hard-boiled scientific ideals' and how this has 'spread confusion and led eventually to sinister results'. In this essay Polanyi discusses the influence of Freud as a thinker who in accounting for man showed that he belonged to a tradition of naturalism. Helvetius and Bentham reduced man to a 'bundle of appetites feeding themselves according to a mathematical formula'. Freud's man, too, is impelled primarily by a 'pleasure principle'—

Freud's libido is restrained by society. But no noble features are ascribed to it: on the contrary, morality is imposed on the libido externally, and this restraint is actually condemned because it produces sickness. Good and evil are replaced by health and sickness.

'The Two Cultures' in *Knowing and Being*, page 43

A belief in naturalism may be found among thinkers of the Enlightenment in the eighteenth century who held that man's moral sense could be grounded in Nature. ('One impulse from a vernal wood . . .', etc.) However, with Freud naturalism is no longer a 'moral command' but a doctrine of moral scepticism. Polanyi continues—

Yet it is not this scepticism by itself that is distinctive of the modern mind. For moral scepticism, and the ensuing hedonism, libertinism, Machiavellism, etc., have been current before now, and are only about as effective today as they were in former times. The decisive step in forming the modern mind takes place at the next move, when *moral scepticism is combined with moral indignation*. It is the fusion of these two—logically incompatible—attitudes that produces modern nihilism.

op. cit., page 43 (my italics)

The consequence is that, in our time, we are likely to meet the revolutionary whose *'measure of his own moral force is the degree of evil he is prepared to commit'*. Moreover, such an individual will 'recoil from a straight morality', feeling that his inversion is a sign of a 'more intense passion for social justice'. Thus it is possible that even in such an inversion, there may be found a positive germ. As Polanyi says—

The line of modern writing descending from Dostoevsky undertook to explore the limits of nihilism, in search of an authentic residue of moral reality. While this quest has sometimes led to meaningless despair, the movement has, as a whole hardened the moral tone of our century, and cleared the ground for re-laying the foundations of morality.

A parallel inquiry has explored the chaos created by the rejection of all existing forms . . . as in Dadaism and surrealism . . . towards the vigour of a new primitive culture. Such rejuvenation has, I believe, never before been achieved without the previous intermission of a long Dark Age.   op. cit., page 45

At best, the 'progressive' position rests on a belief that the present 'Dark Age' is the interim moment on the way to a new ethical reality. At worst it simply tries to see the predominant aspects of the Dark Age as beneficial in themselves: for Sartre, Simone de Beauvoir and Susan Sontag, hate, violence and pornography are signs that man is recreating himself.

In the meantime, however, it is important, says Polanyi, to recognize that some of our assumptions about culture, ethics, and society are quite fallaciously supposed to follow from the 'objective' criteria of science, when in fact they can have no such basis. Science is today the 'only uncontested intellectual authority', and so arises the absurd inclination to base upon it ethical critieria that it cannot support. There can be no occasion to base (say) the claim for 'total permissiveness' on science, for—

it can as little sanction the claims of nationalism, religion, or natural ethics as ever it could before. In fact, its criteria of objectivity must deny reality to any moral claims. No chemical analysis or microscopic examination can prove that a man who bears false witness is immoral.

op. cit., page 46

For this to be seen, says Polanyi, we must first emancipate such biological sciences as psychology from the 'scourge of physicalism': 'the absurdities now imposed on the science of life must be discarded'.

The task is difficult, for it calls in question an ideal of impersonal objectivity on which alone we feel it is safe to rely. Yet this absurd ideal must be discarded.   op. cit., page 46

Earlier in the same book, Polanyi discusses the influence of nihilism further. He points to a type of individual who becomes an 'armed bohemian'—

The personal immoralist bohemian converts his anti-bourgeois protest readily into social action by becoming an 'armed bohemian' and thus supporting absolute violence as the only honest mode of political action.
op. cit., page 17

Every bookshop now displays the concomitants of this 'armed bohemianism' in the sphere of symbolism. Immoralism and 'armed bohemianism' meet in French Sartre-led existentialism. Sartre and his mistress have elevated individuals of extreme immoralism to the status of saints—

Mme. de Beauvoir hails the Marquis de Sade as a great moralist when Sade declares through one of his characters: 'I have destroyed everything in my heart that might have interfered with my pleasures.' And this triumph over conscience, as she calls it, is interpreted in terms of her own Marxism: 'Sade passionately exposes the bourgeois hoax which consists in erecting class-interests into universal (moral) principles.'
op. cit., page 17

In the field of culture a fervently moral immoralism is now moving beyond being manifest, to becoming immanent. Yet there is little recognition of the logical contradictions at the heart of the position. A good deal of what is happening in the theatre, in New York or London, belongs less to the theatre than to the brothel or to 'acting out' in the mental hospital. Yet this is all offered fervently in the name of art, with solemn philosophical vindications. One of the quotations offered recently by the *Journal* of the Drama School of New York University to justify way-out activities was from Nietszche—

We must also be capable of setting ourselves above morality; not with the uneasy rigidity of the man who constantly fears to lose his footing and fall, but with the practised ease of one who can float, disport himself above it! And how should we achieve this without art, without the madman's aid ... ? And as long as you are in any way ashamed of yourself, you cannot possibly be of our number ...
from *Die Fröhliche Wissenschaft*

Here, with intense moral fanaticism, is expressed a 'schizoid sense of superiority', in the recommendation of a stance which holds itself to be above morality, towards 'perfect nihilism'. Those who fail to achieve this sense of being above morality, it is implied, are really morally inferior. The origins of such fanatical moral inversion are obvious to anyone who has studied Fairbairn's analysis of schizoid modes. What Nietszche is saying is that anyone who cannot establish an intellectual moral system on hate is inferior. It is highly moral, he implies, to seek complete inversion of the basis of normal morality in love. We may, in the light of the insistence of psychoanalysis on the fact that the mind always exists in a body, see Nietszche's pronouncement as implicitly denying the existence of that moral dynamic which is created in the body and being—in the 'psychic tissue', in the 'true self' of the infant. Such fanatical amorality as Nietszche's could only exist in a split-off mind or schizoid intellectual system. Those who idealistically follow his lead use his words, as a fervent motto to vindicate activities based on depersonalized hate in the realm of sex, which amount to the acting out of primitive phantasies, and such activities exclude as 'dangerous' all love and truth of 'being'.

Because such activities belong to primitive mechanisms, such organizations as The Living Theatre have, as Dean Brustein has indicated,* been moving rapidly towards anti-intellectualism, sexual obsessiveness—and ultimately a fascist-like collective psychopathology.† Instead of art in the theatre—

mass love-zaps and petting parties were organised on the stage among couples of various sexes and sexual dispositions . . . endless, loveless sexual groping . . .
Dean Brustein in the *New York Review of Books*, 13th February 1969

The ideology that was 'marketed under the name of anarchism' in all this had fervour, in the name of 'brotherhood' and 'love'—but no tolerance. 'No spectator was ever allowed to violate the pattern of manipulated consent.'

At Yale, we saw a female student launch into a passionate denunciation of the Living Theatre, only to be hustled offstage by a group of performers who embraced her into silence—unbuttoning her blouse, feeling her legs, and shutting her mouth with kisses . . .   ibid., loc. cit.

---

* *New York Review of Books*, 13th February 1969.
  † The same is true of poetry readings in England. 'When the Austrian Ernst Jandl read . . . the audience successively turned football crowd, Boy Scout rally, and wolfpack . . . As his Sound-poems rose to a crescendo, a rhythmic furore aided and abetted by the claps and cries of the crowd, so, suddenly the destruction of words and their conversion to a shouted, half-hysterical series of sounds, seemed sinister—took on a Hitlerian aspect: the Hall became a Babel. It was perhaps the most extraordinary event of the evening. . . with its own logic, rational collapse of reason, and despair of communication communicating itself'. Alexis Lykiard, *Wholly Communion* (ed. Whitehead, Film Books 1966).

This 'acting out' of a kind of rape, as Brustein says, manifested an aggressiveness that aroused in him 'disturbing memories of the youth rallies in Hitler's Nuremberg'. (See a more full comment in the present author's *The Masks of Hate*, page 358 ff.) This horrifying contempt for the person combined with intolerance, fierce with fanatical puritanism, seems now an immanent component of 'progressive' politics, and *avant-garde* culture. It is difficult to see why the degradation of the human person should be accepted thus as the mark of a desire to change the world for the better.

So 'immanent' have these fanatical trends become, however, that any 'progressive' who wishes to dissociate himself from the obligatory pattern has to do so apologetically, with no hope of being influential. For instance, in a recent book, Dr. Benjamin Spock said that, while he was in favour of erotic episodes in genuine art—

those works in which the primary aim is to shock, revolt or embarrass by explicitly depicting sexual intimacies—especially those of a loveless, perverse or brutal kind—and other works which horrify with vivid details of a non-sexual kind are in a special category ... I think that such works are unhealthy for society because they assault the carefully constructed inhibitions and sublimations of sexuality and violence that are normal for all human beings (except those raised without any morals at all) and that are essential in the foundations of civilisation ...

from *Decent and Indecent*

Yet he feels bound to add—

I realise that almost no liberals or intellectuals, young or old, would go along with me.   op. cit.

Spock condemns what he sees as the tendency in youth to depersonalize and deny sex its 'spirituality'. He sees a decline in the romantic aspects of love—in tenderness, in the conviction that the beloved is uniquely attractive, in the desire to serve and please, in the wish of the couple to be always together, and in the heightened appreciation which he says idealistic love gives to all forms of beauty and spirituality. Of love affairs, he says they have the—

superficial appeal of romantic sexuality without family responsibility and family grubbiness.   op. cit.

Those who can only enter into 'affairs' are cut off from 'the life-long satisfactions that people demand from marriage'.

In his excellent book for adolescents, *A Young Person's Guide to Life and Love*, Dr. Spock also says, too early dating 'has a tendency to dehumanise love'. (Inevitably, so far has the brutalization of sex and sex education gone that some reviewers found this book 'old-fashioned'.)

Similar views are put forward by Viktor Frankl, and here it is important to emphasize that we now have a strangely dissociated situation between philosophical anthropology and philosophical biology on the one hand, and the arts and commercial entertainment on the other.

Fanatical moral inversion has now become the orthodoxy of the *avant-garde*, and even of the Arts Council Working Party, when it comes to sexual depiction. In commercial entertainment the cry continues to be, 'Abolish censorship!' while the contents of magazines, films and television become increasingly full of dehumanized sex.

Yet in object-relations and existentialist psychoanalysis, in which we may suspect no vested interests in the profits to be gained by further permissiveness, voices may be heard warning us of the dangers. We have seen above how Viktor Frankl warns of the dangers to psychic health of the commercial exploitation of sex.

Elsewhere he refers to a survey the observations of which we may take as relevant to the rapid changes which are taking place in the behaviour of young people under pressure from the fanatical immoralists who are putting out powerful propaganda through 'pop' magazines and other media—

Where sexuality threatens to take precedence over eroticism and become dominant, the psychiatrist or the sex educator must raise his warning voice. A large-scale statistical psychological study of the Charlotte Buhle School has shown that serious sexual relationships of very young girls (in whom we may assume no proper erotic relationships have yet developed) led to a distinct shrinking of general interests, a limitation of the mental horizon. Within the structure of a still incomplete personality, the sex-instinct, holding out the promise of easy pleasure-gains and vehemently demanding gratification, swallowed up, as it were, all other concerns. As a result of this deviant development, inner preparation for the generally esteemed and culturally valuable state of marriage must naturally suffer. For the happiness and duration of marriage are guaranteed only by attainment of the ideal aim of normal development: the maturity for a monogamous relationship, which means successful synthesis and congruence of sexuality and eroticism.   *The Doctor and the Soul*, page 174

Such views today have to be put forward hopelessly in the face of orthodoxy of belief in 'freedom' in the sexual realm which, because of its fanatical moral inversion, is scarcely prepared to grant them a hearing. Who can listen to such careful and measured arguments, between the noise of orgasm on records, the naked couples on the latest record sleeve, the lesbians putting tongues towards one another's mouths on the cover of film magazines, the advertisements for books such as *The Sensuous Woman* ('ways to drive a man to ecstasy ... the Hoover ...') pictures of 'group gropes' in the *avant-garde* magazines, the voyeurist sequences in nine-tenths of the films on show in London at any time? All these seem so much larger than life. Who can hear such gentle, quiet insistences as Spock's in the general hullabaloo of the 'sexual revolution' and the buzzing of auto-vibrators at Danish Sex Fairs?

But that, in a way, is an aspect of the whole problem. Moral inversion seeks a situation which puts it beyond the access of ethical debate—and tries to drive us towards what even progressive people are now calling the 'ultimate'—as if there were a 'final solution'. Haven't we heard that phrase somewhere before?

6

The truth about perversion

ᏬᏬ

The pressure in our time from those who are devoted to fanatical moral inversion may be linked with a newly arrogant pressure which is coming from those of the schizoid minority who are also sexual perverts. Society has, valuably, given at least nominal tolerance to the pervert. But, of course, mere removal of social guilt does not alter the inner problem of the pervert. So he seems to have turned to seek something more than tolerance. He wants perversion to be accepted as 'good' ('Gay is good') or even as superior to normal sex. (Groups of perverts are even seeking to persuade schools to give them time to 'counter heterosexual education'.)

A typical article on perversion was published in *The Times* of 2nd November 1970. The article consisted mainly of quotes from lesbians, and was described by a doctor writing to the Editor later as 'a recruiting advertisement for lesbianism'. It told those interested, curious, or merely experimentally-minded, he said, where to go so that they 'may be casually picked up'.* It quoted members of clubs who commended lesbian relationship as being 'more open, honest and satisfying' than a heterosexual relationship, and spoke of a group of lesbians as being 'more resilient, more self-sufficient and more composed' than a 'matched group of heterosexuals'. It countered possible inhibiting fears by speaking of the 'light-hearted atmosphere' and 'much laughter', and by describing lesbian gatherings as 'reminiscent of nothing so much as a midnight feast in the dormitory of a girls' boarding school'. It conveyed an atmosphere of respectability by reference to 'quiet social evenings with cups of coffee—just like the women's institute'. Dr. Sutherland's letter to the Editor said it conveyed—

an aura of moral superiority by a misuse and degradation of the word

---

* The magazine for teenage girls, *Valentine*, published details in January 1971 of how it is possible to get 'picked up' in London.

liberal (in its reference to the 'liberal circles' in which lesbianism is accepted as normal).

This doctor insisted that lesbianism is a 'pathological . . . abnormality' which 'creates grave problems for those who have acquired it, and wreaks havoc among those emotionally close to them'. The letter to the Editor said it was 'unforgiveable that any responsible person or organization—let alone a newspaper of the standing of *The Times* should do anything to encourage the spread of lesbian propaganda'.

The Times article was inadequate because it relied too easily on the comments of lesbians: and there is substance in the doctor's criticism that it gave details of where groups of 'attractive young girls' could be seen at a lesbian club. More suspect, perhaps, was a similar article directly aimed at young people, and telling them that—

Lesbians can only be considered 'abnormal' in that a minority of women indulge in it. It's certainly not 'unnatural'—homosexuality can be observed in animals from mice to elephants . . . Just as it's a mistake to despise homosexual people for being 'perverted' it's wrong to pity them as 'sick'.   *19* Magazine

It is worth examining this article as one typical of enthusiastic propaganda put out for the young on the 'new sexual freedom'. Quoting Kinsey, the writer tells us that it is just that lesbians are just a 'small and misunderstood section of society'.

The rest of the article is, of course, 'frank': 'The idea that we fake-up male organs to enjoy sex is ridiculous!' said one girl. 'I suppose you could describe lesbian love-play, in heterosexual terms, as "heavy petting"—accent on the heavy. Some girls might use aids, but I'd say this was a male myth . . . men are just so conceited that they can't possibly believe that any woman could ever get any kick out of sex without them around.'

Such writing may itself be suspected of titillation, stirring up 'bad thinking' that could possibly convey to others that to be a pervert was to be at least 'alive' and 'on the scene'. It also seriously distorts human truth. As we shall see in a moment, what perverts seem to tell the analyst is that sexual relations between members of the same sex are of their nature unsatisfactory. But this underlying problem is turned aside by trying to involve the girl reader in a hatred of the male.* The article discusses an organization which campaigns for lesbians called Kensic and in it someone speaks of being a 'true lesbian'.

---

* See my discussion of the 'technique of intimacy' and Khan's work on this (pages 100ff.).

'We don't want anyone to think we're corrupting anyone,' Cynthia said. 'Also until a girl's twenty-one I don't think she can really know for *certain* if she's a true lesbian or not. After all, nearly all girls go through a period of homosexuality at one stage, having crushes on the gym-mistress or whatever.'   ibid., loc. cit.

The latter comment is true. But reference to it in connexion with the lesbian club seems doubtful. As we shall see, from the re-searches of psychoanalysts, the pervert, whose every venture is a failure, is insatiable. He or she sometimes needs a continual supply of fresh objects—and such a club could easily be a source of new contacts among young women going through a period of homo-sexuality. There is surely a great difference between the 'crush' of adolescence and a lesbian relationship with a member of such a club?

If the pervert is to succeed in making new conquests, he or she must dissipate prejudice against perversion, and break down the defences of those who might be enlisted. So, those who wish to proselytize and put out propaganda for perversion argue that homosexuality is not a 'sickness' but a valid and 'natural' life-style. This, as we shall see, is to endorse what the pervert knows to be a false solution—

'You can't be psychoanalysed out of being a homosexual any more than you could psychoanalyse a heterosexual into being a homosexual. It's like putting an Englishman in Finland and saying "Right, you're a Finn. Get on with it".'   ibid., loc. cit.

Psychoanalytical theory, based on psychotherapeutic experience with perverts, shows this to be false. In such a comment (made by Esmé Langley of the Minorities Research Trust) there is an implicit denial of the truth, which is that homosexuality is a manifestation of a failure to achieve the capacity for normal relationship. It seems impossible to foster compassionate understanding of this problem unless one begins by accepting this, and then perhaps goes on to see how best to enable the pervert to find such relationships as he is capable of making.

The journalist in *19* wanted perversion and normality put on the same plane—yet this is not how the pervert sees perversion once his defences have broken down and he consults the therapist, as we shall see.

Of course, there is a gain in the tolerance of homosexuality: as the writer says here—

In a permissive society like ours (and thank heaven it is) girls are bound to be franker about their problems than ever before . . .
                                                             ibid., loc. cit.

But there is now the problem that sexual realities are themselves falsified, even in the way individuals conceive them, as a consequence of such highly suspect propaganda put out by perverts on behalf of their own false solutions while they can sustain them. As Masud Khan makes plain below, it is possible, if very difficult, to help the pervert to find what he himself tells the analyst he deeply desires—a cure. Unfortunately, we do not know very much about perversion, as yet. Significantly, however, such articles do not ask for more research.

In the article in *19* the concepts of how people become homosexual belong to the absurdities of the 'enlightened' view that sexual problems are 'created' by the taboos of society—

While women are in a hideous state of transition between inferiority and equality (a situation that sours many good relationships with men) it is possible that more girls will turn to their own sex in desperation . . . a typical case is Paul, a dolly girl . . . (who lived with her boy friend and had an abortion) . . .

'I suddenly thought—well, I've done all these socially unacceptable things, why should I suddenly become prudish about admitting I've got lesbian tendencies . . . life is altogether so wicked that if two people care about each other it shouldn't matter what sex they are. I would never wish that I didn't feel like this. I can't see anything wrong with it . . .'

ibid., loc. cit.

The degree of protestation perhaps indicates the uncertainty: but the effect of the article is to try to persuade the reader to accept what is, from the point of view of a serious concern with psychosexual problems, very misleading and possibly disastrous. The intention may be to lessen 'social guilt': but the effect could be to cause deeper anxiety, in a girl (say) who felt lesbian tendencies, and knew they were part of a whole life-problem. She could be persuaded that there was 'nothing wrong' (so she should just *enjoy* being a lesbian) and that there was no cure. Though she would know, deep down, that something was wrong and that what she needed more than anything else was to fulfil herself in a heterosexual relationship, a girl with lesbian tendencies could be encouraged by such writing to pursue activities which, in others, are a 'defence against psychosis' and a hopeless attempt at self-cure. In being enlisted in their perversions she could be led further away from the possibility of satisfactory engagement with her own problems.

The effect of such articles is to trivialize attitudes to very deep problems of identity. The writer did not consult any independent authority on psychosexual disorders: she merely consults *lesbians* —especially those who are most vociferous in defence of the lesbian solution, in defiance, and in hatred of the male. She does not concern herself with the need to find out more about this problem which causes many people anguish. Yet it is by such propaganda in dozens of periodicals every week that young people's attitudes to sex are being educated today.

It is time our suspicions were aroused by the evident way in which 'permissiveness' is being exploited by those who wish to exert certain doubtful persuasions on the young before they are mature enough to develop their own judgement. Publishers of 'sex' books do not seem concerned about the effects on the young of their books.* Magazines for the young not only offer continual advice about sex. Such articles are often forms of titillation, and are sometimes perverted or propaganda for perversion. They increasingly urge depersonalized sexual activity. One magazine (*Honey*) in a recent issue, contained a 'sexual game' in which the forfeits were forms of sexual activity: another had an article on 'how to get a man into bed as quickly as possible—and if not a man, then a woman companion.' A recent issue of *Vanity Fair* contained an article based on *The Sensuous Woman* urging the reader to masturbate. *The Little Red Schoolbook* and *Oz* have both encouraged children to 'try' sexual perversions.

In the light of 'enlightened' attitudes to sex, and the present cultural treatment of sex, there would seem little to object to. If shame is a restriction, it had better go. But what if it is a protection as philosophical biology argues? My strictures are based on psycho-analysis—on the work of those who know perverts, and have studied them over a long period. Here I would like to invoke a whole group of papers by Masud Khan, the Editor of the International Psychoanalytical Library. Khan has made a special study of perversion based upon twenty years' experience of a dozen pervert patients. His main essay is a chapter on 'The Function of Intimacy and Acting Out in Perversions' in an American book on *Sexual Behaviour and the Law* (see Bibliography, page 221). Another paper is 'Reparation to the Self as an Idolised Internal Object', published in *Dynamic Psychiatry*, Vol. 2, November 1968.

The importance of these studies is that they make it unequivo-cally clear that *perversion is perversion*, and that ethical problems are involved, because of the impulse of the pervert to exploit others. Perversion is not in itself to be 'condemned', but it is certainly a form of false behaviour.

What right have we to call perversion 'false'? Is this a mere semantic trick? The answer is that, when he has tried everything

---

* The Running Man Press sent out 300,000 circulars advertising *The Mouth and Oral Sex*, and many of these fell into the hands of children. The publisher was fined for publishing an indecent circular in March 1971.

possible through his perverted activity, and when these auto-
therapeutic attempts have broken down, it is *the pervert himself*
who tells the analyst that his perversion was a false attempt to
cure himself. As Khan says—

Clinically, we see perverts only when their auto-therapeutic attempts
have totally failed . . .
'The Function of Intimacy and Acting Out in Perversions',
from *Sexual Behaviour and the Law*, page 404

That is, the psychotherapist discovers that the aim-inhibited
sexual behaviour has a meaning, part of which belongs to an
attempt to fulfil the true self in its need for relationship. Such
behaviour cannot ever achieve fulfilment of the true self, since it
takes a false direction. In the end, the falsity of the auto-therapeutic activity is exposed even to the pervert himself, and his
truth can become the basis of a new *ethical* view, founded on the
recognition of inward reality.

Masud Khan's papers are based on the developing insights of
ego-psychology and studies of infant-mother relationships—especially those which are coming from the study of schizoid states.
The latter insights are concerned with 'distortions' or 'abnormali-
ties' in consciousness in its dealings with experience, and in terms
of their meaning. With the kind of ethical statement to which Dr.
May refers in the background, it is possible to see 'distortions' not
as something we must reject as 'immoral' but rather as manifestations we must try to understand as what R. D. Laing has called
'strategies of survival'. That is, they are modes of behaviour in
which the individual feels he cannot survive unless he clings to the
patterns of life, however false, he has created for himself. These
may differ completely from the ways of living established by 'those
manic-depressive people we call normal' (as Winnicott puts it).
Their ways of treating others may differ totally from those forms
of relationship by which we may satisfy the 'true self' and its need
to relate. Yet it should be remembered that, according to Winnicott and others, this true self is there in everyone; hence where
there are false patterns of behaviour there is always a basic
conflict.

Khan's paper is relevant to those of us who are concerned with
culture because he reveals how the pervert becomes preoccupied
with *libidinized erotic activity*, because he can neither find himself,
nor the 'significant other'. Since this conclusion was reached from
what perverts in analysis told the therapist, it is *their* truth, not
one imposed on them. Moreover, these insights expose that many
'confessions' of perversion in literature are themselves falsified—
idolizing body activity and making it all seem much more exciting,

and much less drab than it really is. The confessions of perverts are not true confessions but rather desperate rationalizations, and attempts to glorify behaviour which is essentially a mark of the failure to find meaning. Perverted culture, in this light, like porno-graphic films, can be seen as attempts to celebrate a false reality by those who behave in meaningless ways, in a desperate but futile attempt to 'find reality' and yet who must try to persuade themselves and us that it is meaningful.*

Moreover, Khan regards perversion as belonging to the *psychoses*: that is, to madness or, to be more accurate, to the flight from madness and collapse of the identity. He is concerned with the meaning of the 'technique of intimacy' by which a sexual pervert involves the object of his attentions in his own problems and his attempts to deal with them. Fundamentally, Khan claims, the pervert's sexual acts belong to the attempt to cure certain deep-rooted psychic problems which originate in the mother-infant relationship in the individual's personal history having proved inadequate. Such a person, whose developmental processes failed to complete themselves in infancy, tends to revert to primitive ways of dealing with experience, not least relational experience.

Not only is this primitive infantile behaviour inappropriate in an adult. Despite the fact that his acts are a desperate attempt to feel real and to find a path to development, because of the develop-mental failure, they tend to take forms which inevitably mean that the individual must try to *live at the expense of another person*. Yet this person is really nothing to him. He is never 'found' and for him the pervert has only something like contempt, or even a voracious impulse to devour or destroy.

Khan sees sexual perversions as attempts to 'still mental pain associated with anxiety and depression; and to neutralise, suspend or sidetrack the impulses of hostility and aggression'. Perversions, as Khan says, are 'a social acting out of the infantile neurosis in the pervert'.

Through this technique another object is appealed to, involved, seduced, and coerced to share in the enactment of the developmental arrest and cumulative trauma resulting in identity confusion which constitutes this infantile neurosis.   op. cit., page 399

Khan traces perversion to problems originating from childhood experience of being handled, and the effects on the individual's *cultural* capacities. From the point of view of object-relations

---

* Frankl has an illuminating note on the experience some schizophrenic patients have of feeling they are 'being filmed'—that is, they experience themselves as *objects*. Pornographic films simply 'negative' this objectifica-tion. See *The Doctor and the Soul*.

psychology such as that of D. W. Winnicott, culture emerges as a human employment of symbolism starting with the child's first play with his mother, as an infant. This play has a large *reparative* element—an element of the capacity to find 'the significant other' and to give to her, and to find satisfaction in pleasing or enriching 'the object'.

It is a significant aspect of the pervert that he cannot *find* the other and cannot *give to* the other. This has immense implications for our culture now that it is so much dominated by the 'confessions' and other forms of 'showing' of the schizoid pervert. As Khan says—

very subtle and discreet inhibitions of emergent aggressive potential in these children as infants play a role here too. Such mothers distract, diffuse, and negate the aggressive gestures in the infant-child's reparative drive that draws on his body-musculature. This leads to expressions of aggression in rage-reactions mostly to precocious developments of defensive ego-mechanisms. When these patients sought out accomplices they had, as it were, a latent wisdom in choosing objects who would not involve their ego too directly and explicitly, otherwise their phobic and paranoid anxieties and defences would come precipitately into action and spoil the whole venture.

'Reparation to the Self as an Idolised Internal Object', in *Dynamic Psychiatry*, Vol. 2, November 1968, page 96

Perversions are similar to 'acting out' in analysis. This is to enact in actual life unconscious phantasies which cannot, for some reason, be worked on by insight, or expressed and discussed. Such acting out is full of dangers because it is so full of falsification (since, say, those equated with the parental imagos are not the patient's parents). According to Rycroft, acting out makes the patient 'less accessible'—and so to encourage it drives a patient further and further away from genuine insight towards false solutions.

But the pervert's activity of acting out arises from a need which is life-or-death to him, and so he develops a special magical power to charm and influence others. As Khan says—

The pervert's talent at enlisting reality and external object as an ally in the service of his ego-needs and instinctual exigencies is what gives him a spurious and exaggerated sense of his own sensibility and its potentialities. The pervert's subjective experience of the technique of intimacy and its achievements can be categorised as sense of over-valuation of self and object, insatiability, a solitary game, and envy.

'The Function of Acting-out and Intimacy in Perversion', from *Sexual Behaviour and the Law*, page 402

The pervert's over-valuation and idealization of his perverted activity is in lieu of the genuine capacity to relate in a committed way to another person—

The sense of insatiability derives from the fact that every venture is a failure for the pervert. The internal anxieties relating to the ego's dread of surrender never allow for a gratification of the impulses involved. At best there is mere pleasurable discharge . . . even though two persons are involved . . . it is all the invention of one person.   op. cit., page 403

Khan does not shrink from using the word 'surrender'—a word with clear ethical implications. He knows that perversion is a matter of one individual making use of another, to the latter's disadvantage. Moreover, the self-respect and sense of values in the other have to be broken down—

This invitation to surrender to the pervert's logic of body-intimacies demands of the object a suspension of discrimination and resistance at all levels of guilt, shame and separateness. A make-believe situation is offered in which two individuals temporarily renounce their separate identities and boundaries and attempt to create a heightened maximal body intimacy of orgastic nature.   op. cit., page 402

But from his inside knowledge of this kind of intimacy Khan knows that in perversions there is no real 'meeting'—

There is always, however, one proviso. The pervert himself cannot surrender to the experience and retains a split-off, dissociated manipulative ego-control of the situation . . . Hence, though the pervert arranges and motivates that idealisation of instinct which the technique of intimacy aims to fulfil, he himself remains outside the experiential climax. Hence, instead of instinctual gratification or object-cathexis, the pervert remains a deprived person whose only satisfaction has been of pleasurable discharge and intensified ego-interest. In his subjectivity the pervert is *un homme manqué* . . .   op. cit., page 402

Here, again, obviously, we have ethical statements, which have considerable cultural implications, in a psychoanalytical document. Khan goes on to argue that the pervert treats his object as an infant treats his 'transitional object'. This is the name Winnicott has given to the infant's first symbol, his cuddly toy or whatever, which symbolizes for him his internal possession of the mother and his growing independent personal culture. This first object, at this primitive stage, lends itself to be 'invented, manipulated, used and abused, ravaged and discarded, cherished and idealised, symbiotically identified with and de-animated all at once'. But whatever happens between the pervert and his 'transitional object' in sex, *the 'other' person is never found*, so that there is inevitably a reductive effect on the person who is in the transitional object role—

envy derives from the actual perception and suspicion that the other person has got more out of it than the self. It is this element of envy which makes most perverts behave viciously and meanly to their objects and compels them to jilt and hurt . . .   op. cit., page 403

Yet while the 'solitary game' of the pervert inevitably leads to such exploitation, the elements of magic and dream in his approach lead the pervert to project himself and his 'technique of intimacy' as larger-than-life. Here we have insights which reveal a great deal about our present-day culture: we can see much of it as emanating from the intense needs of perverts who are terrified of 'ego dissolution and disintegration'. They must exert their 'technique of intimacy' as a defence against this, while the *confession of their sexual activities is almost as important—*

The pervert's talent at enlisting reality and external object as an ally in the service of his ego-needs and instinctual exigencies is that it gives him a spurious and exaggerated sense of his own sensibility and its potentialities.   op. cit., page 402

Despite his sexual failure the pervert's own view and the picture he tries to give of his state is quite different. Khan says—

Confession is another basic function of the technique of intimacy. It is a remarkable feature of the pervert's behaviour that he confesses with a singular unrestraint, lack of shame and guilt—both to the sexual object and in the clinical situation. Even in literature the extravagant sincerity of writers like Oscar Wilde, André Gide, Henry Miller and Jean Genet are outstanding for their intensity and absoluteness.
op. cit., page 403

Yet this kind of confession, despite its 'extravagant sincerity'—

is nearer to dreaming and a hallucinatory mode of psychic activity than an organised ego-activity . . . it is a confession doomed to failure because the accomplice can only help to dramatise the theme, give it a concrete reality in behavioural experience and a body-compliance without being able to meet and make known the true ego-need and the latent distress in the pervert . . .   op. cit., page 403

Here we have a clinical conclusion which offers us useful insights for dealing with problems of sex in culture. When the pervert 'confesses', this is virtually in the service of his own need to seduce others into becoming his accomplice in an activity in which there can be no true meeting. The element of confession cannot really bring the meeting between two human beings which might help advance the auto-therapeutic attempts of the pervert. Instead it all becomes part of the magic by which the object 'becomes a sort of thing in his dream'.

The same is true, I believe, of the confessional element in the kind of culture of which Khan speaks. In responding to it the audience at large merely become the willing collaborators of the

pervert and in a sense his 'victims'. Because of his exaggerated
sense of his own sensibility, and because of his idealization of his
technique, we are seduced into accepting something which is
larger-than-life and a grand hallucination, but essentially objectifying. Our mental excitement or our masturbatory response is
analogous to the 'body compliance' in which the pervert finds what
satisfaction he can.

But behind the mask there is *un homme manqué*, seeking to cure
himself of a sense of meaninglessness, and with a deep fund of
latent distress, whom we are masked from meeting. He keeps his
distance, and avoids 'meaningful surrender' at all costs. We can
never reach the true condition of the man through his confession.
All we experience is what Khan calls a 'charade'. All we get from
much modern 'sex' culture is 'mere expertise in the technique'
itself—while the idealization of sexual activity and discharge
merely leads us further and further away from the essential problems of love and meaning. It moves towards a generalizing clarity,
while love moves towards 'concealment, half-light, and silence' in
unique intimacy.

The pervert hates the private. As Khan says of the pervert—

The failure to achieve any form of ego-satisfaction is then compensated
for by idealisation of instinctual discharge-processes, which in turn lead
to a sense of depletion, exhaustion and paranoid turning away from or
against the object. This vicious circle gradually reduces the positive
strivings and expectancies implicit in the technique of intimacy . . .

op. cit., page 409

Culturally, we may extend this, to suggest that because of the
predominance of perverted concentration on sexual activity in our
culture, there is now a consequent and inevitable 'turning away'
from sex itself, and a kind of exhaustion, and paranoia—a paranoid
turning away from our relational needs, and from our humanness.
People are in consequence turning to increasing dehumanization—
as in bestiality, public acts of sex, and violence (a magazine, *Seen*,
at the Danish Sex Fairs combined pictures of decapitated victims
in Vietnam alongside pictures of sexual activity).

From Masud Khan's paper we may take yet another ethical
statement, about sexual activity which has become separated from
the whole complex of relationship and meaning in an individual's
life. Khan says of his own argument—

My argument here is close to that of Schmideberg: 'With perversions the
fixation is not on an object but generally on an activity . . .'*

op. cit., page 400

---

* Schmideberg: 'Delinquent Acts as Perversions and Fetishes', in the
International Journal of Psycho-analysis, 1956.

From the point of view of the individual concerned with culture and symbolism, such insights have great importance today, because sexual activity, as I have argued, has become separated in this way from human wholeness and creativity. Moreover, our whole thinking about sex has become affected by a parallel separation of sex from the whole human individual who makes his own conscious and responsible choices in life. That is, our thinking has tended to make sex not only a separated activity, but also an impersonal force which determines our psychic life—a force which is itself irresponsible, and over which we need not be responsible nor invoke values. Seduced by perverted culture we are even liable to forfeit our ego-boundaries (as do those who enter into coition with strangers on the stage at Danish 'sex' night clubs), or to lower our barriers of shame about sexual activity on the stage (as the 'enlightened' are nowadays ready to do and as the authorities, even, have been persuaded to do). Yet all this thrusts the 'shrunken existence of persons no longer capable of being immediately touched' into the realms of those who are 'in becoming hidden from themselves,' and are discovering themselves, as Straus points out.

The problem is made more complex by the distinction which Masud Khan sees in his subsequent paper between *benign* and *malignant* forms of perversion. As Khan says: 'Genet has survived the inbuilt fatality of his perversions through the rescue measures of an over-permissive society and its humane zeal.' But can it be possible that Genet has been saved at the expense of the sensibility at large? 'Confessional activity' to do with sex in the realm of culture, can have behind it all the force of a sensibility which seeks 'total annihilation of self and object'. Surely we would be foolish not to recognize the dangers involved here?

Certainly, if we ponder Khan's paper we can see that the truth of perversion is very different from the picture we are given by our culture. As Khan says, of perversion—

It is all engineered from the head, and then instinctual apparatuses and functions zealously exploited in the service of programmed sexuality . . . outside such relationships these people [i.e. the perverts he treated] were all very selfish, impatient, patently unempathic and ungenerous, as well as coldly aloof towards others . . .

'Reparation to the Self as an Idolised Internal Object',
in *Dynamic Psychiatry*, Vol. 2, November 1968, page 96

As personalities his pervert patients—

felt shut-in, almost claustrophobic, rather depersonalised with a distinctly schizoid type of personality and *yet seething with a latent urgency towards life and others which they couldn't actualise in life-experience or contemporary object-relationships*. Hence they felt eager and disregarded, intensely subjective and yet dull and depleted, full of themselves and with nothing to offer others, and above all else special. They had a distinct secret sense of waiting to be found and met. It is in such an inner climate of strangulated activity and instinctual tension that an opportunity or encounter with someone would provide them with an opening into life.   op. cit., pages 94–5

This is a truly profound comment on the anguish of those whom the newspapers call the 'hell-stirrers'. Their hell is that of waiting to be found: of wanting to *begin*. The above can also be read as a comment illuminating the appeal of the schizoid psyche in the perverted predicament: it is the *seething* of the pervert that can be commercially exploited—and thrust at us all. The urgency of love moves in different directions and dimensions. Normal people can actualize their sexual life: perverts cannot. Normally reparation, and the discovery of a sense of meaning can come from *giving*. But perverts have 'nothing to offer others'. They are sealed in a certain inescapable narcissism. Yet they cannot bear to see love as an activity that really exists between others in their independent life: that is, perverts seek a form of togetherness which is dehumanized, while real human meeting evokes only their malignant hostility. Perverted culture is often an attempt to *stop us loving*, and to fill our 'love-in-being' with hate where it can. Cultural perversion wants to make of us a 'sort of thing in the pervert's dream': In the light of Straus's analysis and Khan's we need protection.

The pervert's private world of idolized sexual activity is out of touch with reality, and is especially separated from ethical values.

This is a problem we get stuck with quite often in the treatment of schizoid characters with acute selective sexual inhibitions ... The sexual intimacies anticipate a privacy and seclusion from public view and allow for private symbolism and rituals to be tried out, learnt and thought. They are relatively at one remove from the exigencies of ordinary reality and value-systems. Another factor is that in all perversions there is a definite lack of elaboration of body-experiences into psychic reveries. The overt fantasies of perverts are patently banal and repetitive ...   op. cit., page 96

Some of the predominant figures in our cultural scene today are 'schizoid characters with acute selective sexual inhibitions'—and now, with *Oh! Calcutta!* on the stage, we have perverted sexual rituals transferred to the public area, dissociated from 'the exigencies of ordinary reality and value-systems'. Everywhere we have 'banal and repetitive' overt fantasies, thrust into books, films and plays, to what is now a quite obsessional and preponderant degree.

In cultural perversion we have private symbolism and rituals employed as Masud Khan says they are employed, as a form of reparative *play*. The sexual gratification is only a 'screen-experience' in these patients, directed against anxiety states: 'the basic use of the sexual apparatuses and instincts is of a reparative kind'. What is being enacted by perverts is 'a very special type of early relationship from their childhood'. Khan describes this relationship from his observations of his patients—

This relationship, in spite of all the overt and ecstatic awareness of what they were doing, was hidden from the patient himself, and in its essence was a repetition of the mother's idolisation of the infant-child as her created-object, which the child had internalised and hidden.

op. cit., page 95

One characteristic of this type of perverse sexual intimacy and relatedness, Khan says, is that—

both parties have a silent ritualistic acceptance of the *play* quality of the relationship. In spite of all their vociferous remonstrances to the contrary it is understood that the whole venture is transitional and uncommitting . . .

op. cit., page 95

From our point of view, in the concern with culture, we may note that the 'vociferous remonstrances' extend to an insistence that transitional and uncommitted relationships are superior and that such implications tend to contain a *hatred* of those committed relationships which are feared. Thus, under the influence of such propaganda for perversion in our culture normal love and marriage are implicitly debased in value, while what Straus calls 'immediate experience' which 'makes the erotic possible' is threatened 'by the world of outcomes'.

For instance, in the article in *The Times* on lesbianism referred to at the beginning of this chapter, the journalist quoted a member of a lesbian 'club' thus—

Caroline, a 38-year-old actress with two children was married 'very happily' for 12 years. She left her husband four years ago to live in Bayswater with another woman who had also been married and had had only one previous heterosexual experience. 'At the time I didn't sense any inadequacy in my relationships with men, but now I would never go back to a heterosexual relationship because this is so much more open, honest, and therefore satisfying . . . no more boosting someone else's ego . . .'

The Times, 2nd November 1970

Here we have 'vociferous remonstrances', translated into journalism, which the pervert at the time knows, inwardly, in all probability judging from Masud Khan's insights, to be false.

Of course, there are positive elements in perversion which can make it benign. Khan says—

the relationship in its true detail is private, secretive and something very special between the two persons concerned . . . each in fact is doing it as a reparative gesture towards the other . . .

'Reparation to the Self as an Idolised Internal Object',
in *Dynamic Psychiatry*, Vol. 2, November 1968, page 95

In benign perversion, says Khan—

. . . each will grow larger and more whole as a person from the venture . . . in spite of protestations of perpetual fidelity and devotion, each knows that separation and loss are inevitable and will not be too traumatic . . . a basic shared sense of gratitude at the time at having been allowed a mute and unsharable experience.   op. cit., page 95

In the benign form of perversion, then, 'the element of hostile and sadistic exploitation of the other is kept at a minimum'. But there are other malignant forms of perversion from which come hostile, destructive and nihilistic elements pouring out into the world, through the cultural media, so that the benign and reparative elements are lost sight of.

Very little is known, still, about perversion: as Khan says, 'the predicament of the pervert is still far from clear'. Yet the psychoanalytical approach begins to help us understand both the positive trends hidden in perversion, and its deeper meanings. Only thus, believes Khan, can we find—

true clues to the predicament of the pervert, without all the mystifications of moral approbation, or the envious adulation of the seemingly liberal social approach.   op. cit., page 96

The situation has now been reached in modern culture, in which these 'mystifications' are predominant, and the 'liberal social approach' has spread abroad an 'envious adulation'.

There seems to be an irreconcilable conflict between the ethical implications of such insights as those of Masud Khan and the implications of articles and advertisements in student journals, left-wing magazines or underground newspapers calling for 'more pornography', or the advocacy of such *avant-gardists* as Susan Sontag who wants more 'sensuality'. Masud Khan implies a human truth and an 'ethical statement' in the light of which the 'progressive' ethos only seems likely to leave society too much open to exploitation by those who seek to falsify and to harm sexual creativity itself. Where 'progressives' are actually selling, printing or performing matter for scopophile perversion they are actually spreading falsifications of perception which have their roots in the disturbance of communication, and may well be glibly spreading psychic ill-health abroad. That the deliberate dissemination of psychic disease should be part of 'protest' is impossible to accept for anyone who tries to grasp the implications of philosophical anthropology and philosophical biology.

The consequent dilemma is not easy to solve. Many works, considered to be 'modern classics' such as Genet's *The Thief's Journal* are now to be found on the bookshelves of intelligent adolescents in England, yet no-one would deny that such a book is an obscene work describing as it does forms of sexual perversion in enthusiastic (and idealized) detail. Toleration of such a work, and the acclaim of Genet as an artist both seem based on assumptions which derive mostly from arguments put forward by such thinkers as Sartre who dominate contemporary thought about culture and society. Yet in fact there are some areas of thought in which profound doubts are expressed about these assumptions. As Polanyi indicates, there is always that danger of the appeal of 'stability' in moral inversion: hate and perversion may seem more secure than our normal weak moral confusion. So, it is the works of the Sartres, and those they endorse, like Genet, that one finds at the ends of the earth, receiving more deference, acclaim and attention than those of Winnicott or Buber, Binswanger, Polanyi, Buytendijk, or Merleau-Ponty. Caliban casts out Ariel, in the excited schizoid atmosphere in which, to feel alive and real, one is encouraged to 'give oneself over to the joys of hating'.

If we examine the essays on perversion by Khan, it is obvious that what links the interest of the psychotherapist here with that of the individual concerned with culture is this question of meaning. For instance, the literary work of a pervert, such as Genet, may be tolerated because it can illuminate our understanding of the pervert, and thus promote a useful sympathy. But this inevitably raises the question of 'good' and 'bad' in the conduct depicted: and there is also the question of the social effect of such work in relation to its aesthetic qualities—that is, the quality of its meaning. This can only be discussed in symbolic terms—and we can only get to the meaning of the symbolism if we listen to someone like Masud Khan who can unravel it. Yet he may find some of it 'malignant' with effects that are likely to cause harm. We need help here from such a 'science of tropes and metaphors' as psychoanalysis may be considered to be. Surely we must also be prepared to take the ethical implications of perversion in literature, and act accordingly?

When a therapist like Khan unravels the symbolism of perversion, he learns from the pervert when his auto-therapeutic attempts have broken down and the 'true self' of the individual in despair is revealed; and so he finds that what is often achieved by such an individual is bound up with an intense energy of moral inversion from which others are bound to suffer. He sees and judges this in the light of the discovery that there is also in every individual a 'true self' which may be sometimes 'fobbed off', but persists in its determined attempts to pursue its own pattern, its 'formative principle'. Moreover, he finds that every human act, however perverted or evil-seeming, contains a motive which is positive, in that it is auto-therapeutic—that is, it is, however misled, an attempt to find a meaning in existence. From subjective disciplines one may also discover something very disquieting, which is that the search for meaning may take totally negative inverted courses: 'Evil be thou my good' and 'Good be thou my evil'.

However positive may be the auto-therapeutic impulse behind this, and however much it yields existential satisfaction for the individual in terms of a 'pleasurable negative identity', such a development may also be tragic, and dangerous and even criminal to others. Thus, while there is implicit faith in human nature in such an approach as Khan's, there is also an indication that sexual activity and the cultural depiction of sex can be harmful, unethical and destructive.

As Khan makes clear in his discussion of the Marquis de Sade, Genet and others, the 'technique of intimacy' by which the pervert exploits others can extend into the cultural realm—so that all of us, in a sense, may be exploited by mean, egocentric, and destructive personalities. We may be as much the victims (even 'willing victims') of such people as those they exploit in life itself by malignant acts of sex.

Moreover, because of their primitive nature, the sexual acts of the pervert (and, by implication, the cultural manifestations which arise from them as in 'confessions') can never solve the existence problems to which they are directed. The implication of this is that forms of 'confession' from the sexual pervert, which are becoming a dominant feature of contemporary culture, whatever they seem, may actually serve to endorse false solutions to the problems of life (and sex) and to divert our attention towards primitive attitudes and modes of behaviour belonging to hate. They can solve none of our existential or relational problems, and may spread evil abroad. We go to them in trust, expecting some contribution to our living dynamics, only to be urged by their 'technique of intimacy' towards false solutions, moral inversions and the shrinking of the inward life of others.

Once the considered statements of psychoanalysis have made us aware of the dangers in cultural manifestations such as these, there are certainly no grounds for an 'amoral' or 'shameless' view, nor is 'total permissiveness' the solution to our cultural problems.

Masud Khan's prefatory summary of his paper sounds like a series of ethical statements—

The technique of intimacy is described as an essential modality of the pervert's relation to his sexual object. The functions of the technique of intimacy are discussed as a defensive exploitation of eroticism against depression, internal anxiety-situations and object-relations; as a specific sexual variant of manic defence; as a vehicle of the anti-social tendency and the transitional object-phenomenon; and as a corrective auto-therapeutic emotional venture. It is postulated that acting out is the preferential mechanism of choice in the realisation of the technique of intimacy. The psychodynamics of acting out are discussed. The relation of the technique of intimacy and acting out in ego-pathology derivative from the pervert's disturbed early relationship to the mother is elaborated.

'The Function of Intimacy and Acting Out in Perversions'
from Sexual Behaviour and the Law, page 397

As Rollo May recognizes, behind such theories there are truths and values based on the kind of human 'fact' established by this kind of philosophical anthropology derived from 'reflection' and 'indwelling'. They seem to me to endorse all those insights one may derive from a study of creativity whether in children or the art of adults. They seem at odds with much that is fashionable in the world of art and thought. So it is on these ethical statements and this kind of human truth emerging from 'philosophical anthropology' that the present work attempts to base its rejection of the bigoted assumptions of 'enlightenment' about the ethics of sexual behaviour and sex in culture.

7
Ethics and sex

Masud Khan's analysis of perversion makes it plain that the origins of 'aim-inhibited' sex are in failures of creativity in life. The individual has not been able to create, out of the 'play' and 'reflection' between himself and his mother, either a meaningful world for himself, or a sufficiently independent sense of self to be able to bear the pains or enjoy the satisfactions of genuine relationship. So, his body-activity, and his idolization of body-activity are a form of desperate play, in which the 'other' is treated like a 'transitional object'. The 'other' may be a part of a person or a symbol like a teddy-bear or cuddly rag, and is subjected to all kinds of manipulation, objectification and even annihilation in the desperate hope that this may cure the individual, at the expense of his whole existence, if need be.

Obviously, ethical problems are involved here, as when one individual exploits another, jilts him, or is mean to him, or even when the pervert creates an atmosphere in which others become his 'envious collaborator', or in which his objects become 'a sort of thing in his dream'. Ethical considerations are still relevant. Where a pervert is schizoid and malignant, the other may become involved in a dream which ends in his death. Obviously, for the victims of de Sade, this meant becoming a 'willing victim' whose end could be horrible. These processes can be translated into the cultural sphere.

The association between the insistence of the sex reformer on pleasure at all costs and the philosophy of de Sade does not seem to trouble the liberal, the reader of the underground press, or the sexual emancipationist. The Marquis de Sade was one who so hated his own nature that he wanted to destroy all Nature. Yet this seems to be the ethical basis of the 'sexual revolution', which seems to be in pursuit of the 'perfect nihilism' of Nietzsche's Superman.

A good deal of enthusiasm for the sexual revolution seems to be based on a misunderstanding of the ethical implications of existentialism. It has picked up its rejection of social obedience, but without taking into account its emphasis on self-examination. In truth, from the existentialist point of view, as George Kneller writes—

Moral freedom is neither gratuitous nor licentious. It is not even synonymous with happiness. It implies an acceptance of dreadful responsibilities, because all other men must be morally free in the same way. Existentialism considered in this light cannot be thought of as a doctrine of moral anarchy . . .

Existentialism and Education, pages 94-5

Moral freedom does indeed involve an indebtedness towards other persons, arising from our obligation to grant to 'others' what is rightfully theirs—

to recognise the right of every other human being to the kind of freedom and self-expression he demands for himself.   op. cit., page 85

To recognize both what others are entitled to in this way of freedom, and to know what one's own freedom implies surely requires understanding of man's nature. This understanding is coming to us from those who approach man phenomenologically— taking into account his 'inwardness' and the meaning of his acts, signs and symbols. Psychoanalysis is making it plain that the 'healthy moral sense' is an important aspect of our relationship with others and the world, and that in this there are elements of 'reparation', and of the 'formative principle' at work. Phenomenology even seems to be showing that such a moral manifestation as shame may have an essential protective function. For instance, in his *Phenomenological Psychology*, Erwin Straus argues that 'shame is a protection against the public in all its forms . . . Shame is a safeguard for immediate experience against the world of outcomes. It does not constrain the erotic, as is assumed in (Freudian) psychoanalysis, but makes the erotic possible.' This implies that the secret and immediate 'creative becoming' between lovers, such as existentialism might be supposed to wish to promote, may in fact be menaced by the intrusions of pornography—

Those who are in love have no use for the 'dirty joke', pornography or the mirror, for these all belong to the shrunken existence of persons no longer capable of being touched . . . The secret that shame protects is not, however, as prudery makes the mistake of believing, one that is already in existence and only needs to be hidden from outsiders, for those in becoming are also hidden from themselves. Their existence is first made explicit in their first shared immediate becoming . . .

Phenomenological Psychology, page 222

The implications of this by no means lead towards moral anarchy, or even towards 'permissiveness'. They suggest that scopophilia may be a destructive force in our culture, against which shame needs to be upheld as a protection for creativity and erotic potentiality.

The denial of values, and demoralization, then, depend upon ignorance of man's nature. The substitution of hate for love, and the development of an inverted morality based on hate go with the implicit denial of the 'true self' and those ways in which our formative principle may realize its goals. The recognition of the problems of ambivalence and dependency, however, require us also to take into account our emotional vulnerability, and our sensitive 'female element' humanness. The need to accept these elements in our nature comes up against the 'taboo on weakness' in our culture.

In its turn the taboo on weakness is endorsed by a science 'imprisoned in physicalism', which tends to regard man as a machine. Polanyi has pointed out the connexions between reductionist views of man and the logical appeal of moral inversion. The apparent 'stabler state' of moral inversion can only be sustained by the denial of all moral values such as are created among human beings by their civilization—and this process is developing apace in our culture, as a study of the reviews on the culture pages of newspapers will demonstrate.

In the realm of 'philosophical anthropology', between philosophy and psychoanalysis, there would seem to be no endorsement of the position of the moral anarchist. Values at large emerge from the exchange of the sense of 'what seems right' between individuals, so that 'what seems right' becomes 'as absolute as maybe', in the same way that 'what seems red' and 'what seems graceful' can become established—

Just as the redness, the real objective redness, of a red flag is a matter of its redness to nearly everybody today and also tomorrow, unless it's been dipped in ink, so is the beauty of a face, the niceness of a person, and the rightness of an act, a matter not only of how they seem to oneself but also of how they seem to others, not only now but when the band stops playing . . . Real redness is constructed from redness to A and redness to B and redness to C, etc. etc. And redness to A is constructed from seeming now red to A, still seeming, e.g. on closer inspection, red to A. Likewise satisfactoriness is constructed from satisfactoriness to A to B, to C and really satisfactory to A is constructed from seems satisfactory to A after listening to it again, or even now that he is sober, or, etc. Likewise rightness is constructed from really seems right to A, to B, etc. and really seems right to A is constructed from seems right to A at first blush, still seems right to A after review, comparison, etc. It is with the business of the transition from 'seems for the moment acceptable and right to A' to 'seems really right and acceptable to A', that one is concerned ...

Philosophy and Psychoanalysis, page 110

Though such a process might seem to open up the question of the validity of everything, this is not so, because—

To say that right is what at infinity still seems right to everybody and that what seems right to so and so is a matter of what he finally feels, is not to make right more subjective than red (though it is *more* subjective). But it is a naturalistic and anti-transcendental *metaphysic* of ethics, e.g. ultimate description of ethical activity.   op. cit., page 107

The complex dynamic of 'ethical living', between 'what at infinity seems right to everybody', 'what so and so feels (to be right)', and 'what I feel to be right' has its origins in the earliest moral experience with the mother, as John Wisdom points out in another passage in which he says that it is she who draws out in the child his potentialities for what Winnicott would call 'a healthy moral sense'. From this point of view, to be sure that one can know what is right becomes no more absurd than being sure that a dancer is graceful.

This kind of talk suggests that ... goodness is related to stopping on the way from Damascus and cups of water, etc., and our reactions to these, like the grace of a dancer to her movement and our feelings for these. Her grace is a matter of the patterns she gives to our eyes and the lift she gives to our hearts. So there is no problem of how we know she's graceful.   op. cit., page 107

That one can be sure of rightness, taking into account ethical values that exist in the world, is not the approach of some of those who are most influential today, and who are notable free-thinkers in the realm of sex.

One of these is Dr. Alex Comfort, who is now Editor of the explicit magazine on sex, *Man and Woman*. As we have seen (in the quotation from *Nature and Human Nature* discussed on page 56) Dr. Comfort has only recently become aware of the reality of love: but this reality is not prominent in his magazine, which is essentially concerned with the outward realities of sex.

From the point of view of philosophical anthropology, love is the primary fact of human existence, because it is bound up with *meaning*. And it arises not from some excess of the quantitative fluxes or mechanisms of the organic body, but from consciousness —the way in which consciousness is created and developed, and consciousness as a quality in man that quests for meaning. This reality can only be discovered by what Polanyi calls 'attending from'. The trouble with Dr. Comfort's scientific point of view is that it is imprisoned in 'attending to'—that is, looking at the 'outside' of things.

Dr. Comfort's disciplines cannot bring him face to face with the 'true self', nor with 'reparation', nor with man's ethical flame, nor his formative principle, nor his values—and certainly not with his will-to-meaning. It is true that he speaks of 'personal responsibility'—yet, when one asks 'responsibility to what?' he cannot, with his objective approach, point to anything.

So, in the end, as so often with enlightened advocates, we are left with nothing but the advocate himself. He seeks to thrust aside all other sources of ethical values, and to supplant them by his own writings or broadcast talks. We are thus invited to live by Comfort and his 'sex instruction' magazine, and not from our own centres at all!

This seems evident from Dr. Comfort's reduction of all sexual problems to two 'commandments'. (These have now become embodied in the Report on Morality of the Church Council.) These are 'Thou shalt not invade the feelings of another' and 'Thou shalt not bring an unwanted child into the world'. It would, of course, only be possible to obey such commandments if one lived entirely at the 'explicit' level, and if sex were a pure biological, zoological function. The approach is too rational, and calls the irrational levels of our being too little into account.

As we saw above, Dr. Comfort now admits in spite of himself that somehow 'sexual love' has 'spilled over'. But as we see from Merleau-Ponty, sexual love and existence are indivisibly bound up, and are not to be seen as an 'overspill' from a bundle of organic functions (which is how *Man and Woman* presents the human image). 'Sex' exists largely in the area of 'being' and can only be approached by the 'tacit elements' in understanding. The sexual life, as is obvious from the comment of psychotherapists like May, is thus only minimally affected by culture and intellectual belief, or even by intuitive insights; it is created by the mother and the creativity she draws out, and belongs to the intractibility of the psychic life, with all the stubborn inflexibility of our 'psychic tissue'. Beneath all explicitness there is a spiritual daimon in every human being. Comfort's over-simplification is itself a disguise of these deeper problems which emerge, for instance, in the sort of case Rollo May describes, when a woman has an 'unwanted child' which is unconsciously very much wanted because she *wants* passion and creativity as aspects of the meaning of her existence.

It would, in fact, be possible to fulfil Comfort's commandments, while still frustrating one's primary needs, and ignoring the realities which philosophical anthropology has brought to our notice. As the work of Masud Khan shows, it is perfectly possible, for instance, to bring about a situation in which 'invading the feelings of another' is made to seem perfectly acceptable. May shows how we may easily be blind to invading another's feelings. In publishing *Man and Woman* Dr. Comfort is, in the light of Straus's essay on shame, invading the secret feelings of others.

Also, the injunction 'not to bring an unwanted child into the world' could be interpreted in terms which could lead to the destruction of another life, through abortion, even though the child's genesis was originally in the deepest desire of its mother to create life, and to find love and significance in the cosmos.

What is lacking from Dr. Comfort's simplistic morality is the whole problem of one's relationship with oneself—and the underlying problems of the unconscious and its symbolism. Such enthusiasts of the 'sexual revolution' see the scopophile exploitation of sexual symbolism, as in 'girlie' magazines, as a new breakthrough into liberation. I see it as a form of symbolic dehumanization, reducing the image of woman, by schizoid hate, to a less-than-human status. The explicitness of sex emancipationists I see as an invasion of our inwardness. Sexual symbols like the naked couples in the magazine *Man and Woman* are used to arouse primitive anxieties. In the light of Merleau-Ponty's comments I see all this as a manifestation of hate abroad in the world, by which we are threatened with objectification, while our concepts of ourselves are abused. All these ethical problems would not be seen by Dr. Comfort.

Dr. Comfort's co-editor is John Wilson, Director of the Farmington Trust in Oxford for research into moral education and author of *Logic and Sexual Morality*.

John Wilson's purpose is set out in his brief preface. He tells us that 'it is now some time since philosophers stopped being sages who told us about Ultimate Reality or The Meaning of Life'. They no longer, he says, even tell us what moral principles to adopt.

The philosopher is not able, and should not try, he says, to 'take the weight of moral decision off our shoulders'. What he can do, Wilson declares, is to 'help us make our own moral decisions for ourselves'.

In the sexual sphere Wilson believes we have 'a situation of malaise, anxiety, breakdown, or even chaos . . .' He says: 'Those who have the perspicacity and courage to see that we have got to make up our own minds must go back to first principles'. John Wilson's book is an attempt to go back to first principles—and he obviously supposes himself to be among those who have the courage and perspicacity to do so.

When there is a breakdown we have to overhaul the whole machine . . . No longer blindly accepting authority, we have to go back to the beginning and start again: and for this we need the philosopher, since starting again means looking with fresh eyes at arguments and opinions which we may have too casually accepted or dismissed . . .

Logic and Sexual Morality, page 7

John Wilson offers himself, as we shall see, as an 'analytical clarifier' in this realm. When he speaks of overhauling the whole machine, he means the machine of *communication about sex*.

This work can only be done properly by the use of more honest, realistic and effective forms of communication about sex than those we now use. Writing books is a large-scale but rather primitive form of communication: our society needs more person-to-person discussion, questions, broadcasts, lectures, seminars, classroom periods and so on. Provided they start from first principles, and are not incompetent attempts to indoctrinate, it is these methods that will benefit us the most; and I should judge the success of this book by whether it encourages the reader along these lines rather than by any other standard.

op. cit., page 8

Man and Woman is presumably one of the new methods of 'communication': in its first issue it printed a photograph of a couple having sexual intercourse, a set of graphs of sexual arousal from the Masters-Johnson sexology findings, a close-up drawing of the female sex organ, and an alphabetical encyclopedia in which one item was 'Artificial Penis or Dildo'.

Without denying the gains we have achieved by reaching a situation in which open discussion of sexual problems has become possible, I believe we may have doubts about the confident implication that such 'improved communications' are all we need. In 'communications' theory we already take too much for granted, not least the problem of communication with ourselves and all that initiation of perception which may be called 'intentionality'—and, indeed, all that belongs to meaning and our creation of a meaningful world by imagination.

Here we need, I believe, to go back to the 'first principles' not of communication, nor even of modes of thinking, but of the nature of thought itself, and its relationship to living a whole life. The philosopher may have given up trying to tell us the meaning of life; but philosophy has certainly not given up its preoccupation with *meaning*—indeed, it is making a fundamental transposition from the analytic to another co-ordinate system, or to a new key. As Marjorie Grene says, speaking of Suzanne Langer: 'What is the "transcendental unity of apperception," the "I think" which unifies all phenomena and makes the categories and principles, and through them experience, possible?' In Marjorie Grene's discussion of Kant the emphasis is very much on the particular.

The activity of mind is not like the 'activity' of a strong acid, it is not a bare event, but a *doing*, and it must be done by *someone*. And someone is always someone in particular, born somewhere at some time of some parents, possessing some innate aptitudes, moulded somehow by the setting of his family, society, time.

The Knower and the Known, page 143

It is this emphasis which we must take from 'philosophical anthropology', from forms of philosophy very different from that to which John Wilson subscribes. These do not offer us Ultimate Reality or the Meaning of Life, nor do they tell us what moral principles to adopt. But they *do* present us with certain inescapable facts of being-in-the-world, and of the nature of the human pre-occupation with meaning. Such forms of philosophy take us beyond a concern merely with 'communication', because meaning emerges from one's creative engagement with one's inward world, by dream, phantasy and symbol, and is bound up with bodily orientation and the 'psychic tissue'.

These human facts are worth emphasizing alongside some of Mr. Wilson's points. First, where there are sexual difficulties, these must be seen as emerging from the whole complex living experience of an individual, not least that formative experience of infancy to which Marjorie Grene refers, in which the capacity to relate to others is drawn out by the mother and family. Secondly, where there are sexual difficulties, these can never be engaged with by intellectual effort alone. If we are to help individuals to develop morally, or to become more effective in their whole complex of living, then no amount of 'communications' alone, however 'clear', will suffice. The ability to communicate itself depends upon the degree to which an individual has developed the capacity to find meaning in his world.

To help overcome 'sexual difficulties', there needs to be slow change and development of the whole psychic life, to enable the 'someone' to grow those capacities which were perhaps never grown, or inadequately grown, during the formative years of infancy, when he was learning to love. Only love, or a version of love, can help us to grow, in our relational capacities.

In invoking 'communications' and logic alone, John Wilson surely fails to take into account the intractable nature of such a problem which belongs to a whole life-pattern, and one's 'communication' with one's world. Above all, he suggests from the beginning that this kind of problem is tractable, through the medium of intellectual communication such as logic is concerned with. This is implicitly to deny 'psychic reality' and its essential inaccessibility. In consequence of this denial, it may be that, since 'an unbridled lucidity can destroy the meaning of complex matters' as Polanyi has argued, the explicitness of *Man and Woman* and other forms of 'analytical clarifying' in fact help destroy meaning here.

John Wilson and Alex Comfort sound from the blurbs on the jackets of their books as if they belong to a new 'scientific' approach, untrammelled by all the old bogies of superstition and prejudice. Of Wilson's Pelican book the blurb says 'A highly unexpected approach by a philosopher via fact, logic, and science, to the problem of morals and sexual behaviour in society'.

From the point of view of philosophical anthropology, there would seem to be no more reason, just because he is a logician, to pay any more attention to John Wilson's views on sex than any one else's. (Nor should we pay special attention to Dr. Alex Comfort because he is a zoologist.) However, as we shall see, it is as an Editor of *Man and Woman* and author of a Pelican book on sexual ethics: it is as an expert on sexual conduct that he offers himself (despite his disclaimers, his book *Logic and Sexual Morality* ends with a section of 'advice'). Though he pretends to 'objectivity', he is in this being highly subjective. It is only by some strange quirk of our intellectual history that we should be prepared to consider a logician as a 'scientific' specialist from whom we could learn to deal with such a complex aspect of living experience as sex, for logic is the most narrow-minded of specializations. As Marjorie Grene says, discussing Kant's *Critique of Pure Reason*, Kant felt that the character and content of logic were established once and for all in Aristotle, and that this was so because the achievement was so easy—

it is the very narrowness of the subject which permitted its once-for-all formulation. Logic is concerned only with the pure form of thought. It 'abstracts' Kant says, from all objects of knowledge and their differences, and so in it the intellect is concerned with nothing but itself and its form . . .   *The Knower and the Known*, page 124

Kant considered it much harder for reason 'to take the sure road of science when it had to do with objects'. How much harder, then, for logic, when it comes to take account of psychic, inner reality! All logic can do, faced with a problem of such substance, is to substitute one kind of narrow-mindedness for another.

Yet it is obvious that ours is an age in which one is inclined to give assent to such a specialist when he offers himself as an 'analytical clarifier' who is going to help us form our own moral judgements, even in the sphere of the intimate dialogue by rational or 'objective' methods. We are inclined to give him more assent because he is claimed to be 'scientific' than we would give, say, a poet or even a psychotherapist who might perhaps be more able to recognize 'the category of life'. As Marjorie Grene says, philosophers themselves have not—

wholly overcome, in the grounds of their own thinking, the dualism of Descartes, and the concept of wholly explicit knowledge that goes with it. Therefore they still seek a pure and independent Reason exempt from the hazards of life. op. cit., page 146

John Wilson, as we shall see, pays tribute, on the face of it, to the fact that 'logic and situation, the ideal and the factual, reason and history' live as aspects of our lives in tension with one another, in 'ineradicable ambiguity'. Yet this attitude seldom inhibits his clarifying enthusiasm.

The whole appeal of such a book as his, and the magazine he co-edits, is that they seem to offer us rapid and easy possibilities for this 'ineradicableness' to be overcome, and the hazards to be avoided. On the other hand Wilson seeks to persuade us that 'there are no ultimate, unquestionable criteria by which truth can be recognized and labelled and stored away forever apart from human aims and interests', and so goes too far in suggesting that there are no values on which we can rely. While questioning all values, he is at the same time too enthusiastically concerned to set up his own criteria, as one having 'perspicacity and courage', while other criteria are suggested by the existence of his magazine alone.

Wilson is keen to dispel all deference to existing values and truths—

'Be sensible!' or 'be reasonable!' are commands usually intended to stop people doing things. *Since we don't know what is really sensible or reasonable in sexual behaviour, there is no point in pretending that we do . . .*
Logic and Sexual Morality, page 261 (my italics)

But we *do* know, from the collocation of 'naturalistic descriptions', from the 'ethical living' of each individual, as suggested by Professor John Wisdom. We *do* know, from those values which have been created between individuals over centuries of civilization, some of which 'at infinity . . . still seem right to everybody'— such as that rape is wrong and that love is a dimension utterly remote from, say, the devouring and distance-keeping looking of the voyeur. I believe we also know, because we still *feel*, for instance, that sexual activity in public is wrong, despite the attitudes of the *avant-garde*. The existence of feelings of shame and modesty, and the need for privacy as described by Merleau-Ponty and Erwin Straus also indicates an intuitive knowledge of 'right' and 'wrong'. We know such things are 'right' or 'wrong' from *within ourselves*, because in our history, in the body, through the creative reflection of the mother, we have developed a 'healthy moral sense' which has been drawn out in ourselves in complex with the culture and values of civilization.*

By contrast, John Wilson's ambitions, so far as we can see, seem to be to attempt to deal with the world by the 'male elements' of analytical intellect and 'doing' exclusively, while denying that 'other' ways of dealing with the world exist and can only be 'lived'. He seeks to persuade us that we are only minds, and can deal with this realm by mind. This is absurd because in such a realm as that of sex, obviously, the 'female element' capacities of emotion, meaning and 'being' are pre-eminent. It is the one area where no amount of conscious intention, intellectual analysis, or mechanical 'doing' alone can overcome difficulties, bring satisfaction or create meaning. Looked at from the diagnostic insights of psychoanalysis, John Wilson's position seems to offer a parallel to the problem of the individual who has split off his female element because he fears it, and cannot embrace it. Such a theory even seems a defence against 'going with' sexual experience itself: we must never flow into the realm of 'female being' of intuition and spontaneity, but always be 'sensible'. We must choose according to conscious ethical precepts, in a situation in which all values are relative. But as I have suggested, this is to remove us from the necessary risk in time by which alone creative living is possible.

It is not sensible (in this society) to have illegitimate children, seduce minors, bring up children *before you know that* you and your wife (or husband) can produce a happy family . . .   op. cit., page 261 (my italics)

Since it is impossible to 'know' anything of the kind, the phrase in italics imposes an impossible qualification on our sexual lives. If one were so unwilling to take 'risks' one could never have *any* experiences. Instead of fostering intentionality, such an injunction would seem likely to promote impotence and ineffectualness since it puts one's capacity for choice at the mercy of an impossible desire for certainty. Moreover the way in which the logician frames his sentence allows that it might be acceptable to seduce minors, if only society removed a 'taboo'. In such an implicit relativism one may detect an impulse to undermine values, out of a failure to recognize the primary realities of the inner life, and values which are as near absolute as possible. We know from the philosophical anthropology arising from case histories that the damage caused by such a seduction is a consequence of the violation of the integrity of the 'true self' in an immature creature. Such an invasion of one individual's 'secret core' by another impinges a basic ethical

---

* See also the paper by D. W. Winnicott on 'The Location of Culture', discussed in the present writer's *Human Hope and the Death Instinct*.

principle which is 'right to infinity', and it is merely destructive to suggest that we could perhaps ignore such insights and values.

To accept one's inner core of being is to accept one's vulnerable 'female element', and one's dependence—one's need to love and to commit oneself to love's creativity. The limitations of John Wilson's thought here may be seen in the way in which family life is dealt with in his book. No-one, for instance, could bring up a baby by the injunction that one should not start until one *knows* that one can bring up a happy family, since the crucial needs of the situation involve a forfeiture of the mother's identity and an emotional commitment in the realm of 'being' *for* the child. The mother has to 'go with' an experience, before she knows whether she can deal with it, and in any case how she deals with it does not depend upon *knowing*. The same is true of the sexual life. Until one accepts and enters a relationship whole-heartedly, or actually has children, one cannot know how one is going to react, and certainly not whether one is going to be 'happy' or not: reactions to these experiences arise from deep, unconscious factors not stirred until the life-situation actually presents itself, and they are only involved *once* one is committed. Love demands 'emotional surrender' (such as the pervert, who sticks to an 'activity', cannot give). Until one 'goes with' an experience one cannot know how one's 'being' will respond to it. It is true that Wilson says 'Say "Yes!" to life'—but the total effect of his work is to suggest to us, as does his magazine *Man and Woman*, that we can only say this 'Yes!' in an explicit and intellectual way—by analytical clarification rather than by living through an experience, or entering into the creative mysteries of love in a committed way. As Straus says, 'The behaviour of the voyeur is not an inherently meaningful surrender to fate, like that of lovers'. It is this creative committed surrender that John Wilson's approach threatens. He does not make the erotic possible, because he threatens 'shared immediate becoming'.

This again may be related to the question of how we think of learning and knowing. As Marjorie Grene says—

Our cultural heritage comprises, as Polanyi remarks, 'the sum total of everything in which we may be totally mistaken.' That is the risk inherent in being alive . . .   *The Knower and the Known*, page 146

She quotes Price—

'It is the capacity of making mistakes, not the incapacity of it, which is the mark of the higher stages of intelligence.'   op. cit., page 83

There is a kind of 'knowing' that is obtained only through giving and suffering. As Viktor Frankl says—

We cannot live with Baedekers in our hands; if we did so, we would overlook all chances in our life that only come once; we would skirt our destiny and pass by situational values instead of actualizing them.

The Doctor and the Soul, page 60

Only by 'going with an experience' can we exert, as Marjorie Grene says, 'the creative imagination through which we shape the time that we are'.

The existential nervousness of John Wilson's position is evident from his way of writing—

If you use your reason properly, two things should happen: first you should not be carried away from what you know to be true; and second, you should not be hoodwinked into believing things that you don't know to be true . . .   *Logic and Sexual Morality*, page 261

If one could be as much in control as he suggests, however, life would simply prove emptier, because one might not be presented with the need to endure successfully the kind of dilemma which promotes growth, discovery of possibilities—and satisfaction. Unless we 'go with' an experience and allow our struggle with it to bring out our creative potentialities, we may never discover that daimonic union of love and will which Rollo May sees as our much-needed source of intentionality. We would fall into that dissociation and apathy—that loss of integration of will and passion—which May diagnoses as our basic ill, schizoid in itself.

It is never possible to know beforehand if one is going to be happy, or whether one is to be 'hoodwinked' or not. On Wilson's pattern no woman could go over into Primary Maternal Preoccupation. No-one could ever teach. No-one could ever be in love. We may suspect that his doubtfulness here arises from the fact that fundamentally he lacks confidence in the capacity of a woman, of the mother to *be* for her child. He can say 'we cannot know what is right' because he does not *know* 'female knowing', from experience at the simplest level. Yet if we really followed his advice, we could not even learn to ride a bicycle, for even this we do by 'indwelling', and 'going with an experience'.

Wilson says, 'You can't change yourself as much as you think'; but all he offers as a positive in the moral quest is a simple hedonism: 'Does this relationship make me happy?' He adds that one should 'find out what the other person wants', and urges us to 'treat people as equals'. These are valuable injunctions, but Wilson surely reveals the difficulty of obeying them by his passage—

I myself prefer *contracts with women who like to regard themselves as equals* . . . who take the initiative as much as I do, who are sexually generous rather than 'modest' or 'reticent', and who do not demand constant attention or wooing . . .   op. cit., page 263 (my italics)

The phrase 'like to' surely implies an attitude to 'the other' which inhibits her freedom? The astonishing plural surely itself disqualifies any relationship in advance from becoming committed? It is very difficult to deal in a serious argument with personal 'confessions' like this, in books about sex. All one can say perhaps is that one is astonished that the declaration doesn't take the form, 'If I fall in love with *a woman* . . .' To speak of the 'contracts' one would like to have with 'women' seems to the present writer to reveal a somewhat primitive concept of love.

We must, however, stick to the argument, rather than engage on any *ad hominem* speculations about John Wilson's own personal attitudes. Again, we need to invoke the insights of psychoanalysis into the nature of love. Michael Balint distinguishes, in *Primary Love and Psychoanalytical Technique* (Hogarth Press, 1962) between immature and mature love, and indicates that considerable efforts are needed to attain the capacity for mature love. When individuals develop a deeper sense of personal reality they come to realize that—

our needs have become too varied, complicated and specialized, so that we can no longer expect automatic satisfaction by our objects . . .
Primary Love and Psychoanalytical Technique, page 126

John Wilson's argument all along seems to me to rather vindicate a more oversimplified approach to the problem—as if we didn't have to go through considerable struggles to love. As Balint says, we have to become able to 'bear the depression' of realizing that we cannot find satisfaction through merely 'omnipotent' or 'greedy' love. Immature love cannot find the reality of the other person: 'no consideration or regard can be paid to (the object's) interests, sensitivities or well-being', and the 'object' must be 'taken for granted'. But isn't this just the effect of an attitude, if we accept it, that what we shall look forward to is 'contracts' with 'women' who do not make too great demands upon us?

Balint points out that an individual who takes the point of view that 'only one partner is entitled to make demands' is, in fact, by no means 'free', but is really showing over-dependence. He may even have a 'fundamental contempt for the object'. I believe that many people are influenced by 'enlightened' books on sex, to believe that a non-committal attitude to relationship represents 'freedom': yet in the light of such an essay as that of Balint, this kind of detachment is really a form of defence against emotional surrender—

Such hate is a last remnant, the denial of, and the defence against, the primitive object-love . . .   op. cit., page 128

That is, where we find individuals remaining 'sexually disposed persons' as Frankl calls them, shrinking from deeper eroticism and emotional commitment, we may suspect that they are motivated by a kind of hate, that tends to exploit the 'other' in a primitive way, and avoid creative commitment—

(to be mature) we must accept the fact that we have to give something to the object, something that he expects from us, in order to change the object into a *cooperative partner* . . .

Primary Love and Psychoanalytical Technique, page 126

It is this recognition of the need to 'find' and to 'commit' oneself that I find so lacking in *Logic and Sexual Morality*, and this seems to me a fault emphasized by the occasional lapses of tone ('the occasional blonde') which indicate a certain superficiality of attitude to personal relationships.

The capacity for relationship, as we have seen, is bound up with the capacities of the individual for 'ethical living'. Thus, in John Wilson's work, the failure to recognize the full complexities of emotional surrender go inevitably with the denial of values— 'there are no experts in sexual morality', 'all moral questions are . . . ultimately matters of your own decision. Nobody can form our own values for us. Nevertheless certain disciplines (including religion and psychology) can help us to arrive at the most *rational* decision.' To this, I believe, we would need to add that only by what Balint calls 'reality testing', that is, living through experiences and developing one's creative capacities to be in touch with one's 'ethical flame' and the created values of one's civilization, can one engage creatively with the experience of loving another person.

The more we study the philosophical anthropology of 'object-relations' and 'existentialist' psychoanalysis, the less confident we shall be, I believe, in Wilson's emphasis on 'rational' decisions. As Leslie Farber indicates there are moments of immense importance in our decisions when barely anything is conscious, and certainly not explicit.* But John Wilson insists that 'improvement can only come by better communication', and he adds nothing to qualify the word 'rational' as Professor Wisdom tries to (for him one chooses by 'what really *feels* right'). The 'tacit dimension' again is disastrously missing from Wilson's work.

John Wilson goes on to make it plain that he really believes that knowledge, of the explicit kind alone, can bring us towards perfection in such a realm. He wants to influence human nature.

---

* 'In spite of their conscious will to consummate their longings into a clear proposal of marriage, Varenka and Koznyshev both will to do otherwise in a manner in which they are not even conscious of willing' On a passage from *Anna Karenina*, in *The Ways of the Will*, pages 12–14.

'In the not-too-distant future we shall be able to influence human nature far more than we now can . . . as knowledge advances.'

Such a hope would seem to manifest a kind of belief in magic or a divinization of science, rather than a true recognition of human truth.

A philosophical anthropology which recognizes our existence in the body realizes that rational insights can never determine completely or be in absolute control, and would be very hesitant about even considering that human nature can be changed by knowledge alone. It could perhaps hope that knowledge could help people to alter the circumstances of lives in such a way as to bring some improvements in the 'psychic tissue' of future generations. Here, I believe, the effect of such arguments as those of John Wilson could even make things worse—as by encouraging individuals to avoid that creative commitment in which alone they could find the sense of meaning they essentially seek.

From the point of view of such writers as Rollo May or Frankl, who believe that man's primary needs are love and the need to satisfy the will-to-meaning, the injunction to ask 'Does this relationship make me happy?' would seem trivial and superficial unless 'happiness' could be defined in more subtle and complex terms. A definition of 'happiness' could only be given body and form in a discussion of man's totality which included assumptions about his quest for meaning in a love that is stronger than death. This kind of discussion, serious in tone, Frankl gives us, also certain forms of creative symbolism. Logic cannot help us here. The value of logic is in helping us to examine the steps in an argument. If the terms and premisses are inadequate, logic cannot help us. If one term is 'happy', and this word is given no full living definition, however logical the argument, it will still be trivial—without roots in 'whole being'. Wilson's way of discussing sex, whatever his gift for logical debate, is nearly always too trivial to engage with the deeper problems. So his approach is inevitably to trivialize sex— which is, of course, what his magazine does too with its thousand-word articles unnecessarily asking 'What is male orgasm?' and such absurdities.

As director of the Farmington Trust John Wilson published a revealing article on moral education in *The Times* of 7th October 1965. His article shows some odd tricks for a philosopher. He says of his centre 'we hope to point to those contexts and methods which have *real* importance' (my italics). Isn't the word 'real' here somewhat question-begging? 'Real' to whom?

Though Mr. Wilson speaks of the way in which 'authorities' are nowadays questioned, it is obvious by his confident tone, in this article again that he feels his ideas alone to have any authority.

There are no standards but his standards, and they are those of a fervent need to remove ethical debate into a realm of intellectual dissociation. From his point of view, which seems to be that of a relative approach to all values, 'the gap left by authority' is to be filled only by 'communication', with the teacher as 'analytic clarifier'.

Surely anyone with experience of the education of children must be aware that to be merely a 'clarifier' would simply be to abrogate one's function as an adult in relation to the child? A child needs love to reflect his moral growth. Just as Wilson refuses to commit himself to relationship, he seems to want to encourage teachers to refuse to commit themselves to the 'creative reflection' role, in which they both embody their own ethical position, and yet allow the child to extend his own moral sense by nurturing his creative dynamics, and by allowing the child to 'make use of him' (which will include making use of his—the teacher's—own moral code). As Melanie Klein has demonstrated, identification is here a powerful influence, while what happens between teacher and child includes many subjective complexities which belong to intuition and the emotional life.* This Wilson fails to see. Missing too from his picture are the 'healthy moral sense' of the child, and the adult's recognition of the ethical values which exist in the world.

Wilson says 'children are to be enabled to make their own morality'—but by analysis and logic! While it is true that (as Winnicott says) 'civilization begins anew in each child', no child can create the whole of civilization anew from within himself without interplay between 'union and separateness', that is unless his own moral sense is able to draw on inherited values in his culture. He will, of course, already have taken much from his mother, his home and his early education: these will have drawn out in him latent capacities to be humanly ethical. As Winnicott emphasizes, a child needs 'moral codes lying around' and he needs to feel committed to an engagement with these, in a 'felt' way. There seems a real danger that if an analytical clarifier merely presents him with explicit 'outside' knowledge of moral codes, and a few rules for reassuring, the child will gain nothing, or even feel that the implications of such an approach is that all values are relative, and so are 'debunked'. As with riding a bicycle, learning to be ethical is a process in which there is much that is tacit and subsidiary and which has to be *lived through*. Roots need pressure against which to grow: to take an 'analytical' relative position to all authority with children would be simply to betray one's role in fostering

---

* See also *Adolescent Process and the Need for Personal Confrontation* by D. W. Winnicott, *Playing and Reality*, Tavistock 1971.

their independent growth. There are certain moral codes which need to be conveyed to a child, in a 'whole' or 'felt' way. It is important for one thing for the child to experience the human fact that adults have strong views on moral issues and this is a most important and creative experience for him.*

One of the strengths children look for in adults is the capacity to be so secure in oneself that one can bear to tolerate the different and sometimes opposed views of others. But this kind of security implies that an adult has standards of his own, bound up with his own healthy moral sense. Merely to say, 'Make up your own mind' is to let a child down and to leave him feeling insecure. One of Wilson's standards may be to believe that children should develop their own creative centres of conscience; but they cannot do this unless they become aware of strength of creative conscience in the adult—that he is capable of 'ethical living'. If an adult only 'communicates' or 'clarifies' while abdicating his own ethical position and taking the stand of absolute relativism, how shall a child grow his personality by identifying with him, challenging him as a scratching post, using him as a matrix, *giving* to him, rejecting what he has to offer? How shall he ever find and develop his 'intentionality'?

Of course an adult does best to avoid coercion and indoctrination, because this only induces compliance and false socialization. But it seems as unrewarding to abdicate the responsibility of being 'there', and being, if necessary, unpopular and ready to be hurt by the child's rejection or hate at times. Nothing could be more insecure for a child than an over-permissive home in which the adults have failed to take on the authority of adults.† Rollo May finds the roots of such over-permissiveness in fear and guilt—

It is a sound hypothesis, based on a good deal of evidence in psychotherapeutic work, that the unconscious guilt which parents . . . carry because they manipulate their children, leads them to be overprotective and overpermissive towards the same. There are the children who are given motorcars but who are not taught moral values, who pick up sensuality but who are not taught sensitivity in life. The parents seem vaguely aware that the values on which their will power was based are no longer efficacious. But they can neither find new values nor give up the manipulative will . . .   *Love and Will*, page 278

It could be argued that John Wilson's influence urges us towards

---

* 'If the adult abdicates, the adolescent becomes prematurely, and by false process, adult . . .' D. W. Winnicott, op. cit. footnote above.

† As Winnicott says, the adult role will sometimes be painful. See also W. B. Curry in *Dartington Hall* on the original failure in progressive education there; young children became very exhausted by being asked to make every decision for themselves.

mere sensuality. There is no discrimination in his approach between mature love and immature sexual activity, such as we find in Balint's work, or say, in Viktor Frankl's essay on 'The meaning of Love' in *The Doctor and The Soul*. In his essay Frankl distinguishes between the 'sexually disposed person', the 'erotically disposed person', and the individual capable of love that finds meaning only in uniqueness. What Frankl calls a 'thoroughly decadent sensualism' could be justified by Wilson's logic. So too could that new kind of impotence which Rollo May finds in American society as a consequence of that 'will which blocks love'. Winnicott sees that if adolescents are forced into a false maturity by adult abdication we lose their valuable idealism.* In the light of psychoanalytical insight, John Wilson's approach could be seen in terms of a need to deny the 'female' element in ourselves because it is our most *human* aspect, and thus to subdue our creativity to too much 'male' analysis. It is, in the light of Straus's arguments, likely to prove destructive to subject the 'most intimate dialogue' to diagrammatic weekly journalism with voyeuristic pictures that threaten it with the 'generalized', the 'objective', and the 'public'.

We can never live according to an intellectual pattern alone or subdue life to it: we can only live imperfectly, with our unknown selves, while growth and satisfaction require suffering as well as joy, reliance upon the 'tacit dimension', and 'immediacy'.

As Money-Kyrle points out, despite the ambitions of philosophers, it is impossible to create a philosophical system which is both internally consistent and comprehensive. Most philosophers have achieved their systems at the cost of leaving something out: as he says—

Such defects are usually attributed to the immense complexity of the task. *But they may also reflect essential inconsistencies in man which no system can resolve.*

P. D. Money-Kyrle, 'Psychoanalysis and Philosophy' in *Psychoanalysis and Contemporary Thought*, page 108 (my italics)

The 'essential inconsistencies' are the stuff of our essentially human existence. It is in them that we find our meaning and it is they that make life continually creative, fascinating, and mysteriously full of potentialities.

Money-Kyrle adds in a footnote that he does not wish to suggest that it is logically impossible to construct a system which, within its own level, is consistent and comprehensive—

but that it may be psychologically impossible *to achieve the hidden aim*

---

* Winnicott says that 'Adults are needed if adolescents are to have life and liveliness.' *Playing and Reality*, page 150.

of complete self-integration by means of the construction of such a system.
op. cit., page 108 (my italics)

This seems essentially the kind of aim such a philosophy as that of John Wilson has (as is perhaps evident in the title of his book). Such a philosophic picture, because of its yearning for what is impossible, may *seem* a completely harmonious picture of the world—

but some whole section of what ordinary people call reality—it may be matter or mind, or perhaps the concept of evil—is ignored . . .
op. cit., page 108

John Wilson represents the kind of logical mind which seeks to demonstrate that ethical values are 'bad grammar' and may therefore be rejected. As Marjorie Grene points out, it is typical of philosophy to trivialize issues we know from experience to be real enough, dodging them by verbal tricks. Wilson's popular appeal lies in such a superficial 'clarifying' of profound and complex problems of human nature. His intellectual scheme for sex may be seen as a form of hair-splitting. His aim in the pursuit of the 'rational' is a form of pursuit of schizoid 'purity' (use your reason *properly*') from which the inconsistencies—of hate and ambivalence, and the 'daimon'—are eradicated all too easily. The use of logic here seems a rationalization of the wish not to be human, and what are left out are the 'ordinary realities' of love and the body.

The psychoanalyst seems less liable to make such a mistake because, as we have seen, he meets the individual face-to-face when all his rationalizations have broken down. He is therefore compelled, faced with what Khan calls the 'well-grounded despair' of the pervert, to discriminate between kinds of sexual behaviour, on ethical *principles*, as Wilson is not, and to explore the deeper implications of the meaning of the body as a manifestation of existence.

8
The delusions of sexology

ઝઝ

One of the predominant absurdities in the modern world is the divinization of science. Everywhere in advertisements one may find a picture of the man in a white coat, with the tag, 'Science says . . .'. The scientist above all other men 'knows'—he has access to a body of objective knowledge, by which all complexities of life may be untangled. He is the new witch doctor, and his science is the new mumbo-jumbo.

As a number of philosophers are now pointing out, our genuine belief in science itself is based in passionate subjective feelings— and science only derives its authority from the way in which we are prepared to believe in it. No layman can check the conclusions of science for himself: he simply gives science his credence, from inward conviction, without demanding proof. A measure of our faith is the launching of vast rockets to the moon.*

The situation can arise, however, that 'science' seems to be telling us something that inwardly we know to be false. This kind of problem arose, of course, over child care, in the days of feeding by the clock. A woman would know the 'milk was in', and might hear her baby crying for it. Yet she would lie on the bed crying with pain and frustration, watching the hands of the chronometer, because 'science' had told her that she must not break the laws of baby-minding as determined by science. Then along came a Winnicott who said, 'Only the mother knows. Other people, doctors and nurses, only think they know . . .'. So, we were restored, properly, to intuition, to confidence in another way of knowing.

Today, in the realm of sex, we have a situation in which, especially in America, individuals are tending to disregard what they themselves know, even about their own experience, and preferring to believe what 'science' tells them they should know. Here we may now, however, confidently expose philosophical

---

* See *Science, Faith and Society* by Michael Polanyi, Phoenix Books, Chicago.

absurdities. Polanyi refers to experiments which show that all knowledge has roots in the tacit dimension. That is, what we inwardly know, as whole beings, is primary. We should always remain aware that this is so and refer back continually to our own unique experience, 'from the inside', to check whatever explicit theories we may encounter. Moreover, in looking at the nature of knowledge, we should always remain aware of the subjective elements in the endorsement of 'science'—not least if what 'science says' seems to have the effect of falsifying 'whole being'. There is never any 'objective', non-human 'truth' which exists outside human beings knowing, to which we must give absolute deference. To believe as much is obscurantist.

In her discussion of Aristotle in *The Knower and the Known*, Marjorie Grene discusses Polanyi's concepts of 'indwelling' and says—

This analysis Polanyi has . . . elaborated in reliance on psychological experiments on 'subception', which seem to confirm the subsidiary elements in perceptual behaviour . . . My awareness is not a separate subjective 'in-itself', but at one and the same time an assimilation of what is beyond and an extension of myself into the things beyond. This interpenetration of 'self' and 'world' is not only a central characteristic of mind: it is what mind is . . .   *The Knower and the Known*, page 56

To apply the 'mind' to 'sex' properly is thus to extend oneself into 'the things beyond'—but since these 'things' are 'inward' experiences of people as well as physiological 'facts', sexual reality can only be 'known' by 'indwelling' that is, by imaginative means such as projective identification ('putting oneself in the shoes of others'). Yet, as we shall see, the 'scientific' approach to sex tries to exclude this kind of 'indwelling' from its disciplines. It also implicitly denies that, even in its own methods, the 'tacit element' is predominant.

For instance, the sexologist does not sufficiently investigate his own reasons for wanting to observe others in sexual intercourse, functioning. To do so he would have to examine the way in which his 'seeing' belongs to Cartesian modes, and so implicitly violates those aspects of 'whole being' to which anti-Cartesian science is now pointing. That is, sexology violates those meanings of the body to which Merleau-Ponty draws our attention. Even in his kind of attention to sexual encounter, the sexologist not only objectifies man but makes him into something dead. As Straus says—

The relation of the subject to sensing (in behaviourist thinking) is mere 'having': the subject 'has' sensations, but he does not sense. It is a strange world of the dead that is supposed to be the beginning and the foundation of psychic life.   *The Primary World of Senses*, page 19

Because of the unseen, tacit elements of which he is unaware, the sexologist fails to see that his approach is not 'objective' at all, but 'totally permeated by unexamined metaphysical and epistemological assumptions' (as Straus says about Pavlov). Among these are the failure to examine the problem of 'acclimatization'. Pavlov's dogs didn't become susceptible to conditioned reflex training until they had been in the laboratory for several days. What about the subjects of sexology experiments? They took part in sexual activities not seeking half-light, silence, and concealment, as normally lovers do, but under the impingement of the kind of 'clarity' the voyeur seeks. They had to be the kind of people who could enter into that laboratory, and they had to endure a scopophiliac 'urge to look' from third persons, the effect of whose observation on the naked body, as Merleau-Ponty says, is to threaten 'enslavement' and objectification. We may say of these 'preparatory requirements', as Straus says of the requirements of the animal laboratory, that 'they present problems in themselves'. The apparent simplicity of sexological experiments is thus a fake—

The simplicity is but a superficial one. It owes its sham existence to a scotoma* for the actual problems, resulting in a naive anticipation of theoretical decisions . . .   *The Primary World of Senses*, page 34

The laboratory, compared with the usual life-situation of sexual love, is, like the laboratory of Pavlov, 'characterized by a complete monotony and barrenness'. In these aspects of such experimentation there are problems which may be examined under the word 'significance'—the very conditions under which the experiments were conducted had a significance. But this word is not one in the methodology of the 'objective' scientist, who is even incapable of examining his enthusiastic belief that 'all good is expected to come from ever-new test arrangements' and 'boundless experimentation'. Straus's criticisms of Pavlov offer many devastating criticisms of the kind of approach to behaviour manifest in the sexology laboratory: yet the thinking of such people is simply not accessible to his kind of doubt.

These insights are of great importance, for at the moment, in the sphere under discussion, a certain 'generation' or group are trying to gain the assent of the whole community, and have gained it in America, for their 'consensus of professional opinion' as 'scientists' in the realm of sex.† They wish us to judge them as,

---

* Scotoma: a blindness, turning one's blind spot forwards.

† Large cultural decisions are made on the conclusions of those who make 'scientific' studies of the effects of pornography without considering meaning, symbolism or ethical values.

competent to judge what is 'truth' in this realm, and to give endorsement to their conceptual framework. Yet, in the light of the analysis of the nature of knowledge by Straus, Marjorie Grene and Polanyi, they do not deserve this authority, however much they appear in white coats in laboratories, for their extension of scientific method to the realm in question is absurd.

Not only may one say of them, as Polanyi says of the behaviourists, 'Behaviourist psychology depends on covertly alluding to the mental states which it sets out to eliminate'. One may also say of them that they are essentially destructive, because they implicitly reduce the nature of 'whole being' in this sphere, by excluding recognition of the tacit dimension and by failing to question their assumptions. Their 'knowledge' excludes that which belongs to the 'whole person', and so is itself destructive of its object, by explicitness and analysis. As Polanyi says—

... an unbridled lucidity can destroy our understanding of complex matters. Scrutinise closely the particulars of a comprehensive entity and their meaning is effaced, our conception of the entity is destroyed ... the damage done by the specification of particulars may be irremediable ...   *The Tacit Dimension*, page 18

The destruction of meaning in the sexual realm which is found by psychotherapists such as Leslie H. Farber and Rollo May may be thus linked with the effects of the 'scientific' approach to sexual phenomena itself. We may examine this problem by studying such a work as *An Analysis of Human Sexual Response.**

When I first came across this book I was cowed; later this came to seem to me the most revealing element in my response. It is symptomatic that, when faced with such a work, we feel at once, 'What have we, from the subjective discipline, to do with such a project?' But this is the first step in a diagnosis, just as the sexologist's first step is to exclude the subjective realities of his subject though he is quite aware of them.

The work summarized in this book is based on the 'objective' observation and measurement of body phenomena, using nearly 700 volunteers under clinical observation while in the act of masturbating or having coition. The scientific instruments used included moving cameras, using colour film, and electrical stimulators, including one machine with a transparent plastic penis to simulate intercourse.

Our first response, when confronted by such a manifestation is

---

* A summary of the findings of the work of Dr. William H. Masters and Mrs. Virginia A. Johnson at the Reproductive Biology Research Foundation, St. Louis, U.S.A., edited by Ruth and Edward Brecher, published by André Deutsch, 1967.

that we feel daunted, and this is what we are meant to feel: this effect of overawing us is part of the dehumanization. By contrast, our own sexual experience seems no larger than human, and in any case we prefer not to talk about it. We are certainly not going to bring it up as a counter assertion to the whole movement for 'sexual emancipation'. To do so would have its own effect on our own sexual life, by exposing it with all its 'normal frustrations', and by taking it out of the only realm in which it has significance for us, into the realm of objectification. That is, we know that our sexual life can only happen in the realm of 'being', in the context of love, and only lives when it is neither willed, nor exhibited. We cannot make our sexual experience happen, and if we bully ourselves into sexual 'doing' in the pursuit of significance, sex becomes insignificant, and is absorbed into their kind of reality: if this happens we are lost.

We are, therefore, curiously disarmed by sexology—as we are by so many manifestations of the depersonalization of sex in the modern world. Exhibitions of erotica, Sex Super Markets, Danish Sex Fairs, the orgies recommended by some of our 'scientific' writers, Swedish films in which sexual intercourse is simulated or actually performed by naked actor and actress, books by recognized novelists beginning, 'The only thing Cynthia was good at was sexual intercourse . . .'—all these seem to belong to a world in which sex is larger than human. Yet it is difficult to protest from our own experience, because what we *know* belongs to 'being', while all that exhibitionism belongs to the world of 'doing' and anxious mentality. Love belongs to the immediate and creative: all that exhibitionism belongs to 'the world of outcomes'. If we enter into debate we inevitably expose the world of being and enter into the realm of intellectualization itself, and are so defeated by joining it. Yet, if we study Frankl or May, all that generalized sexuality appears crippled and impotent, beside the essential mystery of love, in the realm of the I-Thou relationship, to use the language of Martin Buber.

There are, it should be admitted, some findings of sexology which are valuable. Some seem to arise incidentally to the main purpose. But what we have to consider is whether the benefits that might come from these could have come from other sources, and whether they outweigh the effects at large of the example and the symbolism of sexology itself.

There were discoveries about the ways in which certain contraceptives fail, about factors of alkali and acid in the secretions, about the 'lethal factor' in some women's organs which destroys the sperms of their partner.

Sex research has helped dissipate some of those strange traditional myths which have their own symbolism. For instance, the sex researchers find that the size of a man's penis doesn't matter—the woman's organ adjusts to her partner's. Sex researchers have also found that breast-feeding is sexually exciting, and that some women can have an orgasm simply by having their breasts stimulated.

Research also discovers that the prostitute often has a painful time of it, subjects suffering from 'chronic pelvic congestion' while 'coital activity became increasingly painful towards the end of (the) working period'. This piece of realism will perhaps help explode the enthusiastic adulation of the prostitute in 'enlightened' comment and even art.

There are valuable findings about sex during pregnancy. These suggest that there is no need to suspend intercourse for long periods before and after birth, so long as medical supervision is maintained in an 'individualized' way. Sex research explodes further the belief of some nineteenth-century authorities that sex feeling in young women was pathological. Even apparently enlightened individuals such as doctors can still be quite barbarous about such matters, and some 'educated' husbands even more indifferent to the woman's enjoyment of sexual love.

It seems from sex research that it is not true that sexual desire and activity in women cease with the menopause, or that sexual activity wanes sharply after forty. 'There is no time limit drawn by the advancing years of female sexuality', while although age reduces the strength of sexual response, 'physically healthy persons continue to be sexually active into their seventh, eighth and ninth decades'. Obviously it is valuable to have this finding, not least in a society in which the sense of identity has become so attached to potency—so that a loss of potency threatens a loss of identity.

It is also apparently false to believe (as many do, including doctors) that sexual activity 'uses up' one's life energy, while continence would conserve one's vitality. The truth seems rather that regular sexual activity maintains potency and keeps the functions functioning. Nor is it true that sexual activity strains the heart.

False beliefs about aphrodisiacs are exposed. It has been demonstrated that an injection of sterile oil is as effective in reviving waning potency as injections of androgen if each is offered as an aphrodisiac. Researchers have found that some aphrodisiacs, famous in lore, like 'Spanish Fly' (catharides), are in truth powerful corrosive poisons, which can cause serious destruction of tissue, and sometimes death.*

---

* 'Aphrodisiacs' are, however, apparently on sale at Sex Fairs and Sex Supermarkets—so we return to irrationalism in 'emancipation'.

Perhaps the most important Masters-Johnson discovery is that the vaginal walls have no sensation (page 120). Whatever subjectively felt differences there may be between one kind of orgasm and another, the physiological nature of orgasm is the same. Such psychobiological findings obviously have a value as a contribution to human knowledge. It is useful for instance, to know that the female vaginal walls are not very sensitive to touch and cannot be the main source of pleasurable sensations towards orgasm. Some unconscious hostility in Freud to women may well have generated his postulation of the difference between 'immature' clitoris orgasm, and 'mature' vaginal orgasm—a distinction for which there appears to be no basis in physical phenomena, though it has been so enthusiastically endorsed by D. H. Lawrence.

However, at this point we may become aware that such a question cannot be divided from the consideration of our whole existence in the body: the crucial question is the depth of experience we have of orgasm, and the meaning it has for us. What is 'seen' of orgasms in general has little or no value for each unique individual in his orgasmic capacities.

So, while it is valuable to have old wives' tales and other sources of anxiety cleared away, the effect of the limited perspective of the sexologist might be to create new anxieties, as by the effect of the setting up of a 'Love Laboratory'. Could not the same results have been achieved just as well by more collaboration between general practitioners in research on a local basis with individuals in their normal life-situations, as 'beings-in-the-world' and without a laboratory? Do these gains justify the claim that the 'importance of this work (i.e. laboratory sexology) to the medical and behavioural sciences, and the health and happiness of mankind is so great ... that widespread support for a broad expansion of similar studies should be widely forthcoming ...'? Could not the 'facts' discovered—amounting in any case to little more than what healthy lovers find out for themselves (as Guntrip has said)—not have been found out by more subtle research that did not require such invasion of privacy, such reduction of human beings to the status of objects, such essential scopophilia, and such dissociation of the spiritual capacities and meanings of love from function?

Consider what was involved. Every morning in St. Louis, the volunteers arrived at the laboratory at 10 a.m., disrobed, stretched out on a couch, and began masturbating or copulating, while the scientists observed. The dissociation involved, at the deepest level indicated by Merleau-Ponty's exploration of bodily existence, resembles the dissociation necessary at a gas chamber, and the suspension of conscience in Nazi 'experiments' on human subjects. Some of the couples, albeit chosen because their sexual life tends to be promiscuous, met here for the first time: did they shake hands before they began? They perform, certainly,

in a businesslike manner, while being measured and photographed . . . (Thank you Miss Brown, see you same time next week. Stop at the cashier's to get your fee.) So, back to one's ordinary existence.
The Ways of the Will, page 83

Miss Brown becomes the faceless torso in the Masters-Johnson film now shown all over the world. Coldly, the scientists observe her moving fingers, the flush on her thighs, her moistening organ, her stiffening nipples, the fine film of sweat covering her whole body afterwards.

If we say 'Miss Brown' of course, the picture becomes pornographic, because a person was depersonalized in the picture and in this reduction of her to an object there is a perverted excitement.* The final product has no head and is utterly de-eroticized, de-humanized and de-emotionalized—the complex image of schizoid detachment necessary for scientific 'objectivity'.

The functions of Miss Brown's body are separated from everything that could make them humanly meaningful, in the intimate dialogue of love. It is in this that we feel the daunting audacity of the enterprise, which is so 'single-minded, so fanatical, and so literal' (as Farber says) that it seems from the point of view of philosophical anthropology an insane nightmare. This impulse to separate sex from the whole of human experience, draws our attention not only to the kind of people who take part in sexology, but the kind of subjects they use. It is not insignificant that they began with prostitutes: a prostitute is one who already needs to separate her sexual activity as doing from her female element of being, and can only relate in this non-relational way. It is not insignificant that many of the volunteers were what Frankl called 'sexually disposed persons' whose way of life included casual sexual encounters, and who were, in Frankl's terms, 'crippled' in the emotional life, or in Straus's words 'shrunken' and 'incapable of being touched'.

The dilemma of our response to sexology arises, as I believe, out of the problem of responding to a form of perversion which marks a flight from psychosis. And our dilemma arises because of a curious schizoid trick with experience that focuses on sex. It is, for those who project super-human sex into our world, a personal 'strategy of survival'. It seems very likely that the sources of the 'larger-than-life' preoccupation with sex in our world are to be found in individuals who have no real capacity for genuine

---

* 'Objectification is the . . . essentially perverse action of the voyeur'. Straus, *Phenomenological Psychology* (Tavistock 1962) page 219.

relationship, and have great difficulty in feeling real as persons. Their frantic, anxiety-stimulated, hyper-sexuality, serves in lieu of genuine personal relationships. They cannot feel confirmed by 'giving' in love, and by meeting another person sexually; they must substitute 'showing' for 'giving'—and this involves them in separating, as far as they can, the outward appearances, functions and symbols of sex from the most intimate dialogue of love, in which alone sex can have any point or validity. As soon as we approach such phenomena as theirs we become involved in their psychopathology.

Here we may usefully recall a patient's dream described in Fairbairn's account of the modes of the schizoid individual. It has characteristic significance for our study of contemporary culture.

A schizophrenic youth, who, while evincing the bitterest antagonism towards his actual mother, dreamed of lying in bed in a room from the ceiling of which there poured a stream of milk—the room in question being in his home just beneath his mother's bedroom.

Psychoanalytical Studies of the Personality, page 14

This dream represents for Fairbairn a symbol manifesting aggression. The youth hated his mother yet wanted to be her baby. He had never experienced the taking in both love and milk from a loving being who was, by her handling, able to enable him to feel real and alive. He had thus never become able to overcome the infant's fears of the dangers inherent in incorporation, by the give and take of secure relationship. Love, having been rejected, was too dangerous to be a source of the feeling of 'I am'. Hate had to be substituted as a means to feel real: yet deep down he still wants to be loved.

The stream of milk symbolizes the need for relationship and love. But in his dream it cannot take the form of any rich satisfaction in personal contact: the detached stream symbolizes a typical need to subject relational needs to separation from the person. Taking is substituted for giving, and hunger and satisfaction for meeting. Libidinal desires must be *depersonalized* and separated from 'the object' of relationship. The image must be that of a 'partial object'—a breast separated from the whole woman. The impulse is characteristically accompanied by a 'regression in the *quality of the relationship desired*' that is, what is desired must be dehumanized. 'The regressive movement is in the interests of a simplification of relationships', and this—

takes the form of a substitution of bodily for emotional contacts. It may perhaps be described as de-emotionalisation of the object-relationship.

op. cit., page 14

The stream of milk in this schizoid dream is the same symbol as the cover-girl, the *sex-bomb*, the bare breast on the magazine cover, and the 'Lady of the Laboratory' in sex research. In this I am drawing attention to the schizoid element in sex research itself and in the intellectual theories, such as Freud's sexual theories, on which sexology is based. The impulse is to reduce human experience to something which belongs to 'bodily rather than emotional contacts', which implicitly reduces human relationships to simplicity, and to something as non-human as possible. 'Taking' predominates in the attention to pleasuring and being pleasured and there is neither love, nor true finding of the I-Thou experience or of the aspect of 'being'.

Here a very wide problem arises, of the very 'life-world' in which we live, the way in which we 'see' our world. This consists not only of the impressions we receive, but, of course, includes also 'the creative aspirations of artists, the vision of saints and prophets, even the delusions of the insane', as Marjorie Grene reminds us (see page 50, *Approaches to a Philosophical Biology*, Basic Books, 1965). While this 'life world . . . stands in contrast with the limited and lucid sphere governed by the operations of the intellect' it also includes the operations of the intellect, and so we live 'in' certain attitudes to nature and man as much as in the life world of all other experiences and impressions.

Some scientists are coming to recognize that in living within a certain attitude to man, the scientist lives in something that may be narrow. As Adolf Portmann has said: 'I emphasize the inevitable narrowness of every image of man that is formed through natural science alone, that does not draw its power from all the sources of man's being' (quoted by Marjorie Grene on page 52 of *Approaches to a Philosophical Biology*).

Michael Polanyi speaks of the 'pathology' of science, and suggests that a science 'imprisoned in naturalism' has itself contributed to many of the dreadful disturbances of moral and psychic health in our civilization. And here, I believe, we have to analyse, from the point of view of 'philosophical anthropology', the life-world and view of man within which the sexologist works.

There are, as Guntrip indicates, schizoid elements in all science—

Where scientific pursuits are concerned, the attraction would appear to depend upon the schizoid individual's attitude of detachment no less than upon his over-valuation of the thought processes. The obsessional appeal of science, based as this is upon the presence of a compulsive need for orderly arrangement and meticulous accuracy has, of course, long been recognised: but the schizoid appeal is no less definite and demands at least equal recognition.

Personality Structure and Human Interaction, page 6

In all science we have both compulsive orderliness and concern for accuracy: when science turns to man we often find a schizoid detachment in the observance of bodily phenomena seen from the 'outside'. The schizoid element in science does not invalidate it of course, but the 'narrowness' should not be forgotten. Sexology also inevitably takes over the schizoid elements in objective science.

So, we find, the sexologists work in a compulsive way—

Masters is said to work eighty hours, including one whole night a week . . . Dr. Kinsey . . . never took a holiday in his life . . . He literally and knowingly worked himself to death . . .
Wardell B. Pomeroy in *An Analysis of Human Sexual Response*, pages 122–3

But they are also energetically concerned to keep the parts and functions split off from whole existence—

A broad, funnel-shaped vestibule leads to the actual entrance (the orifice or introitus) of the vagina . . . One of the major discoveries of Dr. Masters and Mrs. Johnson, of course, is the way in which the motion of the inner lips (minor labia) pulls on the hood of the clitoris . . . In some individuals [in orgasm] the whole body may be thrown or tossed, or rolled over a distance of several feet or yards . . .   op. cit., *passim*

This devotion of sexologists to the pursuit of truth, which, they believe, is to be seen exclusively in the objective phenomena, is confined to a 'life-world' in which insufficient attention is given to the phenomenological understanding of 'man's being'. Inevitably, therefore, there is a compulsive attention that goes with the effect of *objectifying* the human beings under scrutiny. This is not to say that the individuals making the observations are 'schizoid', but rather that the methodologies and theories which govern their work suffer from a schizoid detachment which has been created by generations of those to whom science offered especial attractions because they had schizoid characteristics, and tended to see man in a certain narrow way.

A number of philosophers of science are now examining the ensuing problems arising from the failure to find man's wholeness. Erwin Straus, for instance, discussing Pavlov, shows how passionate was this behaviourist's concern to find the secret of man's personality, so that he could manipulate men, in order to stamp out human evil. But in so far as his assumptions were based upon too great a detachment from other 'sources of man's being', his impulse comes, in the end, to seem menacing, as though he were really seeking to control others, not least by exerting intellectual power over the realm of 'being' itself. A similar impulse seems to lie behind sexology.

Attention to the realm of being enables us to expose the absurdities of the scientific method as employed here. As Erwin Straus points out, the convinced follower of Pavlov will argue that—

(1) There is a possibility of purely objective observations and descriptions, free from any presuppositions (2) (the) experimental design is simple and perfectly lucid (3) the theory directly follows, as an evident generalisation from the results obtained by experiments (4) these results . . . provide ever-renewed proof of the theory.

The Primary World of Senses, page 34

But, as he says, 'all these assumptions, every one of them, are inconclusive'.

the setting of the laboratory is not an indifferent arrangement to be evaluated in merely technical terms. The so-called preparatory requirements of the experiment present fundamental problems in themselves . . . the belief in a lucid pattern of the experimental design is not borne out by the facts . . . The simplicity is but a superficial one. It owes its sham existence to a scotoma for the actual problems, resulting in a naive anticipation of the theoretical decisions . . .   op. cit., page 34

All these remarks can be applied to laboratory sexology, and no-one who has studied the work of Merleau-Ponty, Straus, or Marjorie Grene could accept as valid the methods and theories on which sexology is based. It is, fundamentally, absurd.

Its absurdities are those of what Laing calls 'natural scientism', and belong to that pathology of which Polanyi speaks, and the 'schizoid' element in science to which Guntrip points. Thus, despite the evident integrity of the sexologists, the effect of their work is that of objectifying human beings—in much the same way as the voyeur objectifies them. As Frankl points out, schizophrenic patients have the experience often of feeling as if they are being 'filmed': they feel, he says, the experience of being the object of someone else's thoughts (see *The Doctor and the Soul*). Strangely enough, what is conveyed abroad by sexology is this schizoid kind of experience of being an object. And this, too, is the effect of pornography: as Rollo May has said (in a private communication) a book like *The Sensuous Woman* 'carries to the ultimate extreme the making of the human being into an object'. Doctor Masters and Mrs. Johnson have been most scrupulous in their attempts to avoid lending their work to the pornographer, They have, for instance, refused to publish pictures of their plastic-penis coition machine, for this reason. Yet, willy nilly, because of the very tendency in the whole scientific tradition to which their work belongs, the 'objectifying' effect of their methods contributes to the present tide of dehumanizing schizoid explicitness about sex in our time. In the light of such a study as that by Straus on shame as a device which protects the creativity of love, the inevitable effect of sexology is to menace our essential creativity in the realm of 'whole being'.

Straus's kind of objections suggest that one of the major unseen factors in sexology is the degree to which laboratory experiments are conditioned by the kind of subject that is willing to come forward to be 'objectified' in just this way. What kind of volunteer comes forward? And, between observer and subject, what are the unconscious hazards? Farber indicates the sexologist's problem of involvement, which he can only solve at a certain cost to himself—

Of course, there would be strict rules forbidding dalliance between scientist and volunteer after hours. But should they happen to run into one another in the cafeteria, each would keep his conversation casual, trying not to allude to those more cataclysmic events of a few hours before. Mindful of his professional integrity, the scientist would have to guard against prideful thoughts that he knew her, if not better, at least more microscopically than those nearest her. Most troublesome of his self-appointed tasks . . . would be his effort to prevent his research from invading his own erotic life, particularly if he were worried by the usual frustrations. In this regard, it would indeed be heroic to withstand the temptation of comparing his mate's response to those unspecific, yet perfectly formed, consummations of the laboratory . . .

The Ways of the Will, page 66

If this is the effect on the scientist, what effect is there on the world that is so willing to defer to the scientist's authority?

As Farber points out, behind this research lurks an 'ideal subject' for sex research, and its findings are conditioned by her. If we examine this ideal subject we find that she is essentially psychopathological. She is also schizoid, in that she is capable of depersonalizing sex and dividing it from her whole subjective experience—

her sexuality would have to be autonomous, separate from and un-affected by, her ordinary world . . .   op. cit., page 63

Her 'female element', which would find sexual meaning in sub-jective togetherness, must be utterly subject to being overruled by willed 'objectivity' (or 'false male doing')—

Objectively, her sexuality would be mechanically accessible or 'on call' under circumstances which would be, if not intimidating, at least dis-tracting to most bodies . . . Her lust would lie to hand, ready to be invoked and consummated in sickness or health, in coitus or 'auto-manipulation' . . . in other words, her sexuality would be wholly subject to her will . . . *all that would be unavailable to her would be a real response to the laboratory situation.*   op. cit., page 64 (my italics)

Hence, there is an overall falsification, since such a laboratory subject, because of the nature of the setting and the need to will her sexual function in a depersonalized context, is not normal, and is never allowed to be normal. The sexologist himself is one who 'wishes indifference, which he can invoke at will'.

One's doubts are increased as one finds that over those problems in which it is impossible to avoid recognition of human complexity, *An Analysis of Human Sexual Response* leaves us with some sense of confusion. On page 205 we are told of the 'referral to the psychopathologist of problems of sexual incompatibility'.

There is ample clinical evidence for the observation that sexual imbalance or inadequacy is not confined to individuals who have been identified with major psychoses or even severe neuroses . . .

Later, however, it is stated that—

the marital incompatibility that brings the couple to the physician usually is not primarily of sexual origin . . .   op. cit., page 207

Both remarks suggest that possibly a dimension of approach different from that of the laboratory is required, and that it is problems of identity and relationship which are primary, rather than the mere 'sex activity' under scrutiny. The study admits that—

a wife may be unhappy . . . although very responsive sexually . . .
op. cit., page 148

As we know, marriages often break up even though the couple have been enjoying 'adequate sex' right up to the end. So, sexology's exclusive attention to the bodily responses can only tell us about the bodily responses. It can register physical facts, but not our subjective experiences of them—

psychologically, the experiences may feel altogether different, but the basic pattern of bodily responses remains the same.   op. cit., page 32

Here we have a fallacious duality, in which psyche and soma are divided: yet because they cannot be divided, the sexologist, impinging on the 'functions', is willy-nilly affecting our experience of our own bodies. Though he proclaims he is only concerned with the body, everything he deals with in fact depends upon tacit factors, not least the will of the subjects. Because of this he comes to conclusions which are fallacious because they do not take account of problems of meaning.

Thus, in the discussion of sexual intercourse during pregnancy these research workers, working according to the tenets of impulse psychology, seem to believe that suspension of sexual relations must be the cause of infidelity during pregnancy. The Masters-Johnson data indicated that '. . . an unnecessary sexual prohibition . . . gravely jeopardizes the marriage in a substantial proportion of cases' . . .

However—

Of the twelve who began extramarital sex activity before the baby was born, all twelve continued it after the baby was born . . .

An Analysis of Human Sexual Response, page 93

This would seem to suggest that it is not the suspension of sexual relationships (leading to some kind of build-up of 'hydraulic pressure') which caused the infidelity, but rather the changes in the relationship—that the object of his relationship literally splitting in two at parturition is one of the problems for the husband during his wife's pregnancy, and he often tends in consequence to behave in a split way in his relationship. Thus, it is no solution for the wife merely to continue sexual relationships with her husband: in any case some husbands—

lost interest . . . either because of the gross physical signs of pregnancy, or because they feared sex would be uncomfortable for their wives . . .

op. cit., page 91

These 'reasons' are probably rationalizations of unconscious fears, and other feelings (such as hatred of the foetus as a rival or envy of the woman's creativity), which inhibit the husband's sex, or cause him to split his capacity for relationship.

So, here, the Masters-Johnson approach could prove likely to lead to an even deeper perplexity on the part of a pregnant wife: 'I let him go on making love to me, but still he was unfaithful.' They fail to find the deeper and more complex aspects of failures of object-constancy.

Moreover, if the primary human need is to find meaning through relationship with the 'significant other', the implications of some of the writers quoted in *An Analysis of Human Sexual Response* seem disastrously false. At times a sexual 'smooth functioning' is assumed to be more important than relationship (and so than meaning). Grafenberg, for instance, discusses a patient who had never experienced orgasm with her husband, although she had borne him three children.

Bored by the repeated discussions with her, I finally asked her if she had tried sex relations with another male partner. No, was the answer, and reflectively she left my office. The next day, in the middle of the night I was awakened by a telephone call . . . 'Doctor, are you there? You are right . . .'

op. cit., page 139

The tone is triumphant. But the doctor here seems jubilant about getting quick results in the relief of symptoms even though *at the expense of a relationship* in which four other individuals are involved—and without engaging with the essential problem. Many a partner can be potent in a relationship outside the committed one, while impotent with anyone with whom he has to be 'real'. The problem is surely to enable him to accept responsibility, and thus find meaning in love. To enable him merely to 'function' at the expense of object-constancy seems a false 'solution' which could even mean that the problem of finding meaning was thrust even further away.

On reflection, it seems likely that some of the conclusions about personal relationships are only included in *An Analysis of Human Sexual Response* to give the impression that these derive from from sexology proper. Their hidden origin lies elsewhere—in the subjective experience of the patients in need—in those insights derived from intuition into those tacit dimensions which sexology implicitly denies. Although they *seem* to be drawn from this 'objective research', the conclusions drawn here for marriage counselling are in fact drawn from subjective processes which belong to the counselling situation (for Doctor Masters and Mrs. Johnson also tackle therapy). That is, where there are useful contributions in this book on sexual matters, they derive from a complex in which by intuition 'the physician's love heals the patient' (as Sandor Ferenczi put it) rather than the laboratory work. At times we have an implicit recognition of the healing value of those tacit factors, about which science can say nothing and which sexology denies. There are in this vein some valuable comments on sex education by Dr. Mary Calderone, and a few good pages on the work of Menninger and others (pages 252–7), which reveal some of the new insights of psychodynamics theory.

But in general, however, the conclusions of *An Analysis of Human Sexual Response* do not advance beyond psychobiological 'hydraulic' theory, which clings to such concepts as 'the accumulation of nervous energy', or 'the damming up of biological undischarged sexual energy', and so remain homunculist. The nearest we get to an object-relations view is a reference to Menninger's opinion that some 'frigid' women are those who are 'unable to release themselves' because to do so is interpreted as 'dependency on a man', and the idea is intolerable to them. But Menninger is recognizably talking about 'whole persons', whereas the sexologists are obviously not.

Lurking behind the approach of sexology to human problems is, of course, the Freudian model of human nature. Our libidinal id is constricted by the necessity of having imposed upon it the restraints necessary for civilized social morality. These restraints are embodied in the ego's obligation to 'adapt' and the super-ego's function to 'repress'. For Freud the only way out of this situation is—

to lessen the burden of the instinctual sacrifices imposed on men, to reconcile men to those which must necessarily remain, and to provide a compensation for them . . .   *The Future of An Illusion*, page 7

There is much in the impulse of sex research, of the attempt to lessen 'the burden of the instinctual sacrifices' by offering a new 'objective' point of view which persuades us that the guilt we took into ourselves from our mothers who thought sex dirty or a painful duty, can now be abandoned as 'Victorian' or 'bourgeois'. 'Unnecessary guilt' is removed by a 'rational' approach which explains that culture, traditional morals and religion are merely prejudices. Ethical and emotional problems are merely unnecessary barriers to the free flow of libidinal urge through the sexual organs: so is love.

The exploration of early problems of identity by the 'schizoid diagnosis' of Fairbairn, Winnicott, Guntrip and others has led to a feeling that our belief that man's primary reality is instinctual may be a form of self-deception. Fairbairn's conclusion about human nature that 'the ultimate goal of the libido is the object,' implies that our primary need is to find ourselves confirmed by relating to another in love, so that our sexual potentialities are our means of *expressing* this need. The hydraulic sexual urge is not primary; however, the need to be confirmed in the I-Thou experience is, because it belongs to the human being's primary need for meaning. This reverses Freud's approach to the problems of the erotic life altogether, in psychoanalytical thought.

These conclusions of object-relations theory in England agree with those insights emerging from existentialist psychiatry in America. *An Analysis of Human Sexual Response* includes a dissenting essay by Leslie H. Farber, from whom we have already quoted often in this work. Farber is much influenced by the philosophical anthropology of Martin Buber. His own book *The Ways of the Will* in which the same essay is published, seems one of the most important recent psychoanalytical contributions to our understanding of human nature. Farber's diagnosis of the psychopathology of will, I believe, can provide us with a focus of resistance against the 'pathological moral inversion' which is overtaking our culture, especially in attitudes to sex, and seems also to confirm Fairbairn's diagnosis of the schizoid elements in our culture.

Farber suggests that the fact that we are cowed by the 'perfectly formed ... consummation of the laboratory' is central to the problem of sexology. He believes that the price we have to pay for sexology and the 'sexual revolution' is a loss of spiritual capacity—or, as I would put it, loss of the sense of meaning in life. Farber's conclusion is startling, for it is that 'over the last fifty years sex has, for the most part, lost its viability as a human experience'. This view, like Rollo May's, challenges the optimism of the orthodoxy of sexual enlightenment.

'Willed' sex must always be something less than human. As Farber says—

Before the age of sexology, objectifications of the sexual act were to be found in pornography and the brothel ... both suggesting the relatively limited manner in which will ... could be joined to sexual pleasure—it is only in our time such 'limited' sex can masquerade as larger than sex as part of the whole life of being.   *The Ways of the Will*, page 88

We have already seen how Guntrip speaks of two ways of knowing.

The *male way of knowing* in its highest development is objective, analytical, scientific investigation. The *female way of knowing* in the completest sense is the mother's intuitive knowledge of her baby.
      Schizoid Phenomena, Object-relations and the Self, page 261

If thinking (and 'objective analytical investigation') is an aspect of doing, then it can also be an aspect of 'false male doing' in the absence of an adequate sense of being, in the schizoid individual. Where there is integration, 'doing' and 'being' can go side by side in human experience. So can intuition and analysis, poet and scientist.

But where there is a pathological lack of integration, thinking can be an activity of 'false male doing' which, since it belongs to the False Self, needs to deny and exclude the female way of knowing altogether.

The discomfort one feels when faced with sexology can, I believe, be traced to such unconscious origins, and to its expression of its inherent dread of, and its attack on, that female element of *being* in which alone we may find meaning. Essentially sexology is an activity which belongs to 'false male doing', and to the consequent schizoid tendency to separate sex as an activity from the whole emotional life.

Despite its attempts to serve the highest moral purposes, sexology thus lends itself to promoting those ways of behaving and thinking which belong to 'false male doing' and bad thinking. Because of the tradition it belongs to, it adheres exclusively to 'male knowing' by objective analysis. The complement to this is the impulse to deny and *overwhelm* the female way of knowing altogether. As we have seen, since the female element of 'being' is what is most easily hurt, it is felt by such people to be a weakness to be resisted, denied, and hidden beneath a 'tough' exterior, and the appeal of sexology lies in the way in which this element appeals to those impulses in ourselves to deny our own weakness and vulnerability.

Here the parallel to the 'tough exterior' of the schizoid patient is the 'larger-than-life' image of the 'cataclysmic', 'perfect' sex of the laboratory. The sex which is observed is that of 'male element doing'. For instance, the sexologist is largely preoccupied with 'attending to', say, the sexual organ of a woman manipulating in masturbation—and so he is taking on a male 'activity' role. The inward 'elements' which belong to 'female element' togetherness, as when the man and woman are lying in one another's arms, content, and 'knowing' one another in the dimension of being, after their passionate activity, mean nothing to sexology—nor to the 'sexual revolution'. 'Doing' is all, because it can be seen from the outside. The realms of love and emotion, in which we find meaning, are not recognized because these can only be 'seen' by in-dwelling—by imagination.

Sexology achieves its denial of the female way of knowing, and of 'female element' experience, by adhering to the fallacy that observation and measurement of the external world is the 'only reliable source of knowledge'. Here, in a very significant way, Freud comes on the scene, and the origins of his sexual theory become relevant. Freud is quoted in the book as saying—

If you want to know more about femininity you must interrogate your own experience, or turn to the poets or else wait until science can give you more profound and coherent information.
                    An Analysis of Human Sexual Response, page 127

This is a very significant quotation. How *do* we know about human femininity? There is one central answer, that we could all give—and yet it is not to be found in Freud's theory. This is, we know femininity because it is in ourselves. We are capable of putting ourselves into the shoes of others, imagining the femininity in men, and the femininity in women—and we are able to do so because this capacity was creatively reflected in us *by a woman*!

The existence of this female kind of knowing means that it is impossible ever to know completely a human being as an object of observation and measurement. To strive to do so inevitably tends to reduce the human being to the status of an object of natural science, and thus to reduce him to something less than human, to reify him and dehumanize him. This is the effect of psychology when it supposes that it can be an exact science, and when it supposes that such an exact science does not require imagination.

As Farber says, it is necessary for science to remember that 'the human body is both a natural object and not a natural object'. Science, as Guntrip says, 'seeks to establish what phenomena have in common'. 'This scientific approach is as easily applicable to the human body as any other body.' But problems arose of an epistemological kind 'when science turned to the study of "mental life" . . . and . . . the same approach was automatically made'. That this slide across dimensions of knowing and dimensions of being involved semantic confusions is only just being seen as it is by the existentialists and some psychoanalysts. There is still a struggle to 'equate "scientific exploration" ' with 'the elimination of individuality', so that 'when science begins to treat man as an object of investigation, it somehow loses sight of him as a person' (Guntrip).

In the quotation from Freud above there is a definite implication, the basis of which can be found in nineteenth-century natural science, that science will eventually produce a 'more coherent and profound' account of the origins and nature of our humanness than anything we can be aware of from our own experience, or from the imaginative insights of the poets. Behind this again is the vision of human perfectibility. As Farber says, in this belief of Freud's there is—

one of the chief immodesties of this psychoanalytical age; that one can, instead of imagining, actually know the other in his essence.

The Ways of the Will, page 157

Freud's essential work on the symbolism of symptoms was a *poetic* achievement. But he was driven to proclaim it as scientific because of his religiose divinization of scientific truth, which he equated with what can be seen in the external world as if by a camera.

As Farber says, of Freud's account of patient 'Dora',—

Freud has done something far more interesting and important than to 'trace the whole origin and development of a case.' Instead, he has offered many profoundly useful insights into that human kind of history that has nothing to do with medical or natural history, and into the human kind of nature that has nothing to do with the 'real external world' and may, perhaps, be entirely false to that nonhuman world. Insofar as these insights must be called true, I should like to call them facts: facts that are no less real or imagined than those which science has defined as facts, but which obey different laws and concern quite another subject than do the facts of nature. op. cit., page 165

While he was in truth doing something poetic and imaginative,

Freud was so afraid of these as 'delusions' that he sought to give his insights 'scientific' reason. Reason is 'Freud's God, and truth—which he equates with scientific truth—the only epiphany he recognises'.

At the same time, Freud devised his mythical poetry of the 'instinct' model: 'natural instinct' was in conflict with human civilization, a view which Farber describes as 'pure romanticism' because it accords so little with the observable human facts, which are that man enjoys civilization, and that civilization is the expression of man's primary need for relationship. Yet Freud managed to combine this belief with adherence to its logical opposite—

That is . . . reason defined as scientific truth . . . here the definition was as candidly naturalistic as a camera; truth (for him) was the 'correspondence (of scientific thought) with the real external world.'

op. cit., page 158

One consequence of these fallacies lying behind Freud's concept of truth is that 'behaviour is equated with experience'. And this reduces itself to a kind of symbolism in sexology which it is very important for us to consider. The sexologist begins with an impulse to contribute to human sexual happiness. He finds that human beings are somehow prevented from achieving happiness by all kinds of subjective aspects of their experience. These problems become expressed in the symbolism of the body—in impotence, frigidity, or whatever—as in the hysteric (who cannot hear what he does not want to know). From this a delusion develops, which arises from the bodily symbolism of the personality problem itself.

Winnicott speaks of another kind of delusion, which is found to be widespread in psychiatry itself, that the mind is 'in' the head, while Guntrip speaks of a common philosophical assumption in much psychology that the mind 'is' the brain. Both these assumptions fail to take into account the origins of many of our problems of relationship with reality which arise from phantasy and meanings associated with the body and its modes of ingestion, evacuation, tension, relaxation, and feelings of emptiness and fullness. As Fairbairn says, 'the child's ego is a mouth ego' and in all manifestations of the personality including both emotion and intellect there are underlying problems of hunger, 'taking into oneself', 'giving out' and forms of symbolic play, whose origins are in the lips and other gates of the body and associated with phantasy feelings of wanting to empty, to fill, to repair, to make good, and so forth. This kind of body-life symbolism lies behind many strange manifestations in human sexual life, such as the compulsive looking of the voyeur, who wants to objectify what he sees, because his whole communication with the world has broken down, and he wants to keep sex at a distance as a defence against emotional surrender. His hungry looking is a manifestation of fear of commitment and fate—a fear of love. So he concentrates on the parts, the words, the functions.

By the delusion whereby 'mind' is equated with 'brain' it is possible for the neurological surgeon to enter into an insane delusion with the mental patient, to seek to 'cure' the trouble that is 'in his head' by a frontal leucotomy. That this destroys his personality seems only incidental; the irreversible change is the 'false solution' of removal of a 'nuisance' in the head which the patient demanded. There seems to be a similar delusion in the approach of sexology, when it works on the assumption that the sexual life is 'in' the sexual organs. While this is delusion enough, the sexologist takes it further by drawing from his observation of the external 'facts' of the behaviour of the organs conclusions which belong to the dimension of experience, as when he applies his findings to the realm of marriage guidance,* morality and culture.

It is not difficult to find examples of the sexologists' delusions here. Dr. Kinsey was quite fanatically devoted to 'scientific objectivity'. His insistence was that this work, which has an immense bearing on the most sensitive areas of intimate human dialogue, should be conducted in an ethos of complete dissociation from ethical values, and inner human truth—

Dr. Kinsey was ruthless about it. I recall his turning down one psychologist who applied for a job as interviewer with the remark, 'You don't really want to do sex research.' 'But I do,' the psychologist insisted. 'Well, look at your attitudes. You say masturbation is immature, premarital intercourse and extramarital intercourse harmful to marriage, homosexuality abnormal, and animal contacts ludicrous. You already know the answers, so why waste time on research?'
                    An Analysis of Human Sexual Response, page 117

The implication here is that sexology, to be of any use, must separate itself from the realm of human experience, and from values, in order to find some other more reliable 'truth' in an observable physical 'reality'. Moreover, the implication is that it

---

* The Marriage Guidance Council in Great Britain now advertises and sells books containing photographs of sexual positions, presumably on the fallacious assumption that by 'attending to' these married couples can learn to love! In the light of Straus's analysis of voyeurism, these 'sex technique' books, by menacing love with objectification and generalization, could menace 'shared immediate becoming'. It would be better for a Marriage Guidance Council to support that shame which 'does not constrain the erotic . . . but makes the erotic possible', by reticence—and sell poetry instead.

is also capable of finding 'answers' to problems of ethics and of the meaning of experience *by observing behaviour alone*. This is to claim an omniscience which belongs to the delusion that the experience is 'in' the organs and functions as seen from the outside. As Farber says, such 'ruthlessness' has its own naive adherence to an article of faith, that—

the visible, palpable reactions of the organs themselves, regardless of whatever human or inhuman context they might occur in, would speak a clear, unambiguous truth to all who cared to heed.

The Ways of the Will, page 66

The debate between good and bad is no longer to belong to the world of our existential experience, confused as it is between lust and love, will and desire, give and take. It is to be seen in microscopic terms of the quantitative behaviour of our sexual organs (as if the complexity of experience between mother and child could be observed in the behaviour of breast and mouth).

The questions we are apt to ask about human affairs, not excluding lust, ordinarily have to do with appropriateness, affection and the like—in other words, right and wrong, good and bad, judged in human terms. On the other hand, the ideal Sexologist, as he presses his eye to his research, finds another variety of drama—inordinately complicated in its comings and goings, crimes and resolutions—with its own requirements of right or wrong, good and bad, all writ very small in terms of 'droplets' and 'engorgements' and 'contractions'.   op. cit., page 66

The language of sexology itself has its own significance and its own schizoid quality of delusion. In this book we find 'inadequate erection syndrome', 'controlled penile stimulation', and so forth. The effect is to reduce the problem to a need to make smooth the functioning of the organism, to which all problems of emotion and experience (modesty, reticence, love, etc.) are nothing but hindrances. Besides the underlying philosophical assumption that sex is 'in' the parts, there is also an urge to obtain 'results' without entering into the anguish and puzzlement, the range of experience from the valid to the trivial, which every human being experiences in his actual sexual life. Guntrip says of psychiatry at large—

A good deal of the drive . . . for the discovery of physical treatments, and also to work out a theory of therapy on the basis of 'reconditioning' is motivated as such by this underlying 'philosophy of man' [that mind is in the brain] as by the practical need to find methods of quick relief of symptoms. Such treatments also have the advantage of being less disturbing to the psychiatrist than the attempt to treat the patient at a personal level, entering deeply and in a fully personal way into the heart of his disturbed personality.

Personality Structure and Human Interaction, Introduction, page 17

We can, I believe, extend this comment not only to sexology, but to 'enlightened' attitudes to sex at large. Of course there are some sexual problems which benefit from a 'frank' approach, and serious physical difficulties which can now be dealt with. But most of our sexual difficulties (not least those around which endless books are written) are problems of meaning—of love and relationship. Sexology persuades us to attach these to certain *symptoms* which need to be overcome. We would prefer not to believe that all we can do in the sexual life is to 'enter deeply and in a fully personal way' into relationship in order to discover meaning in our sexual lives. Sexology suggests the solution to our problems is to 'condition' ourselves and our partners to function efficiently. Where we have a sexual inadequacy, instead of regarding this as a symbol of a whole human problem, or the problem of finding a sense of meaning in life in the modern world, we see it as a merely functional problem to be dealt with by itself and in itself. It may be that what we may call a 'problem' is, in fact only one of the 'normal frustrations', while, as May suggests, those who compulsively pursue 'sexual satisfaction' are unlikely to find it, because they have chosen a path which cannot lead them to find meaning. The effect of sexology's attack on problems of meaning and significance to bodily functions surely parallels psychopathological hysteria. However else can we regard such a phenomenon as the demonstration, at a Danish Sex Fair, of female orgasm, by a leading 'feminine emancipationist', on two naked girl models—by an auto-vibrator?

For those who are suspicious of the assumptions and fervour of campaigns for universal sexual enfranchisement, it is a relief to read Farber's conclusion. For he is not naive, but rather speaks from his own experience as psychotherapist, of many patients and their sexual problems—

Little attention was paid to the female orgasm before the era of sexology. Where did the sexologists find it? Did they discover it or invent it? Or both? I realize it may seem absurd to raise such questions about events as unmistakable as those witnessed in our laboratory. But I cannot believe that previous centuries were not up to our modern delights; nor can I believe that it was the censorship imposed by religion which suppressed the supreme importance of the female orgasm. My guess, which is not susceptible to laboratory proof, is that the female orgasm was always an occasional, though not essential, part of woman's whole sexual experience. I also suspect that it appears only with regularity or predictability during masturbation, when the more human qualities of her life with her mate were absent. Further, her perturbation was unremarkable and certainly bearable when orgasm did not arrive . . . orgasm had not yet been abstracted and isolated from the totality . . . and enshrined as the meaning and measure of her erotic life . . .

The Ways of the Will, page **74**

Interestingly enough, there would seem to be some evidence as to the disastrous effects of such 'enshrinement' in *An Analysis of Human Sexual Response* itself. There is, for instance, a quotation from Dr. David Mace, who points out that women who do not experience orgasm are not bothered about it 'until someone tells them'. The problem then becomes a focus of anxieties of all kinds. 'Frigidity' according to others is a term 'that should rarely be applied in the presence of the sexually inadequate female', because the effects of being defined as frigid make matters worse. There is a report on a woman of sixty who was capable of fourteen to fifty orgasms in twenty minutes. However—

The remarkable fact was her ability to achieve full relaxation as soon as her partner did ... Immediately after his ejaculation she relaxed in complete satisfaction ...

An Analysis of Human Sexual Response, page 119

It is true that Kinsey said, 'considerable pleasure may be found in sexual arousal ... and in the social aspects of a sexual relationship' ... so that 'female orgasm should not be used as the sole criteria of the amount of satisfaction in sexual relations'. But this has not been the effect of his kind of advocacy: quite the reverse. Meanwhile these observations seem to indicate that mere function or quantity of function is not the essential goal of our libidinal impulses at all, but that what is primary is the desire to share one's own joy with another, and that what matters about the functions is our experience of them, or the quality of our experience, which of course can never be observed in the laboratory but which is bound up with our whole aspect of being-in-the-world, and the meaning that life has for us.

Merleau-Ponty, Erwin Straus, Buytendijk and Marjorie Grene have made severe criticisms of the way in which behaviourist scientists take animals out of their context as 'beings-in-the-world', and put them in mazes or laboratories, but fail to allow in their conclusions for the unnaturalness of the test environment and for the human element manifest in the test situations which they have invented, while also failing to examine their terms and metaphysical assumptions. As we have seen, Polanyi suggests that mere 'attending to' and 'unbridled lucidity' threaten meaning itself in the life sciences. How much more dangerous is it when all these philosophical errors are transferred to the 'testing' of human sex.

The way in which bodily functions are observed in the laboratory determines the conclusions of sexology for therapy, so that its contribution to 'human happiness' is construed in terms inevitably based on a study of behaviour in a situation which is alienated, from a point of view that cannot see the meaning it is looking for, and may even destroy meaning. That in some sexology experiments the subjects had never even met before surely reveals an impulse to reduce sex symbolically by the unconscious predetermination of the experimenter to its ultimate dehumanized form? In the light of Masud Khan's work, this concentration on sexual activity can only be seen as resembling the 'defence against psychosis' manifest in perversion. If this is true, some of the 'pathological elements' in this 'science' are bound to be found in the consequent approaches to therapy. Thus, 'unresponsive wives' are *encouraged to learn to have erotic phantasies* and to learn to 'focus attention on erotic stimulation and sexual imagery'. They are to be taught to *masturbate*, in the hope of coming to natural orgasm later. They are even to be encouraged to *falsify relationship, in order to pretend to be libidinal*. Thus Marion Hilliard—

I am making a fundamental distinction between loving and making love. A wife loves, therefore she woos a tired mate when she knows he needs her. The pretence is only in her physical reaction to the act itself. There is no greater gift . . . It's the worthiest duplicity . . . Thousands of women who have begun this sort of benign sham have discovered that the pretended delight rapidly became real . . .
An Analysis of Human Sexual Response, page 163

What is not apparently seen is that what is involved is an act of will directed at simulating a satisfaction that cannot be willed: the effect of such duplicity can only be destructive of commitment —and so of meaning—in a quite pathological way. The complex inward issues of love and relationship—the human *meaning*—are brutally thrust aside as 'no more than a subconscious refusal'— '*no more* than'? What is revealed is the implicit mind-willed wish that we were not human and 'woven in the weakness of the changing body'—while the subject is urged into a ('pseudo-male') activity which must become meaningless because not 'meant'.

As Farber says, the effect of such conclusions based on attention to the 'truth' of the organs separated from the human beings to which they belong, is to encourage a kind of 'activity' which turns the experience of love into something else—

what was formerly one of the expressions of relation or love becomes an idolatry, fragmented endlessly in the world of *It*—each article of the sexual act carrying the willful burden. In a sexological age where man is defined by his sexual competence love has been relegated to a device for achieving orgasm . . .   *The Ways of the Will*, page 147

[the lover is caught in the] futile struggle to will what cannot be willed— at the same time as he senses the real absurdity of the whole willful enterprise . . . he learns . . . to prod himself . . . to his task of tinkering with his mate—always hopeful that his ministrations will have the appearance of affection.   op. cit., page 73

The effect of this preoccupation with female orgasm at all costs even at the cost of meaning, is an inevitable outcome of 'laboratory work' in which what matters is that something happens that can be seen. But for the woman it means, says Farber—

The irony that her right to orgasm may perhaps depend for realization upon her willingness to be diddled like a perverse underwater edible whose shell refuses to be prised open . . .   op. cit., page 74

For both man and woman it means that, involved in willing the perfection on earth that cannot be willed, they must 'inevitably suffer the pathos that follows all such strivings towards heaven on earth' (op. cit., page 75).

Instead of finding freedom, 'scientific sex' has in fact become a tyranny and a threat. Such explicitness has not freed us from 'guilt', but has merely changed the way in which the symbolism of our symptoms manifests itself. The hysteric's obsessive pre-occupation with the details of sex has become the predominant feature of our culture, as every film and every fashionable novel now display—

With the idolatry of sex through sexology and psychoanalysis, oppor-tunities for the will have increased, through the appropriation of the details of sexual union. In an age characterized to some extent by the 'tyranny of the orgasm' the choice is no longer between sex or no sex; instead the will joins itself to those particles of sexual behaviour whose sum, it is hoped, will constitute the sexual act.   op. cit., page 109

From Farber's point of view our prevalent preoccupation with sex, separated from other manifestations of the human spirit, belongs to the psychopathology of will, with its roots in hysteria and hate.

Inevitably those delusional elements in sexology affect us, by invading our life in its most intimate spheres. The omniscience and quest for perfectibility belonging to these psychopathological manifestations of intellectual hate become tyrants in our world. As Farber says 'nothing that is observed or undergone in the real laboratory of science is like to escape us'.

Whatever detail the scientific will appropriates about sex rapidly becomes an injunction to be imposed on our bodies. But, it is not long before these injunctions lose their arbitrary and alien character and begin to change our actual experience of our bodies. Unfortunately, our vision of the ideal experience tends to be crudely derived from the failure of our bodies to meet these imperatives.   op. cit., page 68

Any reader inevitably becomes involved in the kind of calculation one makes in reading a *Which?* report: sexually, which is the best buy? In the Melanesian Islands, among 'X group'—

intercourse consists of a prolonged period of fore play, ceasing only when both partners are very close to or absolutely sure of orgasm, insertion with immediate and vigorous thrusting movements, a short period of actual copulation culminating in synchronous orgasm ... fifteen to thirty seconds seems to be the modal duration for optimal satisfaction ...
An Analysis of Human Sexual Response, page 191

Is our sex like this, or is it like that of the patient who 'was particularly pleased that he was able to continue the sex act for fifteen or twenty minutes after entrance'? (op. cit., page 243).

Immediately after studying such a book, that is, one begins to wonder whether one is oneself 'multiorgasmic', and 'self-actualized', and especially whether one is one of those described in this book as 'sexually inadequate'. Could one be, in the stringently objective terms used by one expert, one of those 'marital morons' who 'in their marital relations resemble an orang outan trying to play the violin'?

Despite the delusions of the sexual revolution, behaviour doesn't seem to change very much. Even this book shows that we seem to be concerned with the same old problems—

Americans talk more about sex than they did before, but there is little to indicate that they are actually behaving much differently than they did, say thirty-five years ago.   op. cit., page 283

But there is, it is noted, an increase in anxiety.

So sexology itself is throwing up its own dangerous myths which disguise the reality, which is that the sex of will is perhaps more damaging than the prudery from which we are supposed to have escaped. For instance, in this book we are told that, according to Dr. Reiss of the University of Iowa, who believes that 'Americans will accept permissiveness' increasingly, 'the risk ... of venereal disease has lessened.' How, I wonder, does he reconcile this with such news items as this (which seem to occur more often)—

Gonorrhea is spreading virtually unchecked in the surburban areas of the United States, it was stated at the United States Communicable Disease Centre today.

Dr. James Lucas, assistant head of the centre's programme to eradicate venereal disease said: 'Gonorrhea is pretty much out of control.' It had reached epidemic proportions in practically all areas with large concentrations of population.   The *Guardian*, 1st May 1967

If we examine statistics of sexual crime, abortion, illegitimacy, divorce, rape, marital break-up, venereal disease, mental illness, ill-treatment of children and other such factors which can be associated with sexual problems, and, beneath these, problems of meaning and identity, the bland assumptions of 'enlightenment' and the sexologists, that 'frankness' and 'freedom' are curing all our ills in this sphere, are exposed as absurd. As Rollo May says, despite some gains in freedom from 'external' anxiety, many problems, which arise from deeper inner anxieties, are even being made worse.

Our conclusions about sexology, then, must surely lead us to agree with Farber, that because of its delusions, and its fundamental psychopathological separation of the *It* experience from the *I-Thou* experience, it belongs to—

the degradation of sex that has resulted from its ever-increasing bondage to the modern will . . .   *The Ways of the Will*, page 53

The essential problem of the meaning of love in life does not change, and is little changed by sexology except perhaps for the worse. The essential problem remains what it always has been. It remains what it was to the mediaeval philosopher Duns Scotus—

Love for Scotus does not exhaust itself in self-seeking. There is imperfect love, which Scotus calls 'love of concupiscence', which is imperfect because it seeks the other for advantage. But there is also perfect love . . . which he calls . . . *amor amicitiae* . . . which seeks out the other for the other's sake . . . Hell is not other people: according to Scotus authentic existence is discovered in the relations of unique to unique . . .
                    Eric Doyle, o.f.m., *The Listener*, 11th May 1967

The same is the conclusion of Binswanger, Buytendijk, Buber, Frankl and May—indeed of a whole range of existentialist psychotherapists and philosophical anthropologists. We have two dimensions: that of the common nature of our bodies as natural objects, upon which science is entitled to pronounce, by 'male doing thinking'. There is also our 'this-ness' as unique beings, which is and can only be known by 'female knowing', the province of poetry. Harm can only come from seeking to deny our essential 'thisness', and to subject 'being' to the intellectual will of 'false male doing'—to objectification.

Sexology is more than an eccentric scientific enterprise: it concerns us as an attempt, by the schizoid inversions of hate, to attack and devalue our humanness in the area of the most intimate dialogue.

It is of course ridiculous for defenders of sexology to say that there is no evidence of 'any attempt by the research team to influence attitudes, culture or morality'. The attempt to influence is there in the very terms in which the problem is conceived and discussed, and in its confident energy and lack of hesitant self-questioning. The effects of sexology are inevitable, because of its symbolism and the example conveyed abroad by its own patho-logical elements. All this is evident if we examine the pseudo-scientific tone: 'Throughout these orientation procedures, the calm matter-of-factness of both researchers was a major factor . . .'. This pretence of objectivity is exposed by Polanyi and Straus as a sham. The sexologists' fervour is by no means 'de-tached', and, in the light of Polanyi's (scientific) insights, threatens meaning. Moreover, it seems clear that it *intends* to threaten meaning, as the voyeur intends to keep his distance and to impose 'generalization' on the secret realm of love.

At times in *An Analysis of Human Sexual Response* the tone of the 'scientific' approach becomes quite truculent: 'For some, the fact that sex is being analysed and discussed, that it is, in effect, going public, will rob it of enchantment. This is an area where poets and prudes can be agitated together, and perhaps nothing will agitate them as much as the recently published *Human Sexual Response* . . .'. (John Corry writing on sex research in America, in *The New York Times*, 11th July 1966.) There is nothing unemotional about this fanatical impulse to impose intellectual knowing on the realm of 'being', and the hostility to 'secrecy, half-light and silence' is evident in the tone. If, in the terms of Merleau-Ponty's insistence on the inseparability of sex from existence, the mere intention thus to separate sex forcibly from inward meaning is an attempt to influence attitudes, culture and morality.

The inevitable effect is to prevent us from relying on our own 'felt life' experience, and to substitute 'thinking' for it. Before Masters and Johnson arrived on the scene, Corry says, even workers like 'Freud and Dr. Kinsey had to rely on *what their subjects told them*'. The implication is that what the subject *experiences* (and what he writes in poems or tells his doctor) is less 'real' or 'true' than what can be observed as physiological phenom-ena in the laboratory. 'Attending to' is to be preferred to 'attending from'. What is *seen*, despite the cold-blooded environment, is the whole of sexual truth as it 'really is', while what poets or patients say can be disregarded as 'illusory'. The work of Merleau-Ponty, Straus, Polanyi and others makes it clear that this 'objective' ambition is far more delusory. In the words of Ernst Cassirer—

We cannot discover the nature of man in the same way that we can detect the nature of physical things. Physical things may be described in terms of their objective properties, but man may only be described in

terms of his consciousness. Empirical observation and logical analysis
... here proved inadequate.   *An Essay on Man*, page 5

But because of its vividness, despite its fallacies, sexology has
affected disastrously our thinking about sex, morality, and culture,
at the deepest levels. 'Sex is to be made public' and to be 'disen-
chanted'. One enthusiast in *An Analysis of Human Sexual
Response* actually says that sex research can be used 'to give
people a *real feeling of what is happening to them during intercourse*
... the book can be used to provide *a primer on their own responses*
...' page 289 (my italics).

Factual knowledge of how the body behaves as seen from the
outside as if *by a camera* is to be used as a primer on our experience
from the inside. The way in which the 'insights' of science are to
work, is by making sex 'public', and 'giving people a feeling of
what is happening to them during intercourse'—as if they didn't
really already know, or could know in some other, bodiless, way.
Though some of the pronouncements speak of how man 'seeks to
know himself and face his whole nature' the emphasis is not on
what the 'poets' know—that is, subjective experience which can
only be known from 'within'—but on 'photographic records' and
analysis. 'Persons who have tried to describe their experiences in
orgasm may produce literary or artistic descriptions, but they
rarely contribute to the understanding of the physiology which is
involved.' The implication here is that it is the physiology which is
most real and important, and the true, exclusive source of insight,
not the poetry or meaning of the experience. Yet the researchers
are quite blind to the meanings of the body as explained by
Merleau-Ponty (see also *The Philosophy of the Body*, ed. Spicker).

Such a book as *An Analysis of Human Sexual Response* may be a
'technical work of physiology' but its ambitions to sweep away
'illusion' are only too evident. Doctors Masters and Johnson soon
found that their work became a 'nationwide bestseller', and the
tone of their essay leaves us in no doubt that they confidently
consider themselves to be in the advance guard of an enlightenment which belongs to an 'era of marked change in our cultural
attitudes towards sexual material ...' and which seeks to dispel
'Victorian concepts of sexual taboos'.

This manifests a misguided confidence. From psychotherapy
there seems little evidence that even the removal of inhibition or
guilt over sexual problems can come from mere external knowledge
of 'drops and engorgements'. It seems from such sources that the
solution of sexual problems does not automatically solve an
individual's identity problems, nor give him happiness or a sense
of meaning in his life. Even if a 'sexual' problem can be solved
without a complete regrowth of the weaker aspects of the person-

ality there is often, still, a need to discover a core of being and a sense of the point of life—which 'good sex' alone, whatever the 'enlightened' ethos implies, cannot give us.

Moreover, sexology helps preserve an intellectual stalemate with its roots in the pathological element in science. Under the influence of 'sex research', our world still clings to the Freudian belief that if only the sexual Id-impulses could be freely expressed and fully 'pleasured' we could at last feel fully human—so we should 'release' all sexual impulses. This simple hedonism is the worst delusion of all, for it simply diverts our need for joy and meaning into the pursuit of temporary states of pleasure.

In its neglect of love, *An Analysis of Human Sexual Response* contributes to this false denial of the whole emotional life, and by ignoring the poetry it drives away that power of imagination that alone transcends the flesh and its 'nothingness' in the quest for meaning.

Moreover, besides not being able to find meaning at all, sexology substitutes, because of its methodology, the false pursuit of meaning in body-activity that belongs to perversion. The indirect predominant effect of sexology has been to promote perversion—in film, book, and in sexual activity, by giving the air of social acceptability to dehumanization and 'objective' sex. In destroying enchantment, it has thus led to further destruction of meaning and values. Such are the consequences of its dissociated reductionism. As Viktor Frankl says—

Love is living the experience of another person in all his uniqueness and singularity.
'The Meaning of Love' in *The Doctor and the Soul*, pages 132-3

There are two ways, he says, to 'validate the uniqueness and singularity of the self'. One is active, 'by the realization of creative values'. The other is the way of love. By it—

a person obtains that fulfilment which is to be found in the realization of his uniqueness and singularity. In love the beloved person is comprehended from his very essence, as the unique and singular being that he is: he is comprehended as a Thou, and as such is taken into the self. As a human person he becomes for the one who loves him indispensable and irreplaceable without having done anything to bring this about . . .
op. cit., page 133

Sexology has reduced sex to a sexuality in which the 'indispensableness' and 'irreplaceableness' of the 'other' is implicitly denied as a value fit only to be debunked. (Sex 'works' even if the partners have never met before.) By example it thus undermines those meanings which Frankl discusses as primary—

Love is not only grace; it is also an enchantment. For the lover, it casts a spell upon the world, envelops the world in added worth. Love enormously increases receptivity to the fullness of values. The gate to the whole universe of values is thrown open. Thus in his surrender to the Thou the lover experiences an inner richness which goes beyond that Thou; for him the whole cosmos broadens and deepens in worth, glows in the radiance of those values which only the lover sees . . .

The Doctor and The Soul, page 133

Sexology has, by its 'ripple' effect—that is, the spreading rings of its influence on popular attitudes throughout the world—as well as by its methodology, driven sex as far as it is possible to drive it, out of this realm. And by its activities it has enlisted millions to apply their eyes to forms of compulsive observation, to an area of 'reality' where there is no meaning to be found. Nothing could be more Laputan, deluded, and deluding. 'Sex for the masses' follows in its wake—with all its earnest egalitarianism. Yet in truth, among the millions, there are men and women who find Frankl's kind of meaning in love, and pursue it towards that greatest of all mysteries, the bringing into life of a new person, a child. They know truths, and feelings of merging with the cosmos, which the sexologists, with their eyes glued to the panting bodies in St. Louis, have never yet seen, and never will see, because their fallacious philosophical assumptions have blinded them to these for ever.

9
Sex and culture
ᏕᏕᏕ

The fundamental delusions of sexology then are that the truth of sex is 'in' the parts and the functions, while those problems which attach themselves to the sexual life can be solved without taking into account the whole person as a 'being-in-the-world', and his problems of love and meaning. Its delusions are bound up with a limited perspective 'imprisoned in physicalism' and unaware of its own effects on attitudes to existence. To expose such delusions is urgent at a moment when rapid changes are taking place in the laws governing the public depiction of sex. At the moment this area of public debate is full of absurdities. Of course, in this sphere there are some gains in increased freedom: as Mr. John Mortimer has said, 'A democratic process, subject to public scrutiny and appeal, has been substituted for an autocratic censorship'. However, Mr. Mortimer wants the 'next step' to be reached as soon as possible—which for him is total permissiveness.

The Arts Council Working Committee has recommended, and the Theatre Enquiry has supported, the removal of all legal censorship. Contrary to the belief of some, the Arts Council Committee did not start out pre-determined to abolish censorship; the Committee started by trying to improve the Law. Quite late in our deliberations it became obvious that no amount of progressive goodwill can produce a workable obscenity law, and whether or not a play is obscene is simply not a question which a law court is equipped to decide. There is only one tribunal for obscenity, individual taste; only one punishment, refusal to buy a ticket.

'After the Chamberlain', an article in *The Author*, Summer 1970

As the situation in Denmark shows, there is no evidence whatever that pornography is likely to decline as people become bored with it. What in fact is tending to happen in Scandinavia is an increasing development of this trade, so that it becomes part of the very structure of the economy, and so utterly beyond the access of moral debate.

To counter arguments such as those of Mr. Mortimer, we need to be able to demonstrate that there are dangers—of the kind we recognize there to be in other forms of collective activity which would seem likely to be harmful to the individuals who take part. We now accept that there is danger of this kind in such activities as cock-fighting, public torture or hanging—though there is no 'valid statistical evidence' that these did any harm. What we do know, I believe, is that if any of these were revived, they would not go short of spectators. This means that if there are public activities of a kind which are debasing, then they will always tend to attract people and develop in them a taste for the sensations they offer.

The confusion over pornography arises from the mistaken assumption that the effect of obscene shows is to be considered in terms of sexual arousal, and whether people may then commit immoral acts. The only objection to such shows it is assumed, is that they promote sexual activity—and if you believe it is good for people to 'release their libido', then there can be no objection, unless the sexual activity is really perverse, more perverse than mere masturbation which is 'harmless'. This belief that pornography promotes sexual activity is the basis of arguments offered on both sides—one side believing it is wrong to encourage people to be more sexually active, and the other believing that it is a 'liberation', in a vaguely Nietzschean way.

However, it seems evident from the work of existentialist and object-relations psychoanalysts, and from the philosophical biologists, that the whole problem can be looked at in quite a different light. Here I would like to invoke an essay (which has been already referred to) by Erwin Straus, the psychotherapist and philosopher of the life sciences. Straus is critical of Freudian psychoanalysis, and is also critical of Pavlov and the behaviourists. He belongs to that stream of existentialism (which Binswanger and Buber represent) which is capable of finding love and is not contemptuous of ordinary experience, and so he tries to vindicate the 'unwritten constitution of everyday life'.

The essay is called 'Shame as a Historiological Problem', and appears in Straus's book *Phenomenological Psychology*. Straus rejects other approaches to shame as too static and too negative. He wants to look at shame historiologically, that is, in terms of man's development as a continuously emerging creature. He refuses to accept the view that the primary drive is the will-to-pleasure, so that the sexual problem becomes one of trying to find the degree of 'release' that is socially acceptable. The Freudian and the behaviourist believe that shame and disgust merely inhibit the actualization of innate drives. They are prohibitive: 'Man could be happy only if he could live without shame or disgust'. Most important, Straus refuses to accept that 'it is the drive to consume by looking [scopophilia] that has suffered a painful restriction'. All these beliefs, which Straus rejects, are the basis of the 'sexual revolution' in culture.

Freudian theory sees perversions as the deflection of a partial drive, in a world to which they are offered as merely a source of gratification. Straus sees perversions, as does Masud Khan, as 'modifications of and disturbances in man's communication with the world'. He emphasizes the 'communicative mode' of the problem. The voyeur does not become a voyeur because of some heightened 'urge to look'. He looks in his way because of certain needs—among them the need to 'live continuously at a distance', and to remain alone without a partner, 'an outsider who acts in a stealthy and furtive manner'. The looking of lovers moves towards approaching and uniting. The voyeur moves away into looking at, and he keeps his distance.

But his looking affects others. And we are all affected by the voyeurism of the photographer as reproduced in our morning paper and on our television set, in a commercial culture that is largely based on scopophilia. But as Straus points out, we are annoyed by being overlooked, and this is because being looked at *objectifies us*. This indicates a radical difference between voyeurism and normal sexual activity—

Objectification is the . . . essentially perverse action of the voyeur . . . objectification is only possible with a keeping of distance . . . and . . . it is only the keeping of distance that makes voyeurism possible. The peculiar mode of existence of the voyeur directs his curiosity towards the sexual organs, the sexual function, and the sexual word, continually in search of both clarity and closeness, whereas lovers search for concealment, half-light, and silence.

Phenomenological Psychology, page 219

Here we have an important distinction between the sexuality of love, and that of the obscene stage show, the Sex Fair, and 'sex' cinema. The voyeur is concerned with 'reflected knowledge' that permits 'abitrary re-enactments in phantasy': he does not 'go with' committed sexual experience—

The behaviour of the voyeur is not an inherently meaningful surrender to fate, like that of lovers.   op. cit., page 219

There are thus antipathetic modes—that of 'immediate being', and that of the 'public'—and it is to the latter that the voyeur belongs. He wants to make a furtive entry into the intimacy of others, but he essentially fears that intimacy, and its elements of 'surrender'.

His realm, that of the public, is characterized, Straus says, by objectification, generality, and repetition. The outcome is non-commital, one-way participation. As Khan indicates, this is self-centred and essentially mean. By contrast, 'immediate being is not objectified, it is singular, unique becoming and calls for reciprocal sharing'. Lovers do not know where they are going, but it is towards something new and shared, in time, in their creative moment. To thrust into their committed creativity that which belongs to the pervert's world of 'outcomes' is to inhibit their potentialities.

Shame protects this essential creativity of being, with all the sense of meaning towards which it can lead, from intrusion by the 'public', and from objectification (or what in this book I call dehumanization). This observation Straus backs up by references to various human situations. His conclusion is that—

Shame is a protection against the public in all its forms . . . Shame is a safeguard for immediate experience against the world of outcomes. It does not constrain the erotic, as is assumed in [Freudian] psycho-analysis, but *makes the erotic possible* . . .   op. cit., page 222 (my italics)

Our objection to what is today called 'frankness', is that it may *make the erotic impossible*. On the one hand is pornography—

The word, in the form of 'dirty joke', vivid representation as in porno-graphy, and self-observation in the mirror shows the objectifying character of a self-representation . . .   op. cit., page 222

On the other hand is the world of love—

Those who are in love have no use for the 'dirty joke', pornography or the mirror, for these all belong to the shrunken existence of persons no longer capable of being immediately touched . . .   op. cit., page 222

The intrusive touch of 'the public' however can threaten the creativity of sexual becoming with objectification—

The secret that shame protects is now, however, as prudery makes the mistake of believing, one that is already in existence and only needs to be hidden from outsiders, for those in becoming are also hidden from themselves. Their existence is first made explicit in their first shared immediate becoming . . .   op. cit., page 223

Pornography thus is most likely to harm those who are in the first delicate moments of discovering the possibilities of 'becoming' through love—which also means all of us, who, from time to time, experience the continual rediscovery of love and its recreation in time.

In the light of such scientific insights, it is not only absurd, but improvident, to allow pornography greater and greater freedom, on the assumption that this will bring release to primary libidinal drives. The effect could well be to limit erotic potentialities, and break down the natural protection of shame. There might be justification for greater toleration of scopophilia if those who suffer from it could find release from neurosis by being able more freely to indulge their 'hungry looking'. But it would seem that their breakdown of communication with the world is not likely to be helped merely by more free opportunities for voyeurism. What is likely to happen is that increasing numbers of people will become the subjects of their attempts to objectify, and more and more people will have thrust into their intimate lives energies which menace their creative potentialities in the realm of the sexual, and require energy of them to resist an intrusive objectifying menace.

Deciding what kind of cultural work is likely to threaten us with an unacceptable degree of objectification, however, is very difficult indeed. The Arts Council Working party seems to have given up trying to find a 'workable' law on the subject of obscenity because it was too difficult. The difficulty lies in trying to define obscenity. This they declared impossible. But suppose they had been deliberating the problem of racial propaganda? This too is a difficult problem. Solutions lead to extraordinary situations, as in some parts of America where the use of *Huckleberry Finn* is forbidden in schools because of the word 'nigger'. Yet who would agree that we must tolerate racial propaganda because it is so difficult to define the degree of offensiveness by which we decide a publication must be prohibited by law? Here at least we have become realistic enough to recognize that hate can be spread abroad, and that human beings can be enlisted in the psychopathology of others. So, definitions and decisions must be made, however full of faults they may be.

The difficulty arises round the word obscene. As Mr. Mortimer says—

In the *Last Exit* case, the Court of Appeal made it clear that the Obscene Publications Act narrows the definition of obscenity and confines it to that which has a tendency to deprave and corrupt. In theory, therefore, plays which the Court merely finds shocking or revolting or disturbing should not be found to be obscene unless a corrupting tendency can be proved. No-one has ever defined what that sinister phrase might mean, and the Court of Appeal has said that it is a matter for the jury to decide in any particular case.

'After the Chamberlain', an article in *The Author*, Summer 1970

Our predicament now is that the question of the tolerance or prohibition of works of expression centres round the question of whether a work is likely to deprave or corrupt. And where proof is necessary in a Court of Law, this must be 'objective' proof; evidence, to be acceptable, must demonstrate visible effects on the personal life of the individual who is depraved and corrupted.

This is an impossible situation, as Mr. Mortimer says, not least because the jury is not allowed to hear evidence on the subject of corruption.

Not only does the unfortunate jury have to do this without any legal guidance, but they are not allowed to hear any evidence on the subject. Experts can be called on the literary or social merit of the work, but they are not allowed to say whether they think it would have a tendency to deprave or corrupt ... this is the question for which the jury are expected, as if by magic, to dredge up an answer from the dark recesses of their mind. When Sir Basil Blackwell, an elderly Oxford bookseller, attempted to tell the court that he had never felt the same since he had read *Last Exit* the evidence was later said to have been inadmissable, and the alarming details of Sir Basil's change in personality were, perhaps happily, never investigated.   ibid., loc. cit.

As the literary critic knows, judging whether a work is likely to corrupt, and then judging whether this likelihood is socially acceptable because of the quality of the work, is a very subtle and complex process. The dilemma of democracy is that in law this delicate judgement is handed over to individuals who have no qualifications to judge, and who are not allowed to be advised by experts in court. However, it should not be difficult to devise a system whereby certain individuals, who were qualified, could be given more authority and influence in a court proceeding.

However, Mr. Mortimer does not want anything of the sort. And in his mocking forensic tone we may glimpse another aspect of the problem. In his references to Sir Basil Blackwell we may detect a note of ridicule for the 'elderly Oxford bookseller', and an attempt to laugh out of court any report on subjective experience. The idea that someone might well be altered for the worse in his sensibility by the impact of a work of art is caricatured as absurd—if it were accepted it would challenge the confidence of Mr. Mortimer's total permissiveness—for what he really wants to do is to laugh the *problem* out of court, from quite fallacious assumptions based on 'objectivity'.

He speaks of a 'mind-bending obscurity' in the task of implementing the Obscene Publications Act. What he means is that the task is extremely difficult.

The jury must first find a play or book obscene, that is to say it must tend to deprave or corrupt those unfortunates submitted to it, and then go on to be satisfied that the corruption of a wide number of persons is in the public interest because of literary or other merit. It is small wonder that this is an idea that few judges have been able to explain or juries to grasp: and the procession of novelists, sociologists, lady welfare workers and enlightened bishops who are even prepared to give evidence as to 'public good', has never done much to deter a jury from condemning a book or play they found shocking in the first place.   ibid., loc. cit.

In such a perplexing situation, the Arts Council Working Party opted for complete abolition of legal restraint.

But how far can we ignore the fact that juries are 'shocked'? The law obviously demands that we set aside the degree to which we are shocked and seeks some more 'objective' evidence. This is absurd; the degree to which people are shocked is perhaps the most important evidence. The only reason we banned bear-baiting or cock-fighting is that people were shocked by them. Yet there is a scientific view that shame is a necessary response that *protects* the erotic, as we have seen. Today, 'enlightened' opinion is willing to ride roughshod over people's capacities to protect themselves by shame. But it is also evident today that the natural shame of the public is being undermined by manipulation. In the same issue of *The Author*, for instance, Philip Strick reports of a film that—

The British Board of Censors, as a matter of policy, requested cuts in the orgy sequence . . . which was then submitted instead to the Greater London Council—the censor's policy being that the film would as a result be withheld from general release until any risk of public outcry at provincial cinemas had been safely stifled by the obvious lack of concern shown by London audiences . . .   loc. cit.

Where London is demonstrably demoralized, this may be employed by such tactics to thrust demoralization on provincial communities. This is a calculated way of promoting dissociation, akin to the Nazi assault on humanistic values.

The 'enlightened' view, as is evident from Mr. Mortimer's tone ('the unfortunates submitted to it'—he speaks elsewhere of the Lord Chamberlain as an 'impossibly arbitrary nanny'), is that there is no problem. There is no harm in pornography. This extraordinary blandness needs, I believe, close examination. It would seem to be based on psychoanalytical ideas which have never ever been wholly accepted, and which were challenged long ago. In 1935 Dr. Ian D. Suttie wrote about these 'demoralization' ideas in therapy—

' Cure' is the idea that we must increase the patient's *tolerance* or diminish his censorship of the evil sexual impulses which were at one time imagined to be the main content of the unconscious system. The neurotic was held to be morally hyper-aesthetic, and contact with the broad-minded analyst de-sensitized, or, as many disapproving lay writers held, *demoralized* him to the required extent.
The Origins of Love and Hate, page 164

In therapy this theory was 'never approved by serious analysts', though it was popular with 'rebel temperaments'. But the theory persists in 'enlightened' attitudes to sexual depiction; there is an imaginary assurance inherent in the attitude—

'These evil thoughts and wishes are not really bad after all. Sex is only bad *for children*; that is why it is hidden by adults from them. Now you are grown up and permitted to wish these things.'   op. cit., page 164

This Suttie called 'initiation' therapy; in the realm of culture we might call it 'initiation permissiveness'. Suttie calls another version of this approach 'disillusionment therapy'—

'of course you are bad—if you call sex bad: we *all are* bad in this sense. We are merely hypocrites, and goodness is an illusion.'
op. cit., page 164

If we see this attitude behind 'disillusionment permissiveness' we can perhaps begin to see the nihilism inherent in it. Suttie finds it rooted in Freud's 'pessimism and aggressiveness'. It belongs to that moral inversion which emerges inevitably from the 'homunculist' view of man. As Polanyi points out, even to recognize moral inversion is to challenge this reductive view—

To recognize the existence of moral inversion is to acknowledge moral forces as primary motives of man; it is to deny that 'sublimation' underlies (as Freud thought) the creation of culture. Of course, moral forces are elicited and shaped by education, even as man's intelligence or artistic talent is evoked by education. But this does not imply that morality is a mere rationalization of self-interest, or that science is a sublimation of sexual curiosity. On the contrary, the Freudian interpretation of morality is itself but a spurious form of moral inversion. It forms part of the expurgation of modern language which substitutes objectivist—and preferably appetitive—terms for candidly moral ones.
Personal Knowledge, page 234

Once more, it is a question of escaping from a whole pattern of thought which sees man's primary needs in terms of appetite and 'instinct',* and from a philosophical confusion which supposes that ethical issues can be dealt with by empiricism.†

'Initiation' and 'disillusionment' approaches to the problem of sexual attitudes fail to take into account the primary needs of man, as philosophical anthropology sees them, which are for love and meaning and are therefore bound up with the 'healthy moral sense', the True Self, and values. As Suttie indicates, mere demoralization leaves a patient in therapy 'more isolated than before'.

---

* See my *Human Hope and the Death Instinct*, pages 49–50.
† 'No chemical analysis or microscopic examination can prove that a man who bears false witness is immoral'. Michael Polanyi, *Knowing and Being*, page 46.

From our point of view we may, I believe, say that while there is some gain in being broadminded and tolerant as, say, over the problem of masturbation in children, there is another kind of problem which may be raised by the use of sexual activities, or sex thinking or utterance *in a way which symbolizes a desperate need for meaning in terms of whole being*. That is, a child may masturbate compulsively because this is the only way in which he can still feel alive in the face of an appalling sense of emptiness. This kind of problem can only be understood if we take into account the primary need for *meaning*.

The approach to problems of censorship in our time is bedevilled by our belief in a science 'imprisoned in physicalism'. Effects are compartmentalized, so that the 'effect' of sexual depiction is allowed to be estimated only in terms of consequent sexual behaviour, such as masturbation. Pornography can only be said to 'corrupt' if it is shown to cause 'deviant' sexual behaviour. This simplistic and mechanical attitude to cause and effect in human behaviour has its own implications about our nature: it is essentially quantitative and reductionist, as well as being full of 'carefully contrived perspectives' by which the effects of meaning and symbolism are *not seen*. Take this view for example—

The Committee of Management [of the Society of Authors] has decided not to express official approval or disapproval of the Arts Council's recommendations as a whole but make it known that, if the law were to be revised, it considers that the test of obscenity hitherto . . . should be redefined to establish that sado-masochistic pornography, which might tend to excite cruelty and violence, should be actionable as obscene, where as the frank discussion of sex or the publication of such erotica as would tend only to incite to masturbation, should not be actionable.
Michael Ayrton, 'Obscenity in Committee', *The Author*, Summer 1970

The absurdity of the view may be exposed if we ask whether, for instance, a Dutch still life of lobsters and fruit is to be considered merely in terms of whether it makes us want to eat more, or whether Botticelli's *Venus* merely in terms of whether it makes us want to make love to a woman or masturbate. If a number of nudes in an art gallery have the effect of making us want to have sexual relationships with women in a normal heterosexual way, or to masturbate, this is acceptable, the view implies, while other pictures, if they encourage us to want to try homosexual love or sadism, are bad. Such an approach to the problem of the effects of culture is ridiculous, because it separates its 'influences' into strictly compartmentalized channels, so that sexual stimuli of one kind are held to produce sexual behaviour of one kind, while sexual stimuli of another kind are held to produce behaviour of another kind. This is to oversimplify the human model in an absurdly mechanical way, and falsifies the whole problem of the relationship between the complex being, his perception of his world, and his action in it. In the background, of course, are all those experiments of a Pavlovian kind* in which a single response is supposed to be generated by a single stimulus, such as a bell or an electric shock, producing salivation, or an aversion to sexual excitement. As Merleau-Ponty and Straus argue, such experiments involve such a separation of the subject from its natural state as a 'being-in-the-world' that this alone conditions the conclusions disastrously. As Straus argues, in this behaviourist approach there are many false epistemological and metaphysical assumptions.†

From the point of view of the subjective disciplines, we have to insist that human symbolism, motivation, and conduct are much more complex than is implied by such simplistic, physicalist approaches. A man looking at forms of sexual depiction is not merely directly influenced, as by a 'stimulus'—a bell or a red light—in a psychologist's cage, in his subsequent sexual behaviour, and in no other way. He perceives what is presented to him by a complex process of response and interpretation that involves all his inner life, his imagination, and his powers of projecting interpretations over the world in seeing it and finding it meaningful. These processes in him have a long history—for he was taught in the beginning to see the world by his mother, and his perception of it is therefore deeply bound up with his emotional life and his whole identity. Since this is so, elements of his primitive early responses to the world and primitive phantasies will always infuse his response to sexual symbolism; so the woman in the picture is always to some extent a breast, but also a person. She is an ideal object, but also a libidinal object. She is also a symbol of humanness. Two people in a photograph of sexual activity will be individuals with whom he identifies, but also symbolic of human 'meeting'. And they will also have primitive elements of 'primal scene' phantasy: they will represent, especially in so far as they are physically responding to one another, Mummy and Daddy—and so the phantasies he himself had of parental sexual intercourse

* 'This oversimple paradigm of learning may . . . be misdescribed as it was by Pavlov, when he identified *eating* with an *expectation to be fed*, because both of these induce the secretion of saliva. Whenever we define mental processes by objectivist circumlocutions, we are apt to stumble into such absurdities.' Polanyi, *Knowing and Being*, page 216.
† Not least, that there is such a thing as a 'stimulus', or that subjects merely 'receive impressions', rather than see or sense. The parallel in the realm under discussion is the failure of opinion to consider the expectations aroused by the availability of pornography, and its effect on our seeing and communication with the world.

when he was an infant. Any primal scene phantasy has 'sado-masochistic' elements, with powerful incorporative feelings bound up with these—of eating and being eaten, of *annihilating and being annihilated*.

Thus, all symbols which involve human beings touch on feelings which are not only sexual, but also have to do with hunger, ideal-ism, sadism, fear of annihilation and hurting, envy, anxiety, creativity, 'intentionality', love, and hate. If we consider *meaning*, then we must link symbolism, of whatever kind, with the whole human identity, its means of ego-maintenance and quest for meaningful existence. Sexual symbolism belongs to the whole complex of communicating with the world. We can only consider a man's response to pornography in terms of its total effect on his whole being—of which his sexual behaviour is only one aspect.

This, the sexologists, who base their work on 'objective' ex-perimentation, as we have seen, fail to do. In consequence, so do the enlightened commentators in their approach to ethics and behaviour. The implicit fallacies in such approaches have been exposed by philosophical writers such as Merleau-Ponty, Straus, and Michael Polanyi. However, it seems unlikely that those who cling to scientific 'objectivity' will ever be able to escape from the confines of their physicalism and reductionist thinking, to under-stand how inadequate their approaches are, and how disastrously full of unexamined assumptions. They would find it difficult to understand the difference Polanyi postulates between 'attending to' and 'attending from', or what Merleau-Ponty means by being 'enslaved' by nudity. Yet nearly all 'progressive' approaches to problems of sexual depiction and morality are based on approaches which are believed to be 'realistic' in the objective way, yet which seem in the light of the work of such philosophers to be absurd. Yet governments and government agencies such as the Arts Coun-cil (without realizing it) are taking such approaches to sex and culture as the basis for the toleration of obscenity and porno-graphy, while rejecting other views as 'too subjective'.*

Our perplexity here may be increased by the fact that, even in the terms of their own approaches, the 'objective researchers' have found some connexions between cultural symbolism and behaviour, and this is of great importance. For instance an American team of sex researchers has concluded that boys exposed to large doses of erotic material before the age of fourteen *may develop deviant behaviour*. In a report to a government commission in 1970 on

---

* Yet philosophers within behaviourism itself are deeply critical of the theory of some behaviourists. (See Charles Taylor, *The Explanation of Behaviour*, and W. H. Thorpe on animal behaviour.)

obscenity and pornography Mr. K. E. Davis, chairman of Rutgers University psychology department, of the University of Colorado, reported on a study of 365 men between the ages of eighteen and thirty, ranging from Denver gaol inmates to Negro college students, and Roman catholic seminarists. The men studied were asked to tell if they had engaged in ten activities which the researchers established as deviant, from secretly watching a woman undress, to forcing others to have sexual intercourse, to exhibitionism and transvestism.

Early and ample exposure [to pornography] may affect the youth's view of sexuality and willingness to engage in varieties of deviance.
The Australian, 3rd September 1970

said the Denver Report.

In old-fashioned language, his sexual inclinations may be warped by a very early significant exposure.   ibid., loc. cit.

From the point of view of philosophical anthropology, this conclusion would seem to suggest that we must question seriously the eventual conclusion of the American government commission, which was that laws governing pornography should be relaxed, even though the commission agreed that there should be measures to protect children from such material.

If human beings can be affected adversely at a very early age, they can be adversely affected at any age. There is no definite stage at which vulnerability to cultural influences significantly changes. Significantly, there is an admission here that human beings *can* be affected by sexual depiction in their sexual behaviour. But the criterion of the influence of pornography, surely, cannot be limited to whether or not it encourages 'deviant' behaviour alone. 'Corruption' cannot so easily be measured. If we take, for instance, the item 'watching a woman undress', this could be done in a number of ways—simple curiosity, compulsive voyeurism, attendance at strip clubs as a mania, or in a ballet in which it had high creative content in its symbolism. In any case, watching a woman undress, or helping a woman undress, can be one of the most beautiful and satisfying experiences in life. I am not saying there is not a 'deviant' form of watching a woman undress: I am trying to say that, unless we are to keep to the crudest categories in our 'evidence', we need to take into account the fact that differences in human beings are as countless as the variations and complexities of human symbolism and meaning. To reduce them to categories and statistics may well lead to absurdities.

Moreover, we need to consider in what circumstances the individuals under survey came to have an overdose of pornography in the first place. We may here need to take into account various possibilities. They live in a society much afflicted, as is America, by psychopathological cultural trends (such as the prevalence of pornography) which it is difficult to keep from children, however much parents try, once it is published and distributed. They themselves may have belonged to feckless, disturbed or criminal families in which they were exposed to pornography, or deliberately given it, as part of the psychopathological dynamic of the home. That is, they simply became involved in anxieties which took, as one form, a psychopathological preoccupation with sexual depiction. Also they themselves may have been unstable, and so tended to look for pornography, were more easily excited by it, and more easily affected by it.

The problem cannot be considered without attention to the whole life-process of each individual under survey. What would certainly have been of interest would be to investigate in what other ways these individuals were influenced by exposure to pornography. Here, again 'evidence' could only be gained by exploration of 'subjective' aspects of the lives of these individuals.*
In extensive interviews, what kind of attitude to human nature would emerge from those who had been exposed to a great deal of pornography? What attitudes to women? What ethical assumptions in the sphere of sexual conduct? What ethical attitudes to other forms of conduct, such as aggression? It seems evident that the increasing depiction of depersonalized sex in our time leads to the kind of attitude characterized by Dr. Rollo May, when he reports how college students find it 'too much trouble to say no'. Dr. May asks whether it is wise to reduce one of our greatest sources of meaning and satisfaction, and, indeed, the source of life itself, to such a level of triviality. It would be interesting to know whether the attitudes of the men who had been exposed to pornography at an early age seemed more trivial than those of others. And if so was this triviality associated in any way with a 'diminution of affect'? Were their attitudes to relationship less human? Were their feelings about sex less rich, were they 'cooler', and did sex have less significance for them? Is it true, as Leslie H. Farber says, that our modern preoccupation with sex is gradually taking the meaning out of sex for us all?

But as we formulate such questions, we can see that they cannot be answered by objective research alone, though they could be explored by philosophical anthropology, and by forms of reflection

---

* Moreover, it is also possible to judge the corruption in pornography at its moment of impact, by the same values we would judge any corrupt act which it prompted.

in which individuals report on their own experience in the same way that the literary critic does. So, the position of the Arts Council here is a strange one. While estimating, say, expenditure on opera or music, this official agency will take the considered view of a critic, whose work is all subjective and who can certainly offer no 'objective' evidence, that expenditure on opera is worthwhile. But the same agency will only consider 'scientific' (i.e. behaviourist) evidence, when considering whether or not pornography does harm. This is absurd.

And here a question of authenticity arises. In the sphere under discussion, which agencies are to have our confidence, and whose authority is to be endorsed? As Marjorie Grene points out, scientific 'fact' is only acceptable because in our era we give authority to 'those best qualified to judge'—no man can test for himself even a small range of scientific conclusions and hypotheses. Nowadays it seems evident that some forms of what is believed to have scientific authenticity are encroaching on areas of reality where, by their own terms, they cannot have validity, and do not deserve the authority they are given by the public. The disciplines which should have authority in these realms are philosophical anthropology, psychoanalytical psychology, ethics, cultural criticism and phenomenology.

Thus my 'attitude to sex' involves me ultimately in defending certain forms of insight—such as those gained by poetry and imagination, by the 'encounters' of psychoanalysis, and the phenomenological approach of philosophical biologists—against the encroachment of a science 'imprisoned in physicalism' which is seeking to offer us 'facts' gained by methods, and interpreted by theories, of which devastating criticisms have been made by philosophers and scientists able to find 'the category of life'. We need to assert the primary reality of our unique existence, and to assert the validity of those approaches, not least in science,* which can find these human facts of whole existence, against those who offer us a limiting and reductive 'objectivity'. To put it briefly, they offer us sex which can be seen even on a laboratory test bench, but fail to find the evident 'fact' of love—and so they implicitly dehumanize our concepts of ourselves, and exclude from their view of life everything that makes it meaningful.

The question of our attitudes to sex thus brings us face to face with a wider, menacing nihilism in contemporary thought and culture. In so far as this nihilism has generated a situation in the law courts in which it is almost impossible to bring a successful

---

* See *Approaches to a Philosophical Biology*, Marjorie Grene, Basic Books, 1965.

action against an obscene work, it has laid us open to a mounting tide of assault on our sensibilities, by those individuals who need to live at the expense of others, by thrusting objectifying and dehumanizing influences into the world. That this is a problem to which the 'enlightenment' denies reality is becoming all too self-evident.

It is the opinion of the present writer that the prevalent obsession with sex in our culture, which is a manifestation of compensation for existential insecurity, will, as it proves inevitably inadequate and unsatisfactory as a solution to existential problems, turn to increasingly destructive and nihilistic modes, not least because of the opportunity to do damage offered by the prevalent over-permissiveness. One of the worst effects will be that of damaging the arts themselves as a source of meaning. For this reason, I believe, ethical considerations need to be invoked urgently in this sphere, and supported by legal sanctions.

Yet how shall a 'workable' legal process be devised? For one thing, it is necessary, as in any other case which requires expert advice, for any legal decision on this kind of problem to be based on a thorough study made by those qualified to judge, through expert examination of the evidence. The problem arises, however, as to who shall be accepted as having authority now that the authority of the 'objective scientist' has been shown to be doubtful, since he cannot in his discipline find the problems of meaning and value involved.

The educationist will surely not find this difficult. In such a sphere as education we invest large sums on the assumption (which is by no means based on 'objective' measurements of 'how people behave') that the predominant effect of cultural activity is on each individual's 'inner life'. The cranes and concrete mixers working away on every campus in the world are themselves a tribute to our recognition of subjective realities. The Arts Council itself spends millions on subjective realities. When we enter into debate on pornography, *which is a form of cultural 'teaching'*, why should we be persuaded to distrust all the assumptions we live by in the worlds of culture and education?

If it is 'not proven' that pornography has an educational effect on the attitudes and behaviour of individuals, then it is 'not proven' that cultural effort and education in the humanities bring benefits either, and all our faith in education must be chimerical. If the Arts Council is right in its assumptions about pornography, the Department of Education and Science might as well close its doors where the humanities are concerned.

Obviously, from a concern with culture that recognizes the realities of human inner needs and dynamics, pornography must be discussed in the same terms. The only evidence here is that of the inner life of imagination, and the way in which this is bound up with perception and effective living. And here there can be ethical discriminations—which are bound up with aesthetic discriminations. We make these continually in real life—no-one goes into a Museum to see the latest double-spread from *Playboy* (though things are moving that way with the cult of the empty and ridiculous Andy Warhol).

The essential critieria could be, I believe, based on the theme explored in this book. The question of whether any obscene work should be allowed to be exhibited in public should be decided in terms of the degree to which it might threaten to objectify our concepts and attitudes in a schizoid way, to a psychopathological degree, or whether there is sufficient creative content in it to offset such dehumanizing effects.

Let me discuss this problem round the prevailing sexual symbol of our time, the nude 'girlie'. She symbolizes sexuality separated in a objectified, schizoid way from human wholeness. In the light of psychoanalytical insights, she is a part-object, a breast, detached as an object of appetite, arousing that excited attention from one area of the hungry mouth-ego, such as made us feel alive when we were infants. She is divested as much as possible from her individuality, and with her, as with the prostitute, sexual hunger is separated by will from any possibility of (dangerous) relationship. Dissociated from the possibilities of 'meeting', her effect is thus forever cut off from any possibility of finding 'the significant other'. Her influence, in the light of Frankl's comments above, is to affect our psychic health by recommending mere sexuality and promoting the attitude that sex should be a mere means to the end of pleasure, thus urging us towards a 'thoroughly decadent sensualism'. Though she seems to offer us 'aliveness' her symbolism can never offer us anything which can contribute to the possibilities of finding meaning in a relationship which matters to us, because meaning can only be found in being committed to one unique person, and in finding and sharing experience with that person. She really urges on us ultimate deadness, by associating sex with a temporary state of pleasure in which there is no meaning, and by pressing upon us the objectification and generalization that belong to scopophilia—as defences against emotional surrender and creativity. Genuine erotic art, by contrast, expresses a sense of personal uniqueness and value which is bound up with the true erotic experience—compare, say, the paintings of Bonnard, Marvell's *To His Coy Mistress*, Wyatt's poetry, or Lawrence's *The Rainbow* and *Women in Love*, and Solzhenitsyn's *Cancer Ward*.

This essential difference between pornography and genuine

eroticism is perhaps obscured in our time by the exploitation of photography as a medium, and the concepts of 'reality' which belong to it. From the point of view of the subjective disciplines, a painting of an imaginary woman may be more inwardly true of human reality, more 'real' because it is created by 'indwelling', than a suggestive nude photograph. While no doubt, at first glance, the photograph appears to be more 'real' because its subject was real at the time and actually existed, yet it belongs more to time than creative symbolism which belongs to love that triumphs over time. The obsession with 'outward reality', as in photography, obviously belongs to that objectifying looking which tends to approach 'reality' in a certain external way, as the sexologists themselves do. Moreover, because of its apparent reality, the photographic image has an immediate manic effect, of making us feel excited and alive. It belongs very much to a technological world, and is the technicist image this typically fosters (in my experience the most manic photographs, significantly, are found in the make-up rooms of television studios).

By contrast with this 'instant dish', the truly erotic picture or sculpture may seem too personal, too human. That which symbolizes the uniqueness of the real person after all is likely to burden us with all the old responsibilities, so may merely leave us feeling that we are simply faced with the old relational and existential problems all over again. It draws our attention to the fact that it is only the personal aspects of relationship that are real. The effect of Rodin's *Le Baiser*, for instance, is perhaps even to evoke in us a degree of anxiety, about when next we may be able to experience such a significant and satisfying moment in love such as the sculpture symbolizes, if ever. It indicates that we can only have such a meaningful passion when it *happens* to us in the context of an actual committed relationship in our inward life, between real persons. Erotic art tells us that the true creativity of sexual love is to be found in an 'inherently meaningful surrender to fate', in time, like that of lovers.

This is so because the carved figures are so symbolically evocative, as well as complex and subtle in their humanness: they emerge from 'attending from', from the realities of the inward life. The suggestive photograph, by contrast, evokes immediate 'primal scene' phantasies, and allows us to identify with what is taking place in a primitive, hungry way and at a distance, so that we feel a little more excited and alive at once, and feel as if clarity and meaning here can be willed. Such photographs belong to 'attending to' and thus to mere externals. The partial object, or 'breast', seems real and material even if we cannot grasp the reality of the person. We are able to forget the pains, anxieties, responsibilities and claims of real relationship, in favour of a day-dream one, in which hunger (it seems) can be satisfied immediately, without involvement or responsibility, and in which we can avoid the depression or despair involved in imaginative-creative relationship. Yet this 'objective' imagery leaves us even more exposed to time and nothingness—for only secret, shared love can overcome these.

Pornography is thus an act of intellectual *will*, and so destructive of the realm of *being* in which alone meaningful sex can *happen*. Special problems of will and time are involved here, which are no doubt related to the rhythm of our experience of being fed in infancy.* In the brothel or the 'blue' film, sex can be willed *now*: in any real relationship, one must wait for the time to come, for 'the moment that we are', for 'shared immediate becoming'. Problems of human equality are involved here: willed sex inevitably degrades its object by reducing a person to a 'breast to be taken' without consideration of the desires of the other. To love in true equality we need to project ourselves by imagination into the inwardness of the other.

Between these two extremes of experience lie the criteria for deciding what is permissible, what is merely deplorable, and what should be forbidden, in erotic depiction and behaviour. Coercion must support that valuable shame which protects our erotic creativity from dehumanizing destructiveness.

The belief that, if pornography were permitted without restraints, it would 'fade away' is as unreal as the image of a society which could 'continuously reshape its own life in the pursuit of civic virtues freely fostered in its midst'. The phrase is Polanyi's, and he says that 'in an ideal free society civic life would be improved solely by the cultivation of moral principles'.

But let us remember the facts of power and material ends. Though men be harmoniously guided by their agreed convictions, they must yet form a government to enforce their purpose. Civic culture can flourish only thanks to physical coercion. *It is sown in corruption.* We must now expose the instability of our moral beliefs in the face of this fact . . . coercion is both possible and indispensable in human society . . .

Personal Knowledge, page 224 (my italics)

The 'totally permissive' view in the sphere under discussion belongs to a moral idealism which is not willing to admit the 'instability of our moral beliefs'. It refuses to accept that we have to live always somewhere between tyranny and total freedom, and that our erotic creativity is 'sown in corruption'. It seeks the 'logically

---

* See Leslie H. Farber, *The Ways of the Will*, and Erwin Straus, *Phenomenological Psychology*.

stabler state of complete moral inversion'. Letting everything go would in fact be to give oneself up to the joys of hating—which is what has happened in Denmark. It seems to the 'enlightened' that total permissiveness is a *solution* to a very complex issue. This seems obvious when people reply, on the subject of pornography, 'Who is to decide?' They are implying that *nobody* has any right to discriminate on behalf of all—a position we accept in no other sphere. It is now necessary to insist that the evidence we should consider over obscenity is that which may be collocated by the disciplined attempts of individuals capable of giving an account of their own response to cultural works and estimating this with reference to their own sense of individual humanness and their capacity for ethical living in relation to the ethical values of their society. They should also be capable of comparing their responses with those of others. Of course such processes are complex and difficult; but why should they not be, since man himself is complex and subtle? Why should there be any simple solution in this sphere? To suppose as much is to fall for a merely delusory, 'stabler state' and to refuse to accept that 'civic culture' is only 'sown in corruption'. As for the right of any individual to decide, obviously there are many spheres (such as education) where we continually deal with such complex problems and where individuals are continually obliged to make responsible decisions (as over syllabuses). And no-one in his senses would object to decisions being taken, over, say, racial propaganda, or the exploitation of children in brothels.

Inevitably, if we accept the subjective realities in such a problem as pornography, we are faced with the problem of hate. Some people are obviously driven to thrust anti-human hate into us, by cultural means, because they need to gain a 'pleasurable negative identity', in this way. They enjoy lowering the sense of value in others and breaking down their ego-boundaries. They want to live at the expense of others in this inward way, and want to objectify them—to make them into 'things'.

Because the impulse of the pervert may be an attempt to solve a 'pressing crisis of diffusion of self and identity' it is possible for a perverted work of literature or discourse to be acceptable publicly, as the work of Genet has been accepted publicly, because it can be seen as a contribution to the agonized problems of identity in the modern world. Such acceptance, however, is not without its dangers, as the effect of schizoid influences today in the cultural and moral sphere shows. Those who go to the Danish Sex Fairs speak of being 'stunned' and then of becoming 'immune'. They suffer what the psychoanalysts call 'diminution of affect'—a symptom of depersonalization. They may even lose some of their humanness. Our civilization is tormented by an increasing sense of meaningless. Has this not been increased by the implicit homun-culism and nihilism of *avant-garde* works, which are spreading abroad hate and the depreciation of human value? Here it is most important to hold on to the principle that a nihilistic work is only acceptable if it is of a high creative quality in which benign elements are striving against the malignant. (Unfortunately this principle seems to have been jettisoned in England, for the ob-scenities in *Oh! Calcutta!* can have no conceivable excuse in terms of an overall creative purpose.) But there must be limits, or else nihilism and irrationalism might well breed an incipient fascism once more.

Where the limits shall be, however, is a most difficult problem to judge. One useful exploration of the problem is Eugene Kaelin's study *An Existentialist Aesthetic* which is an attempt to examine this problem philosophically. If we follow Sartre, Kaelin says, we shall find ourselves accepting art as subversive, and as a political act—

once the vision is shared, the value communicated, the social conse-quences of the communication may very well take the course Sartre has predicted for all valid works of literary art: they may become effective political actions.   *An Existentialist Aesthetic*, page 155

Presumably those who urge on us more pornography are following Marcuse, in the belief that such symbolism can release us from the inhibitions imposed by society. Sartre's view is that the authentic man constantly anticipates a social order which is least oppressive and grants full play to his natural liberty. As Marjorie Grene says: 'The revolutionary philosophy turns out to be the philosophy of freedom—not just the philosophy of those who seek freedom but the philosophy of the very free act itself.'

Action against social evils is meaningful only in so far as these evils repress the liberties of men. But in this is implicit a theory of human make-up that sees a dynamic impulse which is being repressed. If we accept this model, then such manifestations as pornography may need 'release'. However, if we take a different kind of model—such as that which is implicit in the philosophical biology of Erwin Straus, or the existentialist psychoanalysis of Frankl or May, we find ourselves in difficulties here. As George Kneller says, the question now becomes—

If other men are mere objects to be controlled in terms of our personal projects, and if mutuality is an illusion [as in the attitude of Sartre], how can personal subjectivity achieve any sort of recognition of another man's liberty?   *Existentialism and Education*, page 8

Another stream of existentialism, of which Binswanger and Buber are representative, finds mutuality a positive force in the development of human identity, as does the philosophical biology of a Buytendijk. From their point of view the 'other' does not inevitably confront us and threaten our freedom, but our freedom is to be found in creative 'encounter' with the other. The recognition of our own liberty, and its fulfilment, is to be found in love. Sartre may have no confidence in benevolence and altruistic love as the basis of society: object-relations psychoanalysis and May's kind of existentialist psychoanalysis see them as primary realities, as did Ian D. Suttie. From their point of view, that is from the 'schizoid diagnosis', they would also see Sartre's position as being one in which it is continually necessary to sustain a posture of 'pseudo-male doing' or 'bad thinking', to feel real. They are aware of another source of an adequate sense of authentic being—which is in that confidence in the capacity to say 'I am' derived from the experience of love, and creative reflection. Since this is bound up with the origins of one's communication with the world, in the first encounters of play, and culture, it is bound up with creativity as we experience it in the arts.

From this point of view, the first creative encounter between mother and infant is the basis of perception and all culture. This is the view of both the philosophical biologist (such as Buytendijk) and of the psychoanalyst (such as Winnicott). The implication for art is that it contributes to those processes of maintaining a self and developing one's creative powers to perceive and create one's world, that are rooted in love. As we have seen, from the same point of view, as in the psychology of Winnicott, Khan and Straus, perversion represents the break-down of love and creativity. To encourage or tolerate pornography, therefore, may threaten the creative modes by which individuals sustain their human identity. The attitude of a Sartre, therefore, may simply be to encourage 'pseudo-male doing' in art, at the expense of that creativity derived from female element being—and so it would offer no genuine revolution at all, no liberation, but a promotion abroad of falsification and dehumanization, with a consequent breakdown of communication with the world, growing irrationalism, and a new incipient fascism. This is in fact what we have in our culture.

Sartre's position would indicate a total lack of confidence in any human institution. In whatever sphere we claim our freedom, the institution for him, embodying the inauthentic collective values of society, is an enemy. From the point of view of philosophical anthropology, however, institutions at their best may embody those values which have been created by love, and by the ethical living of individuals—by their altruism, and their 'encounter'. The philosophical anthropologist is likely to agree with Polanyi that, although we need to keep coercion to a minimum, 'coercion is both possible and indispensable in human society', not least in the realm of culture. One of the problems that coercion has to deal with is the impulse of the individual driven by fanatical immoralism, or a 'pathological morality' to base his dealings with the world on hate rather than love. Sartre may hail de Sade as a moral hero, but society puts itself at risk if it allows a de Sade to recruit as many victims as he chooses, or if it allows a de Sade to thrust into the realm of the most intimate dialogue his utterances of hate which, as he himself fervently hoped, would breed hate in others, and destroy something in their lives.

While Sartre's position has prompted many to seek not only the defiance of social collectivity and values, but also the destruction of social institutions, the position of the existentialist who takes into account the insights of philosophical anthropology is to seek to preserve the institutions, but to make them instruments of the protection of our freedom. For, if we take Straus's remarks about the value of shame, there are certain significant manifestations in our society which need support (as we recognize in our laws concerning racial discrimination).

As Kaelin says—

The decision as to what controls are desirable on truly pornographic works of art is currently being attempted with a modicum of common sense: courts are asking recognised critics for an informed aesthetic judgement differentiating works of art from public obscenities, and so are giving credence to what we have been calling a 'free aesthetic institution'. The assumption is that a well ordered society keeps its institutions in well ordered design, allowing each to function as it is best capable of functioning to permit the maximum development of the human personality ...   *An Existentialist Aesthetic*, page 345

Much of Kaelin's argument centres round the problem of the work of Genet, who represents eminently a schizoid individual whose solutions to the problems of life are based on hate, and whose work is the 'confession' of a pervert, offering vindications of his false solutions, achieved in terms of a 'pleasurable negative identity' at the expense of others.

Genet's case exemplifies Sartre's interest in the bottom-dog. One may agree with Sartre that insofar as Genet's expression is of an imaginary character his books are not crime, and indeed that their reading may produce the kind of sympathy necessary to re-examine the status of existing law; further, it seems apparent that for a society to honour a perverted author but to abhor his perversion is an anomalous state of affairs. If we put aside the question of legality concerning Genet's release from prison, we may even be forced to admit that a work of art may be good because it has bad (disapproved) subject-matter. We use the word 'good' in the last sentence as meaning 'possessing desirable social consequences,' as tending to the community of ends of free individuals. Lastly, it goes without saying that Genet's works may have had this consequence only if they were, in some aesthetically technical sense, good; otherwise we should have to judge them as outrageous pornography. op. cit., page 347

The question arises of course, of on what 'evidence' we base our approaches to such problems.

Kaelin himself is concerned to show that what Merleau-Ponty offers is a form of 'philosophical anthropology' which is eminently relevant in such a sphere—

I have given it the name 'philosophical anthropology' since it is an attempted description of human behaviour based upon an analysis of various structures or formed responses evident in part on the lower levels of evolutionary development, and completely only in man. Its method is not metaphysical in the sense of appealing to 'transphenomenal' realities, but reflective in the sense often intended to include scientific inductive procedures and their critical evaluation. This interpretation of the philosophical method is similar to Heidegger's supposition that metaphysical inquiry (direct personal experience) is a broader concept than the method of science, and the ultimate court of appeal by which the claims of science to validity are judged. Merleau-Ponty calls the method simply 'reflection.' op. cit., page 185

It would seem that our problems here can only be solved if there can be a new recognition of the reflective and inward aspects of our knowledge of the world, and especially our knowledge of man. Where man is concerned, philosophical anthropology can never fail to consider *meaning*, and where meaning is concerned we can discuss, through subjective disciplines, whether any body of expression is human or anti-human, belongs to love or hate, enhances the creativity of others or threatens it. From the point of view of such subjective disciplines it is possible to see such manifestations as pornography as ethically problematic in a way that objective science cannot, since it does not concern itself with meaning. To tackle such problems is immensely difficult, but urgent. Unless we solve such difficult philosophical issues as I have raised in this book we are going to be exposed to a deluge of hate and dehumanization which could destroy democracy, liberal culture, freedom, and, in the end, science itself. What we urgently need is a new social psychology, based on a psychology which is truly psychological. Kaelin sees that Sartre's position is 'extremely naive', because he was so 'poorly acquainted with social psychology'.

As Kaelin says, 'There is hope Merleau-Ponty's writings contain the corrective to Sartre's aberration'. From Merleau-Ponty's point of view 'a work of art is a unique act of introducing a novel significance into human culture', and 'What must be applied to them is not a conceptual or essential analysis, but an existential one'. All the individual can do is to give an account of the effect of the work on himself, in terms of the subjective disciplines in collocation with the values of his civilization. If we accept the existence, then, of the True Self, the inward 'ethical flame' or 'healthy Moral Sense' of each individual, and the existence of values in the collocation of ethical descriptions, then such an account requires commitment of a special kind, and a recognition of the well-being of others such as Sartre's attitude does not permit. This seems a more adequate position than Sartrean attitudes to art: but it requires a special kind of social psychology which still has to be developed.

As Kaelin says—

In terms of the existentialists, aesthetics must become committed, and to something more than the fineness of the aesthetic product. If this means that more emphasis must be placed upon the social psychology of art, then 'tis a consummation devoutly to be wished.

op. cit., page 355

The problem thus boils down to our need to give endorsement to those who can approach cultural problems by 'indwelling' with an adequate philosophical anthropology, employing the 'collocation of naturalistic ethical descriptions'. Unfortunately, in our time, the area of serious minority culture in which such disciplines and such standards could exist exhibits no integrated view of man, is diffuse and divided, and seems threatened with dwindling and dissipation. There is, for instance, in England no journal in which such issues as I have tried to explore in this chapter could be explored seriously at this length. This absence of such an adequate forum for debate, let alone any concensus of opinion, explains why moral inversion and cultural perversion are triumphing.

We cannot, however, wait for a totally new philosophical 'solution'. If the theme of the present work is accepted, then our conclusions require immediate action to be taken, and sanctions to be applied—on behalf of humanity at large—with 'a modicum of common sense' in such 'free aesthetic institutions', as we can establish.

In a leader on the UNESCO Conference in Venice in September 1970, *The Times* discussed 'cultural pollution'—

Pornography always has in it somewhere a hatred of man, both of man as a human being able to respond to ideals, and of man as an animal. Pornography is not an affirmation but a denial of life, and commercial pornography is a denial of life for the sake of money.

The Times, 3rd September 1970

This denial of life, and hatred of being human, is now endemic in the culture of the West.

The 'enlightened' approach fails to take sufficiently into account the delinquent and criminal elements in pornography. Psychoanalysis tells us that the prostitute has a need for prostitution: the normal person has a great resistance to taking on such a role. Those who become pornographers, it would seem, have a need to do so, and this need involves them in menacing the erotic life of others. These individuals can kill two birds with one stone. They can thrust 'objectification' into others (satisfying the schizoid urge to 'petrify' others because they are dangerous, by dehumanizing them) *and*, by the profits they make, they can feel socially accepted in doing so. The gold they amass has its own symbolism—it makes filth clean and hate pure. To tolerate them is to encourage all these false solutions, and to endorse them publicly.

While there are those who exploit sex in various forms of psychic desperation, because of their attempts to overcome the breakdown of their communication with the world, there are also aspects of the dehumanization of sex which are exacerbated by the whole inhuman machine-like process of modern technology. As we have seen, schizoid patients sometimes have a feeling that they are being filmed: as Frankl says, they are experiencing themselves as objects. The very nature of the camera technology of our culture lends itself to making human beings into objects of an objectifying and schizoid looking: in its very nature, it depends increasingly (for economic reasons) on scopophilia.

In this situation, there are some huge futures to be made, and there is a criminal fringe. As *Life* pointed out, discussing 'Pornography: A Gross National Product' (14th September 1970)—

As investments go, this is a cynical business, an intriguing proposition; one enterprising fellow in New York co-authored and co-produced a movie somehow entwining industrial espionage with a good deal of fleshy close-ups. His investment: under $125,000, his expected gross: nearly $10 million. The Swedish film *I am Curious (Yellow)* cost only $160,000 to make and has so far siphoned over $5 million away from competing U.S. film makers. *Life*, 14th September 1970

Commercial journalism, unwilling to forgo any form of 'impact', naturally emphasizes the futility of discrimination in a situation in which economic survival depends upon exploiting a form of psychic sickness. In the same article those interviewed declare that it is impossible to find values—

'You could walk up the street right now and ask the first hundred people you meet to define obscenity and you'd get such a variety of answers you wouldn't ever know they were defining the same word . . .'

ibid., loc. cit.

So, as *Life* says—

on our screens, in our bookstores, and our minds now is every conceivable manner of biological union: heterosexual, homosexual, monosexual, and, for the truly jaded, a whole zoological garden of bestiality.

ibid., loc. cit.

By contrast, those who exploit obscenity know perfectly well what obsenity is: it is only the bewildered public who have such difficulty in defining the term.

Behind this torrent of erotica are some opportunistic businessmen, in the U.S. and abroad, some of them backed by money from organized crime. They keep a watchful eye on the tastes of their customers—with good reason, for it is a $ billion-a-year low-overhead business whose profit margins run up to 10,000%. ibid., loc. cit.

As with the drug problem, the absurd and naively over-tolerant attitude of the liberal-minded, educated person at large has left the field wide open for hate and dehumanization.

Watching *them* is a whole host of largely baffled government officials . . . who can barely stay informed about what's new on their beat, let alone control it . . . ibid., loc cit.

The commercial press with its simple-minded concepts of 'freedom' merely contributes to the paralysis of the community, while the pornographers, often with money from crime in the background, spread cultural pollution rapidly and menacingly. It is this cultural pollution that is spreading so rapidly throughout Britain today, not least because many cultural outlets are owned by American firms. The 'permissive' society is no genuine change, but one created by commerce. At the same time, through 'progressive' journals and the underground press, the 'enlightened' view is being pressed on us that pornography does no harm. This view also comes from America, from whence thousands of Americans come to Europe to gaze at the *Mona Lisa*, Chartres Cathedral and King's College Chapel—in the fervent belief that absorbing culture through the eye has a profoundly beneficial effect in enrichening the inward life! If it is true that the paintings in the Louvre can fill us with humanness, it must surely be equally true that pornography can fill us with hate and dehumanize us.

Yet a young girl can be reported in the same issue of *Life*—

'I don't really think,' she said 'that any film anyone sees will have any effect on their morality or their views.' Besides, she asked, 'Don't you all believe in freedom—you all *do* believe in freedom don't you?'

ibid., loc. cit.

Perspectives here are so astonishingly contrived and adjusted that it seems almost as if people are brainwashed. What, for instance, would this woman say if she read an interview with Barbara Loden?

'Movies have the power to alter us, to change our values, and to influence our ideals ...' *The Times*, January 1971

Speaking of Hollywood glamour Miss Loden said—

I believe people's values were warped by what they saw on the screen and that some of America's present troubles can be related to this.
ibid., loc. cit.

Shall we say, in a few years' time that people's values have been warped by the effects of dehumanized sex in our culture at large? Or must we exclude the possibility of such influences from the consideration of *obscenity* alone? And shall warpers be free?

The inconsistencies around this problem are now becoming grotesque. In the course of his work on this book the author came across the work of G. Legman, who writes copiously on sexual matters. Legman's works seem too pedantic to be pornographic. He belongs to that band of writers who laboriously write down instructions for those sexual games which, when they are spontaneous inventions between lovers, are meaningful and joyful. Written down and made explicit they seem to belong to a realm in which some people seem anxious to imitate actions which have no meaning for them. In print they appear ridiculous and mechanical, because they belong to 'attending to' and not 'attending from', to 'objectivity' and the public and general. What is lacking from such preoccupations with 'technique' is the vision and imagination that make them beautiful to the lover.

The explicitness as we have seen has its own meaning. When I protested that such explicit accounts were unnecessary, Mr. Legman replied, 'Yes, lovers do invent these things for themselves— but they do them *so badly*'. 'To whom', one felt like asking, 'does this matter?' Or is the sexologist now setting himself up in a Godlike, omniscient role? The impulse to control others and keep them in the sphere of the 'public' is evident—and sexual creativity needs to be protected against such impulses to control.

In the course of the same letter, however, Legman said—

cynical and incompetent 'psychological consultants' all over the United States today not only can make an excellent living destroying the lives of desperate neurotic patients with cretinously permissive advice— coming on strong with recommending homosexuality, orgies, and the most dangerous sadistic perversions with children, or whatever else the 'psychologist's' own private perversion may be ...

He went on to say that afterwards these psychologists make even more money—by issuing the accounts of their case-histories as pornographic books.

Exactly! But how absurd of Mr. Legman, to proclaim on the one hand that in the realm of the cultural expression of sexual matters there should never be any question of censorship, and that there can be no harm, while on the other hand he makes it perfectly plain that he recognizes that advice can *destroy*, and that *permissive advice can be harmful*! His paragraph above has behind it an intense moral fervour: but the ethical values that are manifest in the concern must simply not be applied to the realm of cultural expression and publication.

It is interesting to note how often titillating matter is presented as the culmination of arguments which, pitiful as they are, first try to involve us in a homunculist view of man, then try to employ 'naturalism' to encourage us to abandon discrimination—and in consequence find certain perverted attitudes and practices acceptable. It seems evident that those who adopt these 'naturalistic' views know that to win others over to them is necessary, in order that they may proceed with their persuasions towards moral inversion. They know, or hope, that opposition will be paralysed as long as the naturalistic myths can be sustained.

Toleration of pornography thus has its own symbolism: it means that we endorse the homunculist model of man, and that we are inclined to deny the realms of being and existence, and hesitate to defend creative 'becoming'.

It is in this that 'each man's depravity diminishes me'—for unless I object to the implications of the pornographer's reduction of the human image, I tacitly condone his gesture. In doing so I thus implicitly reduce my own relational capacities, my attitude to myself, my own dignity, and my vision of the world as a whole. Surely any individual who has in his mind an image of a public show, socially accepted, at which an audience gazes, amusedly or excitedly, at a woman having sexual intercourse with a stallion or dog, must feel significant inward woundings to his own relational and sexual life, as a 'human being able to respond to ideals'? Even the fact that such a public show is tolerated in a civilized society must wound us all, in our attitudes to 'what it is to be human'. For this kind of reason, many people now are coming to feel (as a correspondent wrote to me) 'I have always been a liberal and am, therefore, by instinct against censorship, and yet *I feel we are now being led down a path of evil*'.

If we are to find a solution, we need first to arouse a genuine humanist conscience that refuses to be cowed into acquiescence by the orthodoxies of enlightenment and arrogant commercial journalism. Roger Money-Kyrle, discussing the ethical problem in relation to the insights of psychoanalysis speaks of a group of individuals who represent a true humanist conscience: those who 'are distressed by any disloyalty to the values or persons who symbolize their good internal objects'. Surely anyone who is capable of feeling, and who has possessed any kind of wisdom based on insights or self-knowledge, must feel that the toleration of pornography represents gross 'disloyalty' to the values of our whole civilization—and especially to the status of woman as a symbol of our sensitive humanness—our creativity, and our idealism?

So immanent has the problem of moral inversion become, however, that it is difficult if not impossible to know where to start. In *The Times* leader on cultural pollution (see also page 188) the Editor said—

We need to return to a higher sense of responsibility . . . we need to oppose the anti-cultures of our age. The counter-attack on the pollution of our physical environment has, thank goodness, begun; the counter-attack on the even more serious pollution of our cultural environment needs to be started. *The Times*, 3rd September 1970

Yet only a few days before, *The Times* itself published a photograph of a woman lying on the ground with bare breasts, having flower-symbols painted round her nipples, together with reports on the 'pop' festival on the Isle of Wight, with definite hints of public sexual intercourse, all described, with a carefully edited air of amorality (the newspaper was careful to select letters suggesting this was all quite innocent). This itself all seemed to me a highly irresponsible adjustment of presentation to secure the attention of a young readership, and a contribution to 'anti-culture' itself. A great deal of work on discrimination obviously needs to be done before such moral confusion can be avoided.

One of the worst confusions of our time arises from the failure of criticism in this field. As *Le Monde* said of *Oh! Calcutta!* the London critics were more than fair *because they feared a prosecution*. We have gained a great deal by the spread of toleration. But at the same time there has been an increasing failure of critical thought. As obscenity is tolerated, it is also absurdly felt to be 'good', and socially acceptable. In consequence, critics have now almost totally abandoned ethical judgements in reviews. But it is, surely, too absurd that there should be a total decline of the kind of criticism which can distinguish between condemnation and prohibition, while also discussing the social effects of culture. It should, surely, be possible to say, 'This is anti-human, but tolerable' as well as 'This is anti-human and intolerable'.

To be 'responsible' in the face of cultural corruption we need to express our determination to preserve human value by defining the problem, speaking out strongly when our ideals are insulted, and taking resort to democratic forms of coercion when 'indecent man' seeks to foster his own 'pleasurable negative identity' at our expense—and certainly when he seeks to live at the expense of the young, weak, or psychically vulnerable person. We need, too, to be prepared to defend the realms of 'being' and 'creative becoming' against destructive assault, and to protect those realms in which alone we can find meaning, hopefulness, and the possibilities of peace from the assaults of a hate which is, essentially, the hatred of being human. There seems to me no doubt, for instance, that the sexual act is so significant, intimate, and personal an aspect of our experience, and such a source of creative meaning, that exhibition in any form of its external appearance involving the genitals should be prohibited by law. I do not, of course, mean its symbolization, as in dance or sculpture, but the performance or simulation of sexual acts by live persons on stage, screen, photograph or gramophone record. But could a law on this subject ever be enacted, in the present state of attitudes to human nature, by which the deeper problems are simply not seen?

The consequences may be deeper than we could imagine. As May says—

Surely an act which carries as much power as the sexual act, and power in the critical area of passing on one's name and species, cannot be taken as banal and insignificant except by doing violence to our natures, if not to 'nature' itself?   *Love and Will*, page 121

10

'Enlightenment'—a new imprisonment?

Holding on to our institutions and using these for the necessary purposes of discrimination, however, is not enough. We need to press the debate towards a new view of man, and so my last chapter must be written from the point of view of the educationist. Here we find an astonishing dogmatism obstructing debate—an orthodoxy of enlightenment. This has led to a ridiculous black-and-white situation around opinions on sex. One is either a supporter of hypoparanoid authoritarian opinion, or one is hypomanic, and 'everything goes'. This is absurd. But what it has led to is a disastrous lack of concern and protest, even as our culture is swamped with features that menace psychic hygiene. As I have also tried to show, there are now voices which cannot be ignored which are speaking of 'over-permissiveness' (Khan), 'a thoroughly decadent sensualism' (Frankl), and the need to 'safeguard' shared experience 'against the world of outcomes'. Will English educationists continue to ignore these?

There is, in England now, as F. R. Leavis has declared, a dangerous *Gleichschaltung*, an 'equal switching' of everyone to the same standard, in such matters, which is intellectually deplorable. Everywhere one meets, as Leavis records, a bland blankness—

Enlightenment—the standard enlightenment of the *New Statesman*, the *Guardian*, clergymen and Members of Parliament—is a formidable aspect of the menace we have to defeat . . . I have found myself confronted by it at the close of a discussion-opening talk addressed to a picked audience . . . My tactical assumption of a general concurrence in my sketch of the world in which school-masters have to do their work was not endorsed—I had in front of me an ostensible unanimity of disapproval, indignant and unconcessive, though (I thought) quaking —not with pure indignation.

*English Literature in Our Time and the University,** page 25

What Leavis is noting, I believe, is a characteristic defence

---

* Published by Chatto & Windus, 1969.

mechanism against intellectual discomfort. People have taken refuge in superficial ideas, and have given an absurd assent to a belief in 'progress' in a technological world, and all the benefits of 'enlightenment', as if man's problems have suddenly become simple and capable of immediate mechanical solutions. Such absurd beliefs with their implicit denial of time and mortality, and their facile denial of guilt and hate, have become the new false myths of our time. They lend their falsity to the 'bustle' that 'distracts man from confronting the problem of existence' (as Buber said). Like this bustle and activity itself these false beliefs are cutting us off from the discovery of our own deepest satisfactions and sources of meaning. 'Enlightenment' is driving our deeper problems underground and menacing our freedom and creativity.

We may usefully begin by taking up the existentialist objections to the 'social collective' and also the insistence in existentialism and philosophical anthropology, that in its rationalist idealism 'enlightenment' has failed to reject the 'homunculism' of 'objective' approaches to man. We need to pay attention to that evidence about man which comes from 'encounter' and from intuition—and which reveals the specifically *human* aspect of man, as through the collocations of reports by therapists on their 'inward' or imaginative insight into *what goes on inside their patients*.

neither . . . psychologists in their laboratories, nor philosophers in their studies can ignore the fact that we do get tremendously significant and often unique data from persons in therapy—data which are revealed only when the human being can break down the customary pretences, hypocrisies, and defences behind which we all hide in 'normal' social discourse. It is only in the critical situation of emotional and spiritual suffering—which is the situation that leads them to seek therapeutic help—that people will endure the pain and anxiety of uncovering the roots of their problems . . . Such data are empirical in the deepest meaning of the term . . .   *Love and Will*, page 19

Those who are concerned with man's nature should surely be seriously interested in the reports made by psychoanalysts in this way, not least because patients often come to them in utter sincerity, when every false solution to the problem of life has been tried—and has failed them.

But such reports inevitably disturb our complacency about 'progress', not least about the effects of sexual 'freedom'. For Rollo May says that—

. . . *internal* anxiety and guilt have increased. And in some ways these are more morbid, harder to handle, and impose a heavier burden upon the individual than external anxiety and guilt.   op. cit., page 41

'External' anxiety was caused in the past by authoritarian attitudes to sex. But though we have gained a great deal through the achievement of much sexual freedom, this alone cannot solve the problem of meaning.

Indeed, in some ways, this very freedom seems to threaten the quest for love and meaning itself—

with rising divorce rates, the increasing banalisation of love in literature and art, and the fact that sex for many people has become more meaningless as it has become more available, this 'love' has seemed tremendously elusive, if not an outright illusion. Some members of the new political left came to the conclusion that love is destroyed by the very nature of our bourgeois society, and the reforms they proposed had the specific purpose of making 'a world in which love is more possible'. op. cit., page 14

Sex always seemed to give at least a facsimile of love. But sex— separated off from feeling—has now become a test and a burden, rather than a salvation—

The books which roll off the presses on technique in love and sex, while still best-sellers for a few weeks, have a hollow ring: for most people seem to be aware on some scarcely articulated level that the frantic quality with which we pursue technique as our way to salvation is in direct proportion to the degree to which we have lost sight of the salvation we are seeking ... Whatever merits or failing the Kinsey studies and the Masters - Johnson research have in their own right, they are symptomatic of a culture in which the personal meaning of love has been progressively lost. op. cit., page 15

Once, as Dr. May points out, the major sexual issue was simple and direct—whether or not to go to bed. In past decades you could blame society's strict *mores* and preserve your own self-esteem by telling yourself that 'what you did or didn't was society's fault and not yours'.

And this would give you some time in which to decide what you do want to do, or to let yourself grow into a decision. op. cit., page 41

Now, the anxiety is all transferred to *how well you perform in the sexual act*. Dr. May finds this deepest anxiety among his patients— 'your own sense of adequacy and self-esteem is called immediately into question, and the whole weight of the encounter is shifted inward to how you can meet the test'.

What we did not see in our short-sighted liberalism in sex was that throwing the individual into an unbounded and empty sea of free choice does not in itself give freedom, but is more apt to increase inner conflict. The sexual freedom to which we were devoted fell short of being fully human. op. cit., page 42

'Freedom' in sexual behaviour has led to a situation in which individuals who have problems of identity and relationship tend to fly too quickly into sexual activity, thus depersonalizing themselves, by separating sex from eros, from passion. Dr. May's accounts of their sufferings, their lack of feeling, their yearning for a tenderness they cannot find, reads like an account of the sufferings of the damned. We need never suppose that the promiscuous individual is to be condemned for following what some sterner commentators have called 'a life of self-indulgent ease'. There must be no-one less at ease than the tormented individual who is driven to frenetic sexual activity to find meaning—only to be faced with a total failure to satisfy his needs to find 'the other'.

To say so, however, is not to condone 'short-sighted liberalism'. In the arts, Dr. May believes, the effect is parallel—

In the arts, we have been discovering what an illusion it was to believe that freedom would solve our problem.   *Love and Will*, page 42

He quotes Edel, who says there has been a dehumanization of sex in fiction, resulting in an impoverishment of the novel. Dr. May's next paragraph should be studied by the Arts Council Working Party—

The battle against censorship and for freedom of expression surely was a great battle to win, but has it not become a new strait jacket? The writers, both novelists and dramatists, 'would rather hock their typewriters than turn in a manuscript without the obligatory scenes of unsparing anatomical documentation of their characters' sexual behaviour . . .' (Taubman) Our 'dogmatic enlightenment' is self-defeating: it ends up destroying the very sexual passion it sets out to protect. In the great tide of realistic chronicling, we forgot, on the stage and in the novel and even in psychotherapy, that imagination is the life-blood of eros, and that realism is neither sexual nor erotic. Indeed, there is nothing *less* sexy than sheer nakedness, as a random hour at any nudist camp will prove. It requires the infusion of the imagination (which I shall later call intentionality) to transmute physiology and anatomy into *interpersonal* experience—into art, into passion, into eros in a million forms which have the power to shake or charm us.

Could it not be that an 'enlightenment' which reduces itself to a mere realistic detail is itself an escape from the anxiety involved in the relation of human imagination to erotic passion?   op. cit., pages 42–3

Sexual 'freedom' thus becomes, in a schizoid society, yet another manifestation of the separation of feeling from activity: a failure of affect and of commitment that is essentially psychopathological, and an aspect of the same kind of horrifying dehumanization and dissociation as we get in megalopolis or a Vietnam war. 'Coolness' in sex runs parallel to 'coolness' and apathy between human beings

—a deadening of 'care', which also, because it goes with a fear of inward emptiness and meaninglessness, boils up from time to time into meaningless violence. Dr. May makes clear the connexions between a society of meaningless and affectless sexual activity, and outbursts of seemingly meaningless violence. Both are false ways of trying to feel real—in a world—

where numbers inexorably take over as a means of identification: . . . where 'normality' is defined as keeping your cool; where sex is so available that the only way to preserve any inner centre is to learn to have intercourse without committing yourself . . .   op. cit., page 32

In this situation, the preoccupation with performance and the mechanics of orgasm manifest forms of escape from the anxiety involved in the relation of human imagination to erotic passion. Covering these anxieties are such myths as are invented by prophets such as Timothy Leary about the supersexual effect of LSD,* or concepts of the 'apocalyptic orgasm' of which Dr. May says—

What abyss of self-doubt, what inner void of loneliness, are they trying to cover up by this great concern with grandiose effects?

op. cit., page 44

Even greater anxiety is caused by the new puritanism of dogmatic enlightenment: as we have seen, it is now *immoral not to express your libido.* We have also seen what Dr. May says about the obligatory use of the 'frank' vocabulary—that it limits our concepts of eroticism.

The importance of Rollo May's book is in its capacity to show from an existentialist position how 'enlightenment' has come to deny biological and emotional differences between men and women, out of an unconscious fear of human nature and its differences. He shows that the over-concern with potency in our society manifests compensation for feelings of impotence of a general psychic kind. 'Impotence is increasing these days despite [or is it because of?] the unrestrained freedom on all sides.' He believes that a 'revolt against sex' is even rumbling at the gates of our cities, out of a sickness with what 'enlightened freedom' has done by 'oversimplifying' sex and love—

By anaesthetising feeling in order to perform better, by employing sex as a tool to prove prowess and identity, by using sensuality to hide sensitivity, we have emasculated sex and left it vapid and empty. The banalisation of sex is well-aided and abetted by our mass communication. For the plethora of books on sex and love which flood the market

---

* Recently repeated in *Nova.* Dr. Masters has rejected this myth, pointing out that the drug caused impotence.

have one thing in common—they oversimplify love and sex, treating the topic like a combination of learning to play tennis and buying life insurance. In this process we have robbed sex of its power by sidestepping eros; and we have ended by dehumanising both.

Love and Will, page 65

Sex has become a drug to 'blot out our awareness' of our needs for passion and for relationship. In 'ostensibly enlightened discussions of sex, particularly those about freedom from censorship, it is often argued that all our society needs is full freedom for the expression of eros'. But what is revealed under the surface is just the opposite—

We are in a flight from eros—and we use sex as the vehicle for the flight.

op. cit., page 65

All this has great significance for those working in education. In such a situation, 'the blanket advising of more sex education' acts as 'a reassurance by which we escape asking ourselves the more frightening questions'. In consequence 'dogmatic enlightenment' 'contains elements which rob us of the very means of meeting this new and inner anxiety'.

In the light of Dr. May's insights, we may feel some dismay about the 'enlightened' approach to sex education in England. We will be disturbed to learn that children are now being submitted to a BBC series of educational films on sex which contain drawings of sexual intercourse, with a commentary describing it explicitly.

Those who leap into such 'up to date' developments (for we must 'beat the clock') never seem to study the work of 'those best qualified to judge': or perhaps they assume that the objective scientist' or sexologist is best qualified to judge, despite the fact that his discipline qualifies him not at all to deal with the emotional life or ethic. D. W. Winnicott has a most sensitive chapter on sex in his book *The Child, The Family, and the Outside World*. He says that, of course children need instruction in biology, but he emphasizes that children 'cannot be classed together and described all in a bunch'. How else can a television programme class them? Winnicott emphasizes the need for sex instruction to take place in the presence of trusted adults, 'with ordinary capacity for human friendship'. You cannot have a relationship of this kind with a face on a screen. He says, 'Quite another thing is the lecture on sex given by a person who comes to a school, delivers a talk, and then goes away. It would seem that people with an urge to teach sex should be discouraged'. Indeed, who can tell how children are affected by hearing about sex—perhaps for the first time—from a stranger on a television screen? Certainly those who wish to promote sex education of this kind should be discouraged.

As Winnicott says, 'There is something better than knowledge about sex, and that is the discovery of it by the individual'. Sexual experience, together with all our capacities for relationship, and for finding value in our own identity, is something we can only discover from 'the inside'. To believe that sex education will cure the woes of ineptitude and waywardness in sexual behaviour is surely a delusion. Television as a medium of communication is eminently 'attending to' rather than 'attending from', so it may even do harm by imposing outward analysis on what belongs to inwardness and 'the most intimate dialogue', thus destroying meaning by over-explicitness.

Winnicott says: 'full and frank information on sex should be available for children, but *not as a thing so much as a part of the children's relationship to known and trusted people'*. Television inevitably makes sex a 'thing', and despite the teacher's presence, the impact it makes is nothing like the sensitive context which Winnicott is asking for. Pictures of sexual intercourse cannot be shown to children, if Melanie Klein is right, without evoking in them emotional disturbances associated with primal scene phantasies, accompanied by deep 'talion' anxieties which arouse fears of the dangers of the incorporation they feel there are in sex. This effect may be associated with the voyeuristic schizoid element of 'objectifying' the humanness which is feared.

There are, of course, those who are even more blatant in wanting to give children sex education *en masse*. Here perhaps the most absurd and menacing statements have been put out by the National Secular Society. Their publication *Sex Education* (1969) has (inevitably) a foreword by Brigid Brophy, who (of course) believes children should be given a 'straightforward description of the act'.

For the authors of this pamphlet, all guilt, complexity and wholeness must be eradicated from sex, together with all moral problems, by sheer secular will. Their own recommendations are, said *The Times*, 'remarkably forthright'. Commenting on sex education books they say—

'We believe that the condemnation of all forms of sexual expression for young people is an attitude totally divorced from reality. Sexual feeling cannot be switched off by cold showers.

Since most young people have always practised, and will continue to practise, some form of sexual activity, these writers should perhaps begin to examine the real alternatives and state openly which they would advise the young to choose: self-stimulation, mutual love-play, or copulation.'

Sexual Education, by Maurice Hill and Michael Lloyd-Jones

The destructive attitude to values and human complexity is

evident from the no-nonsense tone. The assumptions are also absurd: that 'most young people have always . . . practised some form of sexual activity' is not even confirmed by surveys of sexual activity among the young. The authors assert that self-stimulation can no longer be condemned: 'It is natural, completely harmless, and usually very enjoyable.' Discussing homosexual impulses they say—

what may be harmful is the attempt to suppress your desires and to substitute guilt and fear for love, affection and friendship. If you are attracted to a member of your own sex, and if you both want to give physical expression to your feelings, then do so.   ibid., loc. cit

The assumptions behind such arguments appear absurd in the light of philosophical anthropology. Moralizing and prohibitions in the past have no doubt led to much unhappiness. But what is ridiculous is the separation of the problem, in such a generalized and over-simplified way, from the whole life-situation of each individual, while the whole approach menaces true eroticism with 'objectification'.

There are many situations in which we have to 'suppress our feelings' and there is often a great gain in doing so. This is the basis of civilized living—and of our deepest satisfactions. It would be impossible always to give way to 'attraction', and one has often to relate a local or momentary attraction to the quest for deeper satisfactions and more profound relational needs, just as one has to modify one's aggression. While it is valuable to realize and accept that one is sometimes attracted to a member of one's own sex and that this attraction can be erotic, it is ridiculous to suppose that guilt and fear can be eliminated by simply telling a young person that he should simply 'go ahead' in aim-inhibited activity.

The implication that sexual libido must be released is nonsense. As Frankl says—

The shibboleth of sexual frustration is occasionally called forth for purposes of sexual propaganda. In this sense it is a misconception and vulgar misrepresentation of psychoanalysis. The implication is that the ungratified sex instinct itself—rather than the suppression of that instinct—must necessarily lead to neurosis. The harmfulness of sexual abstinence has been preached to youth. Such doctrines have done a good deal of injury by nourishing neurotic sexual anxiety. The slogan has been sexual intercourse at any cost, even among young people, when, on the contrary, sexuality should be permitted to mature tranquilly and to advance toward a healthy and meaningful eroticism consonant with human dignity, eroticism in which the sexual element is the expression and crown of a love relationship.   *The Doctor and the Soul*, page 170

The Secular Society, by contrast with Frankl's realism, begins to look like the Society for Fanatical Immoralism and Dehumaniz-ation. One detects in such urgent 'enlightenment' an impulse to interfere and urge activity on others when it might not be beneficial to them. This is surely as predatory as moralizing. It has its own moral fervour, belonging to the new puritanism, and the absurd belief that one *must* be sexually active. By contrast Frankl says that the doctor ought to be entirely neutral about continence versus intercourse, from the somatic point of view. But in terms of mental hygiene he ought not to be neutral—'from this point of view he must take a stand. He must oppose sexual relationships, must veto them if he can, whenever young people want sexual intercourse without real love'.

Young people may be glad as individuals, to have parents and counsellors to whom they can go to ask for information or opinions, *if they need to*. But this is not enough for the emancipationist, who wants to force them into his brand of sexual activity, and to brush aside the parent-child relationship which is bound up with the child's capacities to love, and the values he has taken in from his home. Such injunctions, in the light of the psychology of Frankl and Straus, could cause harm. Frankl says, 'If the realm of mere sexuality is entered prematurely, a young person is incapable of proceeding to the synthesis of sexuality and eroticism'.

Simple 'enlightened' approaches are often thus misguided. As Winnicott says, it is useless to tell children in large groups that masturbation is harmless, because for some it is a great nuisance. Moreover, whatever point can there be in telling them that it is 'usually very enjoyable'? Again, as Frankl points out in *The Doctor and the Soul*, masturbation may be harmless, but it is 'the sign of a disturbed development or misguided attitude towards the love life . . . The hangover which generally follows the act . . . has a reason . . . that guilt feeling which comes upon one whenever one flees from active, directional experience to passive, non-directional experience' (page 169).

By contrast with the damaging attitudes of the Secular Society we may compare the approach of those who have actually handled children's sexual problems in a truly liberal situation. W. B. Curry who was headmaster of Dartington Hall School can hardly be accused of being a moralizing or authoritarian individual. Yet he says of sex—

I have sometimes been taken to task for not making greater use of group discussion on problems of sexual morality, and I admit that I have done so but rarely. I do not deny that the writers may be right. The problem is certainly extremely difficult, and I sometimes think that at this stage of our particular hypocrisy among adults, the crude debasement of values promoted by so much advertisement and popular entertainment, and the complete lack of any agreement as to what would be an acceptable and also practicable code, not merely among adults in general, but even among Dartington or 'progressive' parents themselves. But however this may be, it seems clear to me that any useful discussion of sexual behaviour with an adolescent must take account of the stage of understanding, particularly emotional understanding, he has already reached, and in any but the smallest group this is likely to vary more as regards sex than in any other subject. I have therefore been inclined to feel that to discuss these matters with a group of any size would be rather like trying to teach algebra to a class, some of whom could hardly count while others had already reached the calculus by diligent private study, and while some were blasé and hard-boiled, others would blush at a square-root sign.   *Dartington Hall*, page 212

Such an individual as W. B. Curry is concerned with the whole situation of the young person as a 'being-in-the-world', and sees that the subject of sex above all needs to be treated, as Winnicott insists, as one that is intimately personal, taking into account the young person's stage of emotional understanding. Moreover, as is obvious from comments made elsewhere by Mr. Curry and from Winnicott's work, the adult's moral standards are significant in the matter, and are part of a confrontation out of which the individual child can develop his own standards—even as he rejects those of the adult. Merely to tell young people that sex is 'pleasant' and they should have it whenever they feel like it is to let them down. Moreover, such an approach, based as Frankl says on a misconception and vulgar misinterpretation of psychoanalysis, threatens the natural and valuable idealism and romanticism of adolescents, and their discovery, for themselves, of the richness of love.

However, the rapidity with which sex education books are produced, and the ease with which they secure publicity, makes it plain that 'explicit' approaches to sex will go on gaining ground everywhere, not least in education. Meanwhile what Curry calls the 'crude debasement of values' is becoming accepted as valid, at large in our culture.

Here, fundamental things seem to change very little, while, as Rollo May indicates, some become worse. Many of the tens of thousands of abortions now being freely performed bear witness to tens of thousands of cases of individuals yearning for passion and creativity, when their own personality and their society make such realization impossible. The problem of hospital staff not being able to face the endless destruction of tiny life-forms is a manifestation of deep underlying metaphysical problems which 'enlightened' thinking does not touch, but which speaks of a deep spiritual distress in our society.

We have made gains in some areas by the lessening of guilt. In

England there seems to be a growing tolerance extended to the unmarried mother. In Australia, by contrast, in the delivery theatre, for an unmarried mother, the doctors and nurses hold up a sheet so the mother cannot see her baby as it is born. They do not even tell her what sex it is, and the baby is hustled away at once. This appears to us now, properly, as brutal and barbarous. It seems more humane to give the mother time to complete psychic parturition, and to have her child to handle and nourish, before making the grim decision as to whether to relinquish her own off-spring for ever. The white sheet in the Australian hospital is a real symbol of sexual guilt.

But the sexual problems associated with childbirth and infant rearing are by no means solved—as all of us who have had children have found (especially anyone who has tried to arrange breast-feeding in a train, for instance). Fear and guilt as there is in the unconscious hostility to breastfeeding, have by no means been eliminated, as we find if we ask mothers about their experience of midwives and doctors.

If one turns to marriage and family life, rather than the beha-viour of promiscuous single persons or perverts, the intractability of sexual problems becomes evident. (Should we perhaps set up an organization called Normsex to defend and issue propaganda on behalf of sexual normality?) There are still many areas in which we find fear, guilt and hatred expressed, as in our divorce laws and procedures which are so much bound up with ideas of culpability, and punitive solutions, and discriminate heavily against women, for unconscious reasons.

Such problems gain nothing from mere permissiveness. And, indeed, as I have tried to show, the 'enlightened' view essentially fails to find the true sources of sexual equality and freedom, in terms of mature individuals solving the problems of mutual inde-pendence and dependence. Only by a close exploration of the reality of sex in terms of 'the whole being' by subjective disciplines can we approach such problems. The 'enlightened' mind cannot entertain such realities, because it is so hypomanic and unwilling to take hate, guilt, fear—and *mystery*—into account. 'Enlighten-ment' has thus become a defence against human reality, destruc-tive of our creativity, and likely to place limits on our freedom.

'Enlightenment' fails because it fails to make the proper diag-noses of the problems of the sexual life. As we have seen, to a therapist like May, an 'unwanted' pregnancy, for instance, may be unconsciously very much wanted, for 'to be pregnant is to be real'. More 'free' abortion may merely mean that a woman goes on getting herself pregnant for unconscious reasons, and then con-sciously frustrates her own creativity, in a *huis clos* of horrifying self-defeat. From such insights, Dr. May comes to conclude the 'new sophisticate' is so afraid of his own procreative powers that he tends inevitably to pour out further dehumanization into the world in the name of humanity.

Here May reaches the heart of objections to 'enlightenment'— behind its mask of freedom and reason such 'liberation' is destructive of life itself.

Sex may be 'the easiest way to prove we are not dead yet', but there are elements in our trivialization of it, and our essential self-defeat in sexual activity, that run parallel to the human destructiveness that manifested itself in the atom bomb. The preoccupation with sexual impotence parallels the paralysis of intentionality that is the curse of our time. May quotes from the film-script for *Seven Days in May*—

The nuclear age has killed man's faith in his ability to influence what happens to him.   *Love and Will*, page 184

In his patients, Rollo May finds 'an inability to construct a future', not least in the sphere of fulfilment in personal relationship. In this, as in culture at large, 'talking about sex is the easiest way of avoiding making any decisions about life and sexual relations'.

Dr. May virtually reaches the position of Fairbairn, who insists that the goal of the libido is not pleasure but the 'significant other'. He finds in his patients that what matters to them, even in the most anonymous sexual activity, is that they should find a *person* there.

In a sense, such insights bring us back to Jane Austen and love poetry—to the proper insistence that what matters most to human beings is their own integrity of relationship, and integrity to their own True Self and its potentialities. (Those who are so keen on sex education might be better off doing imaginative English, dance or drama, and promoting some form of 'philosophical anthropology' in the school curriculum).

To change our approach demands, however, a new kind of capacity in us—the capacity to commit ourselves to experience in a new and more whole way, and to approach knowing and learning in new, creative ways. Dr. May explores the philosophical problems of how we may discover and develop 'a new level of consciousness'. This requires a more adequate combination of love and will in the pursuit of human meaning.

One requirement is that we should cease oversimplifying. The goal seems perhaps simple: it is expressed by Teilhard de Chardin thus—

At what moment do lovers come into the most complete possession of themselves, if not when they are *lost* in each other?'

*The Phenomenon of Man,** page 311

This is not to say that human biology should not be taught nor that there should not be individual counselling. What is objectionable is 'attending to' what only has meaning in terms of 'attending from': to deal with sex, we must restore it to its place in our wholeness, and reassociate it with meaning. For, as Dr. May says, 'the love act can and ought to provide a sound and meaningful avenue to the sense of personal identity.' What makes it possible for us to love is imagination. But before we can begin to understand such problems, the superficial dogmas of 'enlightenment' have to be rejected. Because of 'enlightenment', as Dr. May shows—

many people tend not to give themselves time to know each other in love affairs . . . a general symptom of the malaise of our day . . .

Love and Will, page 282

The violence done to ourselves by sexual activity without responsibility is shown in Dr. May's distinguished book as a deep element in the malaise of our time that helps to defeat our best potentialities. The dehumanization of sex in culture (and 'sex education') drives us further and further away from creativity and meaning.

So passive and apathetic have we become, under the persuasions of 'enlightened' dogma, despite its absurdity, that we both commit violence upon ourselves, while withdrawing our feelings and separating sex from wholeness.

May quotes the director of a student health service at the University of Wisconsin: 'the girls who, in these days of the pill, are promiscuous say . . . "it's too much trouble to say no" '. The implication is that it is too much trouble to be human, and to be oneself, in touch with one's own deepest needs, and one's intentionality.

'Enlightenment' has itself prompted this carelessness about doing violence to oneself, and the banalization which attends it. It has encouraged sexual activity without responsibility to one's innermost 'true self', while endorsing false solutions as valid, as we have seen.

So, the question of dealing adequately with sexual experience in our world depends upon our rediscovering an adequate account of man. At the moment we are falling into cultural disaster, and losing our sense of meaning and values because even the educated mind seems imprisoned in homunculist and fragmentary perspectives. Even the intellectual minority defers to the views of journalists and popular writers, while neglecting more authentic sources:

---

* Published by Collins, 1965.

Desmond Morris has cast out Martin Buber; Robert Ardrey has cast out D. W. Winnicott; H. J. Eysenck, the Behaviourists and neurologists, the human consciousness. So we have to work hard to campaign for attention to May, Frankl, Polanyi and the philosophical biologists who are trying to put the 'ghost' back in the 'machine'.

To find a more adequate basis for our thinking we need to rediscover a view of man as being-in-the-world, and to build a new social psychology on this. Even if, for instance, today a Royal Commission on Pornography were set up, if it consisted of 'homunculist' thinkers,—psychologists and sociologists whose disciplines were 'objective' and 'value free'—we would get no ethical lead from it.* An ethical lead can only come from those whose disciplines can find, above all, consciousness, inwardness and meaning. We need a social psychology which can encompass the I-Thou experience. As Laing says—

The metapsychology of Freud ... has no constructs for any social system generated by more than one person at a time. Within its own framework it has no concepts of social collectivities of experience shared or unshared between persons. This theory has no category of 'you', as there is in the work of ... Buber. It has no way of expressing the meeting of an 'I' with 'an other', and of the impact of one person on another.   *The Politics of Experience*, page 42

The consequence of this has been a reification, in relation to the collective 'social idea', leading to that objectification that Laing rightfully rejects.

We are not concerned with the interaction of two objects, nor with their transactions within a dyadic system: we are not concerned with the communication patterns within a system comprising two computer-like sub-systems that receive and process input, and emit outgoing systems. Our concern is with two origins of experience in relation.
                                                op. cit., page 45

Yet official approaches today to the problem of pornography *do* regard the problem as 'a communication pattern within a system comprising two computer-like sub-systems'. This is why we are now menaced by dehumanization. For—

Natural scientific investigations are conducted on objects, or things, or the patterns of relations between things, or on systems of 'events'.

---

* It was interesting to note in discussions in 1971 on the formation of Lord Longford's private Enquiry and the organization called 'The Responsible Society', that individuals, even those from medicine and the universities, had come to distrust 'research' in this sphere because it never seemed able to find the subjective realities and values involved.

Persons are distinguished from things in that persons experience the world, whereas things behave in the world. Thing-events do not experience. Personal events are experiential. Natural scientism is the error of turning persons into things by a process of reification that is not itself part of the true natural scientific method. Results derived in this way have to be dequantified and dereified before they can be reassimilated into the realm of human discourse.   op. cit., page 53

As we have seen, we now have to dequantify and dereify sex.

That a change is coming is perhaps evident from the success of Rollo May's book on the need to unite love and will. In the face of meaninglessness, people are groping towards feeling and rejecting the reductive effects of Descarte's *cogitatio*: as May says—

The development of psychoanalysis has led to a resurgence of the primacy of feeling. And in academic psychology, a number of papers have come out lately which show the drift of psychologists and philosophers towards a new appreciation of feeling. Hadley Cantril's paper, 'Sentio, ergo sum' is one and Sylvan Tomkins' 'Homo patens' is another. Suzanne Langer entitles her new book, *Mind, an Essay on Feeling* ...
Love and Will, page 303

The rediscovery of feeling is at one with the rediscovery of creativity. May sees psychoanalysis as the 'playground of intentionality', in which patients are brought to be able to construct a future. I believe we can learn from his book how we may translate this into the spheres of education, thought and culture by concentrating on the primary needs of man to find a meaning in his life.

What Dr. May asks of us is that we should 'discover on a deeper level what it means to be human'. He requires us to reconsider the whole basis of learning and cultural endeavour, and to bring about no less than a complete change in our relationship with the world. It involves a rediscovery of our creative power over reality.

We love and will the world as an immediate, spontaneous totality. We *will* the world, create it by our decision, our *fiat*, our choice; and we *love* it, give it affect, energy, power to love and change us as we mould and change it. This is what it means to be fully related to one's world. I do not imply that the world does not exist *before* we will or love it; one can answer that question on the basis of his assumptions, and, being a midwesterner with inbred realism, I would assume that it does exist. But it has no reality, no relation to me, as I have no effect upon it; I move as in a dream, vaguely and without viable contact. One can choose to shut it out—as New Yorkers do when riding the subway—or one can choose to see it, create it. In this sense we give to Cézanne's art or the Cathedral at Chartres the power to move us.

What does this mean concerning our personal lives, to which, at last, we now return? The microcosm of our consciousness is where the macrocosm of the universe is *known* ...   op. cit., page 324

The implications for education and culture are profound—and not least for our intellectual dealings with sex and relationship. We must think of love and meaning, not sex and functions. With Viktor Frankl, May places an insistence on man's primary need for satisfactions of the will-to-meaning—

The meaning-matrix comes before any discussion, scientific or other, since it is what makes discussion—as in psychotherapy—possible. We can never understand the meaning-matrix of a patient, or anyone for that matter, by standing purely objectively outside it. I must be able to participate in my patient's meanings but preserve my own meaning-matrix at the same time, and thus unavoidably, and rightfully, interpret to him what he is doing—and often doing to me. The same thing holds true in all other human relationships as well: friendship and love require that we participate in the meaning-matrix of the other without surrendering our own. This is the way human consciousness understands, grows, changes, becomes clarified and meaningful.

Love and Will, page 262

In therapy, the problem is to get the patient to feel 'I-am-the-one-who-has-these-wishes' and to become able to act in such a way that the whole being is involved in the act. To heal the prevalent schizoid dissociation in tackling our sexual problems, it is the meaning-matrix and the involvement of the whole being with which we must be concerned. In education we must try to restore creativity and intentionality.

One powerful enemy, however, is the acquisitive basis of society. Schizoid dissociation is an aspect of our whole commercial-industrial culture and its symbolic emphasis on ingestion, on pleasure, and the 'breast' detached (as in advertising) from the whole person and his meaningful life. The power of sexual symbolism in popular culture is an immense force assaulting mental health, over which we have no control.

From traditional culture, we should know that frenetic hedonism and mere sensuality are self-defeating. We ought to be able to 'place' decadent sensuality if we are in touch with our values. However, at a time when nearly all cultural media are in the hands of the advertiser, human truth seems unlikely to prevail against the prevalent emphasis on attaching the sense of identity to acquisitiveness and self-satisfaction, which the exploitation of the imagery of sex obviously serves. Offering us continually the image of a 'good feed' may serve commerce. But in its effect on sensibility it makes it increasingly harder to sustain that secret, unique creativity in which true eroticism is developed, and where satisfying meanings are found—and joy.

Viktor Frankl conveys well why mere hedonism is an empty goal—

if this normal reaching out for meanings and beings is discarded and replaced by the will to pleasure or the 'pursuit of happiness', happiness falters and collapses; in other words, happiness must ensue as a side-effect of meaning-fulfilment. And actually man is not primarily concerned with pleasure or with the so-called pursuit of happiness, actually —due to his will-to-meaning—man is reaching out for a meaning to fulfil or another human being to encounter: and it is this that constitutes a reason to be happy.   *Encounter*, November 1969, page 53

This says in yet another form what Fairbairn meant by his insistence on relationship as the goal of libido, and what May means by his 'ethical statement' quoted at the beginning. The dehumanization of sex is a threat to our whole perception of the world. What is threatened by the banalization of sex is a destruction of creative potency, meaning and effectiveness.

In his contribution to the Alpbach seminar, Viktor Frankl said—

Man is depicted [i.e. in homunculist thinking] as being primarily basically concerned with his inner equilibrium or something within himself, be it pleasure or anything else. But I dare say that being human is always pointing beyond itself, is always directed at something, or someone, other than itself: be it a meaning to fulfil or another human being to encounter . . . that is why it cannot be 'pursued', because the more attention we pay to happiness, the more we make pleasure the target of our intentions by way of what I call hyper-intention, to the same extent we become victims of hyper-reflection. That is to say, the more attention we pay to happiness or pleasure, the more we block its attainment, and lose sight of the primary reason of our endeavours; happiness vanishes, because we are intending it, and pursuing it. This makes it impossible for fulfilment to ensue; we can observe this phenomenon in about 95% of sexual neuroses. Whenever a male patient is trying deliberately to manifest his potency, or a female patient to demonstrate her ability to experience orgasm, the very attempt is doomed to fail.
                    Encounter, November 1969, page 53

As May says, 'the emphasis beyond a certain point on technique in sex makes for a mechanistic attitude towards love-making, and goes along with alienation, feelings of loneliness, and depersonalisation'. Yet in our schizoid society, so far as sex is concerned, the question is simply how you perform; 'your own sense of adequacy and self-esteem is immediately called into question, and the whole weight of the encounter is shifted inward to how you can meet the test'. This hell of tormented sexual activity has come about because of the false belief which has predominated our culture— that an impersonal primitive primary mover in our make-up is the 'will-to-pleasure'.

Frankl goes on—

Now what holds for pleasure and happiness also holds for self-actualization. Self-actualization is a good thing; however, we can actualize ourselves only to the extent to which we have fulfilled a meaning, or encountered another human being. But we have no longer any basis for self-actualization at the moment we are striving directly for it. I would like to epitomize this state of affairs by quoting first Pindar and then Karl Jasper. Pindar said you should 'become what you are'. And Jasper's remark, 'What a man is, he becomes only through that cause which he has made his own'. In other words, we may obtain self-actualization by living out the self-transcendent quality of human existence.   ibid., loc. cit.

The answer, as I have always believed, lies in a new approach to education which brings out the creative dynamics of each individual. As George Kneller says—

in the formal education of teachers a greater premium needs to be placed on the 'inner-directed' personality than exists at present and a greater freedom allowed for spontaneity of thought and action. After all, learning is a private matter, a personal creative synthesis and interpretation of one's own experience.

Existentialism and Education, page 145

We need to discover a new integrated philosophy of man to guide both our education and our thought at large about social issues. And we need to find some synthesis from existential thought that brings out an emphasis in our thinking on man's uniqueness and creative dynamics. But at the moment the worst enemy to these necessary developments—and, indeed the worst enemy to those developments showing greatest insight in philosophical biology even—is the simplistic nonsense implicit in the 'sexual revolution' and in 'enlightened' attitudes to sex and sexual depiction (not least as they are embodied in 'sex education').

In a schizoid society, dominated by the homunculist thinking diagnosed throughout the present work, many people are diverted into a desperate quest for sensual gratification and at extremes (as in 'pop' hysteria) into a 'thoroughly decadent sensualism'. This is a diversion from that quest for wholeness of being in which alone meaning and fulfillment may be found. Our objection to the 'sexual revolution' is thus not that individuals are 'indulging' themselves more, but that they are being diverted from the deepest satisfactions of all, and that it is tending to undermine all that those concerned with man's creative potentialities are striving to do, in science, culture and education.

Glossary

ঙঙ

The following notes may help readers who are unfamiliar with psychoanalytical and related disciplines. For further help see *The Penguin Dictionary of Psychology, A Critical Dictionary of Psychoanalysis* (by Rycroft, published by Nelson) and the glossary at the end of Marion Milner's *In the Hands of the Living God* (see bibliography). Each of these has been used in the preparation of these notes, and I am grateful to their authors.

Abreaction 'The discharge of emotion attached to a previously repressed experience' (Rycroft). In the early days of psychoanalysis this 'discharge' was believed to be therapeutic in itself.

Acting out Instead of gaining insight into his problems a patient may act out dynamics which he is unable to verbalize or events which he cannot remember. His activity is symbolic, but 'false', since he is confusing those with whom he is acting out with figures from infancy, e.g. his mother or father. Acting out makes therapy, or true solutions to problems, less possible because of this essential falsity by which elements from the past, or internal objects, are projected into the world around an individual, to distort it, and his dealings with it.

Aetiology the study of the causes of disease.

Affect feelings and emotions.

Alienation '... the state of being, or the process of becoming, estranged from either (a) oneself or parts of oneself or (b) others' (Rycroft).

Ambivalence '... the coexistence of two opposite emotions, especially love and hate, towards the same object' (Marion Milner, quoting Brewer).

Anima the personification of all feminine psychological tendencies in a man's psyche (Jung believed it is a male figure in the case of a woman). See *Female Element*.

Boundary '... of bodily frame, the skin, the feeling of the melting of this' (Marion Milner); or of the interpretation of self and not-self across it.

Castration anxiety 'According to classical (psychoanalytical) theory, all men and male children are liable to castration anxiety . . .' Castration does not mean the removal of the testes here so much as fear of loss of the penis, 'loss of the capacity for erotic pleasure; . . . or demoralization in respect of the masculine role' (Rycroft).

Cathexis 'A neologism invented by Freud's English translators to translate the German "Besetzung" (literally 'investment') which Freud used to describe the quantity of energy attaching to any object-representation or mental structure. A Cathexis is conceived to be analogous to an electric charge which can shift from one structure except in so far as it becomes bound—or to troops which can be deployed from one position to another' (Rycroft).

Defence Rycroft quotes Freud, 'A general designation for all the techniques which the ego makes use of in conflicts which may lead to neurosis'. The function of defence, he adds, is to protect the ego . . . (it includes) 'all techniques used by the ego to master, control, canalize and use "forces which may lead to neurosis" '.

Dehumanization A reduction of those qualities which specifically belong to being human (especially spiritual and emotional experience) and the human sense of values.

Denial 'Defence mechanism by which either (*a*) some painful experience is denied or (*b*) some impulse or aspect of the self is denied' (Rycroft). Psychoanalysts also seem to extend the term to mean denial of aspects of reality, certainly of 'the inner significance of experience' (Rycroft).

Dependence infantile and adult. 'Infantile dependence refers either (*a*) to the fact that children are helpless and dependent on their parents, or (*b*) to the fact that neurotics are fixated on their parents and imagine themselves to be dependent on them' (Rycroft).

Depersonalization Unrelated to the body (Marion Milner, quoting D. W. Winnicott). Feeling that one is not in one's 'self' and not a person. See R. D. Laing *The Divided Self*. See also Sylvia Plath's *The Applicant* and her novel *The Bell Jar* in which 'one's autonomy and existence' often 'come into doubt'.

Depression As Rycroft points out, this may either refer to an emotion or a diagnosis. 'When referring to an emotion it means in low spirits, gloomy. When referring to a diagnosis, it refers to a syndrome of which the emotion 'depression' constitutes one element (Rycroft). Marion Milner says depression differs from grief ('which is realistic and proportionate to what has been lost') by being morbid.

Depressive position 'A Kleinian concept. It describes the position reached (in her scheme of things) by the infant (or by the patient in analysis) when he realizes that both his love and hate are directed towards the same object—the Mother—becomes aware of his ambivalence and concerned to protect her from his hate and to make reparation for what damage he imagines his hate has done' (Rycroft).

Dissociation 'The state of affairs in which two or more mental processes co-exist without becoming connected or integrated' (Rycroft).

Ego-boundary 'Topographical concept by which the distinction between self and not-self is imagined to be delineated. A patient is said to lack ego-boundaries if he identifies . . . readily with others and does so at the expense of his own sense of identity. Analysts who hold that the infant lives in a state of primary identification with his mother postulate the gradual development of an ego-boundary, i.e. the discovery that objects are not part of itself' (Rycroft).

Existentialism Philosophical theory of which existence is the basis rather than essence. As Rycroft points out, Freudian psychoanalysis is an 'essential' rather than an 'existentialist' theory because it tends to explain phenomena in terms of underlying forces. Phenomenology as a study of human experience seeks to confine itself to conscious phenomena and to deny the unconscious and forces of which the subject has no knowledge. They also try to 'formulate their data from the subjects' point of view' (Rycroft).

Female element See also *Anima*. Winnicott believes that in men and women there are distinct male and female elements, the female element belonging to 'being' and the emotional life, the male more to 'doing', action and the analytical.

Homunculist Tending to reduce man to a homunculus, a mechanical model consisting of mere functions, in which 'homo humanus', man himself, with all his spiritual capacities, is missing (See Frankl quoted pages 192, 211.)

Hypomanic Exceptionally manic, especially in the denial of problems of guilt, anxiety, depression and hate. (See *Manic defence*.)

Hypoparanoid Excessively paranoid, and concerned to counter imaginary dangers that threaten from outer reality.

Identification 'A process by which a person either (a) extends his identity into someone else, (b) borrows his identity from someone else, or (c) fuses or confuses his identity with someone else' (Rycroft).

Imago 'Word used by Freud to describe (unconscious) object-representations' (Rycroft).

Introjection 'a defence mechanism operating unconsciously, whereby loved or hated external objects are taken within oneself, symbolically . . .' (Marion Milner).

Libido 'Hypothetical form of mental energy, with which processes, structures and object-representations are invested' (Rycroft).

Manic defence 'Form of defensive behaviour . . . exhibited by persons who defend themselves against anxiety, guilt and depression by (a) denial of the guilt, anxiety and depression, (b) the operation of a phantasy of omnipotent control . . . (c) identification with objects from whom a sense of power can be borrowed, (d) projection of 'bad' aspects of the self on to others. Manic defences purchase freedom from guilt and anxiety at the expense of depth of character and appreciation of the motives and feelings of others' (Rycroft).

Metapsychology   'Term invented by Freud to describe what other sciences call a 'general theory', i.e. statements at the highest level of abstraction' (Rycroft).

Narcissism   'Sexual perversion in which the subject's preferred object is his own body . . . by extension, any form of self-love' (Rycroft).

Object   'That towards which action or desire is directed' (Rycroft).

Object-relations   'The emotional bonds that exist between an individual and another person as opposed to his interest in and love for himself; usually described in terms of the capacity for loving and reacting appropriately to others' (Marion Milner).

Ontology   The science of being.

Paranoia   A form of insanity or mental derangement usually characterized by delusions of either grandeur or persecution.

Paranoid   Relating to paranoia. 'Loosely, touchy, suspicious . . . (Rycroft).

Paranoid anxiety   'Dread of being attacked by 'bad' objects, either internal, projected internal . . . or external' (Rycroft).

Penis envy   'Envy of the penis occurring either in women in respect of men generally or in boys in respect of adult males. According to Freud, penis envy is universal in women, is responsible for their castration complex, and occupies a central place in the psychology of women . . . Jones . . . interpreted the girl's wish to have a penis as itself a defence against anxiety concerning wishes towards the father' (Rycroft).

Perversion (sexual)   'Any form of adult sexual behaviour in which heterosexual intercourse is not the preferred goal' (Rycroft).

Projection   '. . . the process by which specific impulses, wishes, aspects of the self, or internal objects are imagined to be located in some object external to oneself' (Rycroft).

Projective identification   'The result of projecting parts of the self into the object' (Segal, quoted by Marion Milner).

Psychosis   'Mental illnesses which are liable to render their victims *non compos mentis*; in contrast to neurosis for those in which the patient's sanity is never in doubt' (Rycroft).

Reductionist   Science, for the purposes of its methods, treats objects as if they only consisted of what can be measured by apparatus. This is a method only: trouble arises if deductions from this partial view are elevated into an exclusive or total picture of the reality at which we are looking. (See Professor W. H. Thorpe, page 61.)

Regression   'The partial or symbolic return under conditions of relaxation of stress to more infantile patterns of reacting' (Marion Milner).

Reparation 'The process . . . of reducing guilt by action designed to make good the harm imagined to have been done to an ambivalently invested object . . . the process of recreating an internal object which has in phantasy been destroyed' (Rycroft).

Sadism 1. 'Sexual perversion in which the subject claims to get erotic pleasure from inflicting pain on his object. 2. Pleasure in cruelty. 3. Oral sadism: pleasure in biting . . . 4. Anal sadism: pleasure in cruelty of a kind theoretically associated with the anal phase of libidinal development . . .' (Rycroft).

Schizoid '1. Originally, referring to persons in whom there is a divorce between the emotional and intellectual functions . . . 2. By extension, referring to anyone whose character suggests comparison with schizophrenia . . . Hence, by further extension, withdrawn, suspicious . . . 4. Referring to persons whose psychopathology includes the use of defences such as splitting, denial, introjection, and projection . . .' (Rycroft).

Guntrip, however, tends to use the term to indicate profound ego-weakness, and fear of inner weakness, consequent upon failure of the 'maturational processes and the facilitating environment' in infancy: a failure of adequate mothering, leaving a core of profound ego-weakness at the heart of the identity.

In this work I use Guntrip's definition, and use the word to mean empty at the heart of being, and tending to not be willing to accept one's humanness.

Scopophilia Voyeurism.

Talion From 'lex talionis'—the law of 'a tooth for a tooth'. Melanie Klein used the term to discuss the infant's feeling that because he had directed tremendous hunger at his parental imagos, especially at the mother, seeking to 'empty' them, in envy, they might turn in revenge on him, and 'empty' him.

Transitional object 'A symbol of the union of the mother and the baby at the place and time where and when the mother is in the process of transition from being merged in the infant of being experienced as an object to be perceived rather than conceived'. (D. W. Winnicott.)

Bibliography

BALINT, M. *Primary Love and Psycho-analytical Technique* Tavistock 1965

BANTOCK, G. H. *Culture, Industrialisation and Education* Routledge 1968

BOWLBY, J. and FRY, M. *Child Care and the Growth of Love* Penguin 1965

BRECHER, R. and E. (ed.) *An Analysis of Human Sexual Response* André Deutsch 1967

BUBER, Martin *I and Thou* (trans. R. G. Smith) T. & T. Clark Edinburgh

— *The Philosophy of Martin Buber* (ed. Schilpp, R. A. & M. Friedman) Cambridge University Press 1969

BUYTENDIJK, F. J. J. (See passages in GRENE, Marjorie, *Approaches to a Philosophical Biology*)

CASSIRER, Ernst *An Essay on Man* Yale 1944

COMFORT, Alex *Nature and Human Nature* Weidenfeld and Nicholson 1966

ERIKSON, Erik *Childhood and Society* Penguin 1965

— *Insight and Responsibility* Faber 1966

FARBER, Leslie *The Ways of the Will* Constable 1966

FRANKL, Viktor *The Doctor and the Soul* Souvenir Press 1969

— *From Death Camp to Existentialism* Washington Square 1963 (see also his contribution to the Alpbach Seminar under KOESTLER, A.)

FREUD, Sigmund *Beyond the Pleasure Principle* Hogarth Press 1961

— *'Civilised' Sexual Morality and Modern Nervousness* (1908) Beacon Press USA

— *Civilisation and its Discontents* Hogarth Press 1963

— *Collected Papers* (trans. Rivière, etc.) Hogarth Press 1956

— *The Ego and the Id* Hogarth Press 1962

— *The Origins of Psycho-analysis, Letters to Fliess* Hogarth Press 1954

— *An Outline of Psycho-analysis* Hogarth Press 1969

FROMM, Erich *Fear of Freedom* Routledge 1942

GRENE, Marjorie *Approaches to a Philosophical Biology* Basic Books 1965

— *Introduction to Existentialism* University of Chicago Press 1959

— *The Knower and the Known* Faber 1966

GUNTRIP, Harry *Personality Structure and Human Interaction* Hogarth Press 1961

— *Schizoid Phenomena, Object-Relations, and the Self* Hogarth Press 1968

JUNG, Carl C. *Man and His Symbols* Aldus Books 1964

KAELIN, Eugene F. *An Existentialist Aesthetic: The Theories of Sartre and Merleau-Ponty* University of Wisconsin Press 1966

KIERKEGAARD, Soren *Journals 1834–54: Selections* (ed. and trans. Dru) Oxford University Press 1938

KINSEY, A. C., *et al.* *Sexual Behaviour in the Human Male* Saunders 1948

KLEIN, Melanie *Contributions to Psycho-analysis* Hogarth Press 1950

— *Love, Hate and Reparation* Hogarth Press 1935

— *New Directions in Psychoanalysis* Tavistock 1955

— *Our Adult World and Other Essays* Heinemann 1962

— *The Psycho-analysis of Children* Hogarth Press 1959

KNELLER, George F. *Existentialism and Education* Wiley 1964

KOESTLER, A. and SMYTHIES, J. (eds.) *The Alpbach Symposium* Hutchinson 1969

LAING, R. D. *The Divided Self: Studies in Existentialism and Phenomenology* Tavistock 1960

— *The Politics of Experience* and *The Bird of Paradise* Penguin 1967

— *The Self and Others* Tavistock 1969

LAURET, Jean-Paul *The Danish Sex Fairs* Tandem Books 1970

LEWIS, John and TOWERS, Bernard *Naked Ape—or Homo Sapiens? A Reply to Desmond Morris* Garnstone 1969

LOMAS, Peter (ed.) *The Predicament of the Family* Hogarth Press 1967

MAY, Rollo *Love and Will* Souvenir Press 1970

MENNINGER, Karl *Man Against Himself* Hart Davis 1963

MILNER, Marion *In the Hands of the Living God: An Account of a Psycho-analytic Treatment* Hogarth Press 1969

— *On Not Being Able to Paint* Heinemann 1957

MONEY-KYRLE, R. E. See essay in *New Directions in Psychoanalysis*, under KLEIN, Melanie. See also paper on 'Psychoanalysis and Philosophy in *Psychoanalysis and Contemporary Thought* under SUTHERLAND, J. D.

POLANYI, Michael *Knowing and Being* Routledge 1969

— *Personal Knowledge* Routledge 1962

— *The Tacit Dimension* Routledge 1967

PONTY, M. MERLEAU- *The Phenomenology of Perception* (trans. C. Smith) (see also under KAELIN, Eugene F., for his study of the theories of Merleau-Ponty) Routledge 1962

ROUBICZEK, Paul *Ethical Values in an Age of Science* Cambridge University Press 1969

SEGAL, Hannah *Introduction to the Work of Melanie Klein* Heinemann Medical 1965

SLOVENKO, R. (ed.) *Sexual Behaviour and the Law* Thomas, Illinois 1964

STRAUS, Erwin *Phenomenological Psychology* Tavistock 1966

— *The Primary World of Senses* Collier-Macmillan 1963

SUTHERLAND, J. D. (ed.) *Psychoanalysis and Contemporary Thought* Hogarth Press 1958

SUTTIE, Ian D. *The Origins of Love and Hate* Routledge 1935, Pelican 1960

TAYLOR, Charles *The Explanation of Behaviour* Routledge 1964

WARNOCK, Mary *Existentialist Ethics* Macmillan 1967

WESTMANN, H. *The Springs of Creativity* Routledge 1961

WILSON, John *Logic and Sexual Morality* Penguin Books

WINNICOTT, D. W. *The Child and the Family* Tavistock 1957

— *The Child and the Outside World* Tavistock 1957

— *The Child, The Family and the Outside World* Penguin Books 1969

— *Collected Papers: Through Paediatrics to Psycho-analysis* Tavistock 1958

— *The Family and Individual Development* Tavistock 1968

— *The Maturational Processes and the Facilitating Environment* Hogarth Press 1965

— (See also essay on the 'Mirror Role of Mother and Family', in *The Predicament of the Family*, under LOMAS, P.) Hogarth Press 1967

WISDOM, John *Philosophy and Psycho-analysis* Blackwell 1953

YOUNG, Wayland *Eros Denied* Corgi 1968

ZILBOORG, Gregory *The Psychology of the Criminal Act and Punishment* Hogarth Press 1955

Papers

BUYTENDIJK, F. J. J. 'Husserl's Phenomenology and its significance for Contemporary Psychology', in *Readings in Existentialist Phenomenology*, D. O'Connor and N. Lawrence, eds., Englewood Cliffs, Prentice Hall, 1967

DALY, Richard   Review of a book on Rousseau in *Psycho-analytical Review* Vol. 56, No 1, 1969

KHAN, Masud   'The Functions of Intimacy and Acting Out in Perversions', in *Sexual Behaviour and the Law*, ed. Slovenko, Thomas, Illinois 1964

—   'Reparation to the Self as an Idolised Internal Object', in *Dynamic Psychiatry* Vol. 2, November 1968

STONE, Leo   'The Principal Obscene Word in the English language' in the *International Journal of Psycho-analysis* Vol. 45, Part 1, 1954

WINNICOTT, D. W.   'Adolescent Process and the Need for Personal Confrontation', in *Playing and Reality*, Tavistock, 1971

Index

𝕘𝕘

Abortion, 34ff., 117, 204
'Acting-out', 101 (see also 'The Function of Intimacy and Acting Out in Perversions)
'Adolescent Process and the Need for Personal Confrontation', 128n.
Alpbach Seminar, 7, 56, 211
Amis, Kingsley, 5, 6, 6n.
Analysis of Human Sexual Response, An, 132–64 passim, 153, 156, 157, 159, 161, 162
Anna Karenina, 126
Anti-culture, 193
'Applicant, The', 215
Approaches to a Philosophical Biology, 57n., 67n., 141, 178n.
Ardrey, Robert, 54, 208
Aretino, Pietro, 46, 49
Ariel, 82
Aristotle, 120, 133
Arts Council, 58, 92, 165, 169, 171, 175, 178, 179, 198
Atkins, Susan, 39
Aurén, Sven, 19ff.
Auschwitz, 24
Austen, Jane, 3, 4, 13, 14, 206
Australia, 11, 205
Australian, The, 176
Author, The, 13, 165, 169, 170–1, 173
Avant-Garde, The, 24, 91, 108, 184
Ayrton, Michael, 173

BBC, 200
Baedeker, 123
Balint, Michael, 10
Bantock, G. H., 76
Barbarella, 55
Behaviourism, 59, 134ff.
Bell Jar, The, 82, 215
Bentham, Jeremy, 87

Berlin, 22, 24
Bestiality, 192
Binswanger, Ludwig, 109, 154, 160, 166
Biology, 88
Bonnard, 180
Botticelli, 47, 173
Brady, Ian, 86
Breuer, Josef, 213
British Academy, 70
British Board of Film Censors, 171
Brophy, Brigid, 201
Buber, Martin, 50, 70, 74, 80, 109, 136, 148, 160, 166, 184, 196, 207, 208
Buytendijk, F. J. J., 10, 50, 57, 67, 74, 109, 156, 160, 184
Brustein, Dean, Drama Faculty at Yale, 90, 91

Calderone, Mary, 147
Cambridge News, 23
Cambridge University Film Society, 24
Cantil, Hadley, 209
Cassirer, Ernst, 51, 161
Cezanne, 209
Charlotte Buhle School, 92
Chartres cathedral, 190, 209
Chaucer, Geoffrey, 14
Child, The Family and the Outside World, The, 200
Children, 17, 47, 92, 98n., 176, 200ff.
Christ, Jesus, 11
Church Council Report on Morality, 116
Collected Papers of D. W. Winnicott, 67n.
Colossus, The, 82n.
Colorado University, 176
Comfort, Alex, 11, 12, 57–8, 115ff., 129n.
Communication, 118
Confession, of the pervert, 103

Cook, Captain, 39
Cory, John, 161
Couples, 39
Courbet, 46
Cox, Harvey, 46
Critical Dictionary of Psychoanalysis, 213
Critique of Pure Reason, 120
Cultural Conference of UNESCO, 1970, (see under UNESCO)
Culture, Industrialisation and Education, 76
Curious, 36n.
Curry, W. B., 129n., 203–4

Dadaism, 88
Daly, Robert, 48
Danish Blue (film), 23
Danish Sex Fairs, 55
Dartington Hall, 129n., 203–4
Davis, K. E., 175
De Beauvoir, Simone, 86, 87, 89, 109
De Bono, Edward, 56
Decent and Indecent, 91
De Chardin, Teilhard, 206
'Delinquent Acts as Perversions and Fetishes,' 104n.
Denmark, 19ff., 26, 36, 49, 53, 55, 58, 92, 104, 105, 135, 155, 165, 183
De Sade, Marquis, 49, 86, 87, 89, 110, 112, 186
De Sade (film), 23
Descartes, René, 1, 14, 50, 53, 55, 62, 121, 133, 209
Die Fröhliche Wissenschaft, 89
Dionysos, 76
Divided Self, The, 214
Doctor and the Soul, The, 3, 37, 54, 99, 123–4, 130, 143, 163, 164, 202
Donne, John, 7, 8, 14, 39, 45
Dostoevsky, Feodor, 88
Doyle, Eric, 160
Drama Department, New York University, Journal of, 25, 89
Duns Scotus, 160
Dynamic Psychiatry, 98, 101, 105, 108

Ecclesiastes, 6
Edel, Leon, 198
Education, Dept of, 179
Encounter, 7, 56, 211
English Literature in Our Time and the University, 195
'Enlightenment', 195ff.
Eros Denied, 27, 40, 42, 43, 46, 47, 49

Essay on Man (Ernst Cassirer), 162
Ethical Values in the Age of Science, 71
Ethics, 12, 71, 77, 78, 81ff., 87, 88, 89, 99, 102, 106, 108, 110–11, 114–31, 148, 188, 192, 193, 202, 211
Exhibitionism, 41, 52
Existentialism, 89, 112–13
Existentialism and Education, 113, 184, 212
Existentialist Aesthetic, An, 184, 186ff.
Explanation of Behaviour, The, 175n.
Eysenck, H. J. 40, 207

Fairbairn, W. R. D., 10, 75, 84, 90, 140, 148, 152, 206, 211
Fantasia of the Unconscious, 76
Farber, Leslie H., 10, 13, 30, 51, 63, 65, 126, 135, 139, 144, 148, 149, 151, 154, 157–8, 160, 175, 182n.
Farmington Trust, 117, 127
Fascism, 24, 26
Female Element, 79, 81, 83, 122, 144, 149
Fennell, Desmond, 19
Ferenczi, Sandor, 147
Films and Filming, 22
Forster, E. M., 14
Frankl, Viktor, 3, 3n., 8, 10, 13, 14, 15, 24, 27, 29, 32, 36, 37, 49, 51, 53, 54, 56, 63, 72, 92, 99n., 123, 126, 127, 130, 136, 139, 143, 160, 163, 164, 180, 184, 189, 195, 202, 203, 204, 208, 210–12
Freud, Sigmund, 15, 75, 76, 85, 87, 113, 147–8, 150, 151, 161, 165, 166, 167, 172, 208, 213, 216
From Death Camp to Existentialism, 63, 64
'Function of Intimacy and Acting Out in Perversions, The', 98, 99, 101, 102, 111
Future of An Illusion, The, 148

Galileo, 46
Gay Liberation Movement, 94ff.
Genet, Jean, 86, 87, 103, 105, 109, 186
Germany, 22
Gide, André, 103ff.
Godard, Jean-Luc, 23
Grafenberg, E., 146
Grene, Marjorie, 15, 61n., 67n., 118, 119, 120, 131, 135, 141, 156, 168n., 178, 184
Guardian, The, 77, 159, 195
Guilt, 84, 102, 103

Guntrip, Harry, 4n., 10, 26, 30, 44, 47, 67n., 75, 76, 79, 80, 81, 83, 138, 141, 143, 148, 149, 151, 154, 217

Hate, 82, 84ff., 89, 95, 105, 106, 114, 125, 128, 140, 175, 183, 187, 194, 205
Hawksmoor, Nicholas, 41
Hefner, Hugh, 25, 27
Heidegger, Martin, 187
Helvetius, 87
Hill, Maurice, 201
Hilliard, Marion, 157
Hitler, Adolf, 22, 90, 91
Homme manqué, aspect of perversion, 102–3
Homosexuality, 95ff.
Homunculism, 64, 192, 211
Honey, 98
Huckleberry Finn, 169
Human Hope and the Death Instinct, 2n., 54n., 67n., 122n., 172n.
Human World, The, 73
Husserl, Edmund, 8

I am Curious (Yellow), (film), 189
Imaginings, 3
Imprisoned Tongues, 6
In the Hands of the Living God, 78, 213
International Journal of Psychoanalysis, 44, 104
International Psychoanalytical Library, 98

Jandl, Ernst, 90n.
Japan, 47
Jaspers, Karl, 212
Jews, the, 86
Johnson, Mrs Virginia, 132–64 passim, 197 (see also *An Analysis of Human Sexual Response*)
Journal of the Drama Department, New York University, 25, 89
Jung, Carl, 43, 213

Kaelin, Eugene, 184, 186ff.
Kant, Emmanuel, 118, 120
Kensic, Organization for lesbians, 95
Khan, Masud, 11, 16, 29, 30, 41, 48, 77, 97, 98–111, 116, 131, 157, 167, 168, 195
Kierkegaard, Soren, 50
King's College Chapel, 190
Kinsey, A. C., 68, 69, 70, 71, 95, 142, 153, 156, 161, 197, 201
Klein, Melanie, 10, 78, 128, 215, 217

Kneller, George, 113, 184, 212
Knower and the Known, The, 53, 61n., 68, 70, 120, 123, 133
Knowing and Being, 60, 85, 87, 88, 172n., 174n.
Koestler, Arthur, 8
Kronhausen, Eberhard and Phyllis, 26, 47

LSD, 86, 199
Lady Chatterley's Lover, 77
Laing, R. D., 70, 85, 99, 208, 209, 214
Lancet, The, 86n.
Langer, Suzanne, 51, 118, 209
Langley, Esmé, 96
Language, sexual, 44
Last Exit to Brooklyn, 169, 170
Lawrence, D. H., 1, 3, 18, 76, 77, 180
Legman, G., 191, 192
Le Monde, 19ff., 32, 193
Leonard, George, 64
Lesbianism, 94ff, 107
Lewis, John, 54
Life, 189–90
Little Red Schoolbook, The, 98
Living Theatre, 3, 90
Loden, Barbara, 191
Logic and Sexual Morality, 115, 117–18, 120, 121, 124, 126
Logotherapy, 63
Lollobrigida, Gina, 55
Longford, Lord, 208n.
Look, 37, 38
Lord Chamberlain, 171
Love, 57, 67, 74, 79, 85, 87, 91, 106, 113, 115, 119, 121, 123, 124–6, 140, 163, 164, 168, 175–8
Love and Will, 8, 9, 25, 29, 33, 34, 42, 44–5, 64, 67, 129, 194, 196ff., 206 209
Love Laboratory, The, 61
Lucas, Dr. James, 159
Lykiard, Alexis, 90n.

Mace, Dr. David, 156
Machiavelli, Niccolo, 58
McLuhan, Marshall, 64
Macmurray, John, 65
Maidenek, 24
'Male and Female Elements in the Personality', 81
Male Element, 79, 81, 122, 144, 149
Man and His Symbols, 43
Man and Woman, 40, 57, 115, 116, 117, 118, 120, 121, 123

Mansfield, Jayne, 55
Manson, Charles, 30, 86
Marcuse, Herbert, 184
Marriage, 10, 79, 92, 107, 123, 145
Marriage Guidance Council, 153n.
Marvell, Andrew, 14, 180
Marxism, 89
Masks of Hate, The, 2n., 14, 23, 91
Masters, William, 14, 118, 132–64
    passim, 197, 199
Masters-Johnson: see *An Analysis of
    Human Sexual Response*
May, Rollo, 8, 9, 10, 12, 13, 14, 18, 25,
    29, 30, 32, 33, 34, 42, 44, 45, 48, 51,
    56, 63, 64, 65, 67, 68, 69, 75, 111, 116,
    124, 127, 129, 135, 143, 149, 160,
    177, 184, 185, 194, 196–212 *passim*
Mechanism of Mind, The, 56
Melbourne, Australia, 3, 33
Menninger, Karl, 147
Merleau-Ponty, Maurice, 17, 50, 51, 52,
    53, 55, 58, 72, 109, 116, 121, 133,
    134, 138, 143, 156, 161, 174, 175, 187
Michelangelo, 46, 47
Michigan State University, 25
Miller, Henry, 103
Milner, Marion, 10, 78, 213ff.
Mind—An Essay in Feeling, 209
Mona Lisa, The, 190
Money-Kyrle, Roger, 48, 49, 130–1, 193
Monroe, Marilyn, 55
Moral inversion, 81ff.
Morris, Desmond, 54, 208
Mortimer, John, 165, 169, 170, 171
Mother, the, 78, 92, 99, 101, 106, 111,
    116
Mouth and Oral Sex, The, 98
Murdoch, Iris, 14

Naked Ape—or Homo Sapiens?, 54n.
National Secular Society, 201
National Theatre, 45
Nature, 55
Nature and Human Nature, 56–7
Nazis, 22, 26, 86, 87, 138, 171
New English Bible, The, 6n., 7n.
New Statesman, The, 5, 6n., 195
New York, 30, 89
New York Review of Books, The, 90
New York Times, 161
New York University, 25, 89
Newton, Sir Isaac, 15, 53, 62
Nietzsche, 76, 89, 90, 112, 178–9
Nihilism, 63, 64, 89, 110, 178–9
19 Magazine, 95ff.

Nova, 34, 199

Objectivity, 88–9
Obscene Publications Act, 170
Oh! Calcutta!, 32, 33, 49, 51, 52, 106,
    184, 192
'On the Sources of Knowledge and
    Ignorance', 70
Origins of Love and Hate, The, 171, 172
Oz, 98

Paranoia, 104
Paul, Saint, 76
Pavlov, I. P., 134, 142, 143, 166, 174,
    174n.
Penguin Books, 39
Penguin Dictionary of Psychology, 213
Personal Knowledge, 2, 70, 172, 182
*Personality Structure and Human Inter-
    action*, 141, 154
Persuasion, 14
Perugia, 77
Perversion, 94–111
Phenomenological Psychology, 113,
    116ff., 139
Phenomenology of Perception, 50, 52, 55,
    72–3
Phenomenon of Man, The, 207
Philosophy, 48, 50ff., 58–9, 61–2, 70,
    114, 117ff., 126, 130, 187
Philosophy and Psychoanalysis, 78,
    114–15
Philosophy of the Body, The, 162
Physicalism, 88, 114
Pindar, 212
Planned Parenthood Conference,
    Tokyo, 1955, 18
Plath, Sylvia, 82, 214
Plato, 76
Play, 106, 111
Playboy, 4, 25, 27, 32, 34, 64, 83, 180
Playing and Reality, 81, 128n., 130n.
Polanyi, Michael, 1, 2, 10, 12, 24, 46,
    49, 59, 60, 66, 70, 85, 88, 89, 109, 114,
    115, 119–20, 123, 132, 133, 135, 141,
    143, 156, 161, 172n., 174n., 175,
    182, 185, 208
Politics, 91
Politics of Experience, The, 208
Pomeroy, Wardell B., 142
Popper, Karl, 70
Pornography, 19ff., 27, 47, 53, 58, 82,
    83, 88, 99, 102–4, 113, 143, 168, 173,
    175, 176–80, 181–2, 185, 186, 188ff.
Portman, Adolf, 141

Presidential Commission on Pornography, 175ff.
Price, H. H., 123
Primary Love and Psychoanalytical Technique, 125, 126
Primary Maternal Preoccupation, 67n., 82, 124
Primary World of Senses, The, 61, 133, 134, 143
'Principal Obscene Word in the English Language, The', 44
Privacy, 17, 37ff.
Prostitution, 37, 43
Pseudo-Revolution, The, 45n.
Psychoanalysis and Contemporary Thought, 48, 130
'Psychoanalysis and Philosophy', 130
Psychoanalysis, International Journal of, 44
Psychoanalytical Studies of the Personality, 84, 85, 140
Psychology of the Criminal Act and Punishment, 46
Puritanism, the New, 44

Rainbow, The, 180
Reductionism, 56, 61
Reiss, Dr., 159
Religion, 88
'Reparation to the self as an Idolised Internal Object', 98, 101, 105, 108
Responsible Society, The, 208
Roberts, Robert, 6
Robinson, John, 27
Rodin, 181
Roubiczek, Paul, 71, 87
Rousseau, Jean-Jacques, 48
Running Man Press, 98n.
Rutgers University, 176
Rycroft, 101, 213ff.

Sartre, Jean-Paul, 12, 87, 88, 89, 109, 184, 185, 186
Scandinavia, 18
Schiller, 56
Schizoid Factors in the Human Personality, 63, 75, 84ff., 99ff., 105, 106, 117, 198, 210
'Schizoid Factors in the Personality', 84
Schizoid Phenomena, Object-relations, and the Self, 4n., 75, 79, 81, 83, 84, 149
Schizophrenia, 140
Schmideberg, 104 and 104n.
Science, 2, 15, 53, 55ff., 58, 61ff., 65,

68ff., 70, 87, 88, 116, 127, 132–64 *passim.*, 178, 187
Science and Ethics, 78
Science, Faith and Society, 132
Scopophilia, 114, 166–9 189 (see Voyeurism)
Seen, 104
Segal, Hannah, 216
Sensuous Woman, The, 93, 98, 143
Seven Days in May, 206
Sex and Culture, 29
Sex and Dehumanization, 39
Sex Education, 35, 94, 200ff.
Sex Education, 201
Sexology, 60, 69, 70, 132–64, 191
Sexual Act in Public, The, 194
Sexual Behaviour and the Law, 98, 99, 101, 102, 111
'Sexual Fascism', 25, 83, 86
Sexual Regulations and Human Behaviour, 28n.
Sexual Revolution, The (Playboy), 4, 25, 27, 32
Sexual Offences, 41
Shame, 102, 103, 166–9
'Shame as a Historiological problem', 166
Social Contract, The, 48
Society and Sex, 63, 85, 88, 108, 182
Socrates, 76
Solzhenitsyn, Alexander, 180
Song of Songs, The, 7
Sontag, Susan, 88, 108
Spectator, The, 18, 19
Spicker, Stuart F., 162
Spock, Benjamin, 91, 92
Stone, Leo, 44
'Strategies of survival', 99
Straus, Erwin, 10, 13, 22, 42, 47, 50, 51, 53, 61n., 105, 106, 113, 117, 121, 123, 130, 133, 134, 135, 139n., 142, 143, 144, 153n., 156, 161, 166–9, 174, 175, 182n., 184, 185, 203
Strick, Phillips, 171
Surrealism, 88
Sutherland, Dr. (Correspondent in *The Times*), 94
Suttie, Ian D., 10, 26, 61, 171ff., 185
Svenska Dagblatet, 19
Sweden, 18
Swift, Jonathan, 23
Symbolism, 101,

Tacit Dimension, The, 135
Take a Girl Like You, 6

Taubman, Howard, 198

Taylor, Charles, 2, 175

'Technique of Intimacy, and Acting Out in Perversions, The Function of, 99ff.

Thestrup, Dr. Knud, 20, 35, 37

Thief's Journal, The, 109

Thorpe, W. H., 61, 175, 216

Times, The, 55, 62, 94, 107, 127, 201

Times Educational Supplement, The, 22, 69

Times Literary Supplement, The, 57

To His Coy Mistress, 180

Tomkins, Sylvan, 209

Towers, Bernard, 54

Transitional Object Phenomena, 102, 111

Treblinka, 24

Twiggy, 64

Tynan, Kenneth, 45

UNESCO Symposium on Culture, Venice, 1970, 9n., 88, 188ff.

Unwin, J. D., 28–9

Updike, John, 3, 39

Vadim, Roger, 55

Valentine, 94n.

Values, 68–9, 71, 73, 114–15 (see also Ethics)

Vanity Fair, 98

Venereal Disease, 159

Venus (Botticelli), 173

Vietnam War, 198

Voyeurism, 166–9 (see also Scopophilia)

Waddington, C. H., 8, 78

Warhol, Andy, 180

Ways of the Will, The, 30, 126n,. 139, 144, 149, 151, 154, 155, 157–8, 160

Weekend, 23

Westman, Dr. Axel, 18

Which?, 157

Whiting, Charles, 22

Wholly Communion, 90n.

Whyte, L. L., 78

Wife-swapping, 69n.

Wilde, Oscar, 103

Wilson, John, 117–31 *passim*.

Winnicott, D. W., 10, 16, 26, 67n., 74, 76, 78, 80, 81, 82, 99, 101, 102, 109, 122n., 128n., 130n., 132, 148, 152, 185, 200ff., 203, 204, 208, 214, 217

Winsconsin, University of, 206

Wisdom, John, 78, 114–15, 121

Women in Love, 76, 77, 180

Women's Liberation Movement, 33

Woodstock, 21

Woolwich, Bishop of, 27

Wyatt, Sir Thomas, 14, 180

Yale University, 90

Yeats, W. B., 3, 4, 7, 14

Young Person's Guide to Life and Love, A, 91

Young, Wayland, 27ff., 40, 41, 42ff., 45, 46, 47, 48ff.

Zilboorg, Dr. Gregory, 46